The Black Rainbow

Essays on the present breakdown of culture

The Black Rainbow

Essays on the present breakdown of culture

edited by

PETER ABBS

HEINEMANN
LONDON

Heinemann Educational Books Ltd
LONDON   EDINBURGH   MELBOURNE   AUCKLAND
HONG KONG   SINGAPORE   KUALA LUMPUR   IBADAN
NAIROBI   JOHANNESBURG   NEW DELHI   LUSAKA

ISBN 0 435 18025 8

First published 1975

Set in 11/12pt Baskerville

Published by
Heinemann Educational Books Ltd
48 Charles Street, London W1X 8AH
Printed in Great Britain by
Northumberland Press Limited, Gateshead

Contents

Acknowledgements

Chapter 2, Herbert Read's essay 'The Limits of Permissiveness', has previously been published in *Resurgence*, vol. 8/9 1969.

A shortened version of Chapter 12 *The Mechanical World-Picture* has previously been published as *Tract 5* (Autumn 72).

The extracts from *Crow* and *Wodwo* by Ted Hughes quoted in Chapter 4 are reprinted by permission of Faber and Faber Ltd.

From *Two Legends*

> Black is the earth-globe, one inch under,
> An egg of blackness
> Where sun and moon alternate their weathers
>
> To hatch a crow, a black rainbow.
> Bent in emptiness
>   over emptiness
> But flying

TED HUGHES

Song of the Sky Loom

Oh our Mother the Earth oh our Father the Sky
Your children are we
     with tired backs we bring you the gifts you love

So weave for us a garment of brightness

May the warp be the white light of morning
May the weft be the red light of evening
May the fringes be the falling rain
May the border be the standing rainbow

Weave for us this bright garment
that we may walk where birds sing
     where grass is green

Oh our Mother the Earth oh our Father the Sky.

AN INDIAN SONG

1 An Introductory Note

PETER ABBS

Apart from the opening essay by Herbert Read, all the essays gathered here have been specially written for this symposium.

I have decided to both use and open with Herbert Read's *The Limits of Permissiveness* (a lecture given on 1 February 1968, four months before his death) because it prophetically pointed to those forces of nihilism in our culture that now everywhere manifest themselves and which are expressed most generally in our society in a numbing loss of values, meanings and aspirations.

Towards the end of that 1968 lecture, Herbert Read declared:

> The refusal to recognize the limits of art is the reason why as critics we must withold our approval from all those manifestations of permissiveness characterized by incoherence, insensibility, brutality and ironic detachment.

There can be no doubt now as to what sort of anti-art, parading, more often than not, under the guise of 'liberation' and 'breakthrough', Herbert Read was urging responsible intellectuals to be critical of. Nor can there be much doubt that when such disapproval is expressed, especially when it is based on a firm understanding of the nature of art rather than on prurient notions or class-respectability, it is either suppressed or insidiously devalued by the media at large.

There has been for some time now a reasonably open debate in the West on the dangers of pollution. We have seen a spate of books, pamphlets, films, television documentaries, and educational publications. There have been well-publicized conferences, major articles in newspapers and magazines. Society has become aware of pollution and the threat it constitutes to the survival of life. We would not wish to underestimate the value of such discussion or, with the insistence still on industrial expansion, with the need for it to continue, but, at the same time, it can be said that the arguments have tended to overlook an even more fundamental consideration: a consideration as to what makes life *worth living*. We have not asked seriously enough about what sort of cultural and social conditions are needed if human life is not to lose an inner sense of purpose, of genuine well-being, of personal zest. We know that countries which have highly advanced economies, with high levels of production and consumption, countries like the United States of America, Switzerland, Denmark and Australia, have also the highest rates of drug addiction, suicide, and death from violence. It is, thus, the crassest nonsense to delude ourselves into thinking that merely an *unpolluted affluence* would make one iota of difference to the quality of human society. We know it would not, and could not. And yet discussion on all those deeper questions, concerning *meaning* and *worth*, which now confront humanity on all sides, are constantly evaded even, as F. R. Lea points out in his essay, by the university philosophers.

Why, we must ask, hasn't this fundamental debate taken place? Some of the essays in this symposium suggest an answer to the question. Very briefly, it would seem that the debate has not taken place on a large scale because the media themselves have come to depend in various ways on the glittering, nihilistic mode of culture. This can be seen most obviously by considering the way in which the media are dependent for their existence on the seductive images and vacuous slogans of advertising. It can be seen at work more generally by considering the way in which many of our newspapers seek to draw and entertain their audience through a stream of half-manufactured gossip, gutter-stories, and drivel. Nor, as Charles Parker points out in his essay, is this confined to the *News of the World* or the colour supplements: it also informs the policies of the BBC.

For these reasons, the media are the last place where such fundamental discussion about our culture can take place. For the same reasons, many artists and writers have attempted to survive by discarding their own values and adopting the terms of their impersonal patrons. This is too complex a development to describe here but several of the contributors in their essays provide the reader with valuable insights into how this has happened. As a result, much of art now mythologizes the commercial tyranny on which it depends.

In such circumstances, it is difficult for anyone to initiate serious discussion on the state of contemporary culture. Many who might speak out are silent from fear of what they might lose while others secure fame and fortune by publicly indulging their own tawdry interests in perversion and sadism. No man in his sane mind can be happy about such developments or doubt what they portend for the future if they are allowed to continue unchecked.

Yet what is to be done? Herbert Read closed his lecture with these words:

> What we seek is 'a renaissance beyond the limits of nihilism'. We cannot yet determine the outlines of such a renaissance, but we know that they must remain within the limits of art as I have defined them.

Five years later we are in no better position. There *are* developments which may, as some of the contributors to this volume suggest, materialize into a powerful movement. But, at this moment, such developments are still in an embryonic state and only to be found at the very peripheries of social life.

In the meantime, it is important that we become aware of the nature of modern nihilism and barbarism: that we understand it, and refuse to succumb to it. In this way, the fanatical and destructive energies now widespread could, lacking all support, slowly exhaust themselves. A larger space would then exist for the genuine symbolic forms of art such as John McCabe mentions in his essay on contemporary music: a space where a culture based on creativity and trust could again emerge – although, as Fred Inglis makes only too clear, this could not happen without a radical change in our present political and economic structures.

It is hoped that *The Black Rainbow* in however small a way might begin just such a process, beginning with an awareness of what is happening, moving into a stubborn resistance and ending finally in a renewal of our cultural life.

PETER ABBS

1974

2 The Limits of Permissiveness

HERBERT READ

This lecture will be concerned with very recent developments in modern art – including literature, but excluding music which I do not feel competent to deal with – developments that in my opinion are *excessive*, developments that exceed the limits that define the very concept of art. My intention is not in any sense reactionary. The great experimental artists of the modern epoch – Picasso, Kandinsky, Klee, Mondrian in painting; Brancusi, Arp, Moore and Lipchitz in sculpture; Proust, Pound, Joyce and Eliot in literature – these remain our exemplars, pioneers who have established a new basis for the fine arts.

Modernism in art is a very complex phenomenon and our generalizations are more likely to obscure than to illuminate it. But it can be affirmed that one principle, common to all the exemplary artists I have mentioned and to artists everywhere who are distinctively 'modern', is fundamental and cannot be sacrificed without calling into question the whole movement. This is the principle of symbolism as distinct from the principle of realism. The modern artist claims that there is not one level of experience to be presented or re-presented in the work of art, but several, and that some of these levels are even more important than the imitation of phenomena from the outer world.

Subjectivism is, of course, a common feature of the whole romantic tradition in art, but what has been discovered or re-affirmed in our time is that subjective images have their own laws of being, and can be adequately re-presented only by symbols. The word 'symbol', as an American philosopher of art, Richard Bernheimer, has remarked, 'is admittedly one of the most protean in the language. But however it is defined (he continues) ... it clearly suggests a mode of functioning different from that which we attribute to simple likenesses. Transcending the realm of mere visual similarities, all symbols tend to bring us into contact with realities otherwise partly or totally inaccessible'.[1]

A further refinement of this process of symbolization peculiar to the modern epoch is the discovery that abstract forms (by which we mean non-figurative forms) function as effective symbols, a discovery that has been confirmed by modern psychology.

Such is the philosophic bedrock upon which the modern movement in art rests, and nothing I am going to say will in any way call into question this basic principle.

Movements in modern art, such as the Cubist movement, the Surrealist movement, or the Constructivist movement, are usually regarded as attempts by a group of artists to organize themselves to further their common interests. Since the aims of a movement are not always formulated in words, the bond may be no more than the practice of a certain style. Sometimes the movement is first defined and made conscious of itself by critics; sometimes, as in the Futurist and Surrealist movements, a manifesto is drawn up by the leaders of the movement, and adherents are invited to sign the manifesto and follow its precepts. In the case of the Surrealist movement the discipline was strict, resignations and excommunications were the order of the day. Edicts were issued whenever the social or political situation seemed to demand an expression of the group's solidarity.

Movements in this strict sense did not survive the Second World War. In 1947 an attempt was made to reassemble the forces of Surrealism, but after one more manifestation it finally expired. The so-called movements that have followed – Action Painting in the United States, Pop Art and Op Art – have been pseudo-movements without stylistic unity, without manifestos, without common action or association of any kind – the creation of journalists, anxious to find a label for phenomena they do not understand, even anxious to create an order where only confusion seems to exist.

If one looks at a survey of the present scene, such as *The Art of Our Time*, a comprehensive volume edited by the distinguished German art critic Will Grohmann in 1966, one notices in the first place that there is no attempt to classify contemporary art according to stylistic categories: the survey is made country by country, and within each country, artist by artist. If one then turns to the numerous and excellent illustrations in the volume, though these are again classified by country, no national characteristics can be

[1] Richard Bernheimer, *The nature of Representation: A Phenomenological Enquiry*, New York University Press, N. Y., 1961, p. 4.

detected. Instead there is a multiplicity of styles which cuts across all frontiers, so that an extreme geometrical abstraction may be found in Great Britain, Venezuela, Italy or Japan and an extreme expressionistic abstraction in the United States, Spain, Germany or Argentina. But even these categories are meaningless, for there is nothing in common between the paintings in each category except a tendency towards one or other extreme of the formal spectrum.

We must next observe that the extremes are, like the North and South Poles, sparsely inhabited: a Ben Nicholson, a Jesus Soto at one extreme, a Karel Appel or a Vedova at the other extreme. I do not imply that there is any identity of style even between Nicholson and Soto; much less between Appel and Vedova. They merely represent extremes in a spectrum that consists of an infinite gradation of individualistic style. Even the 'pop' artists, Rauschenberg or Jasper Johns, Lichtenstein or Andy Warhol, when seen in a survey of this kind, cease to have any distinctive style – they merge imperceptibly into styles we have been accustomed to call surrealist or dadaist.

The only quality all these painters of our time have in common is eccentricity, their apparently deliberate avoidance of a stylistic unity. Each is an individual speaking a private language, and the total effect is a Babel. But the Babel is not cacophonous: the separate sounds merge into an overall harmony. Since this harmony is not stylistic we must seek some other definition of its total effect.

The only common quality left in contemporary art is perceptual coherence. That is to say, however extreme the permissive freedom enjoyed by the artist, an instinctive visual balance seems to assert itself in his work: the muscular action of the painter's hand as it moves over the canvas automatically conforms to laws of perception. The automatic nature of this control is confirmed by the paintings executed by a chimpanzee some years ago under the direction of Dr Desmond Morris at the London Zoo. I possess two of these paintings and they do not differ in essential characteristics from typical examples of American action painting. This does not imply that the American painters are comparable in their general abilities to chimpanzees, but when they allow their brushes to be guided by instinctive gestures (and they proudly admit that this is what they do) then in that moment they gesticulate in the same manner as the chimpanzee. Of course, the chimpanzee cannot stretch and frame the canvas that has been presented to him: he cannot perform any of the ancillary activities that lead up to and follow the action of a human painting. He cannot, for example, enter a contract with an art dealer. But he can perform the gestures necessary to paint a picture of a certain kind, and the perceptual process ensures that this picture is organized into a significant pattern.

A significant pattern – there we have a phrase that may give us a clue to the unity underlying the diversity of the art of our time. That every work of art possesses a pattern – even in spite of the desperate efforts of some painters to avoid anything so commonplace – is evident from the illustrations in Professor Grohmann's book, or from any international exhibition of art such as the Venice Biennale. If we take two extremes illustrated in the same page of *The Art of Our Time*, such as those by Philip Guston and Barnett Newman or those by Obregón and Soto, the extreme contrast of free and disciplined forms cannot disguise the fact that all four paintings are visually coherent – and this is true of colour as well as spatial values. It was long ago demonstrated by the Dada artists that the more deliberately the painter sets out to destroy the traditional conventions of art the more markedly he reveals his innate aesthetic sensibility. The work of Kurt Schwitters is the best demonstration of that paradox.

Is the good Gestalt (as the psychologists call it) good enough to constitute a work of art? I think it is, if by a work of art we mean what Matisse meant by a work of art – 'an art of balance, of purity and serenity devoid of troubling or depressing subject-matter, an art which might be for every mental worker ... like an appeasing influence, like a mental soother, something like a good armchair in which to rest from physical fatigue'. Matisse's statement has never been very popular with critics of art: it seems to deprive them of their function, which is to reveal spiritual or social or psychological profundities in art. No doubt such profundities exist, or have existed in the past. But the modern artist has proved that the artist can dispense with them. For him the good Gestalt is good enough, and though this looks suspiciously like the old doctrine of art for art's sake, the Gestalt psychologist will tell you that the intelligence itself, and our whole ability to order experience for conceptual apprehension and assessment, depends on this fundamental perceptual process. From this point of view the work of art becomes, not a reflection of experience, but the foundation of experience, the mental event from which all intellection proceeds. From infinite possibilities of form and colour the eye selects images that have visual significance, and though these images may not be matched in the world of appearance, nevertheless they become part of the world of appearance, in so far as man is given

the power to create a visual order out of the confused material
presented to his organs of perception.

The task of the critic remains, unaffected and perhaps clarified
by this reduction of the work of art to its aesthetic nakedness. His
duty is simply to assess the aesthetic effectiveness of any particular
work of art, in relation to human faculties of feeling, emotions and
prudence. This last word may cause you some surprise, but the
work of art is always created in a social context, and it is legitimate
to distinguish between aesthetic permissiveness, which in principle
should be total and unrestricted, and a social permissiveness whose
limits are determined by reason or direction or consideration for
the innocence and well-being of other people. There are many
manifestations in the art of today that are vulgar and moronic, and
there is no reason why, in the sacred name of liberty, we should
condone them.

Perhaps I am only repeating the most important conclusion
reached by Albert Camus in *L'homme révolté*, an idea which I
emphasized in my introduction to the English translation of this
book. It is the idea that excess either kills, or it creates its own
'measure' or moderation. To quote Camus: 'Moderation is not
the opposite of rebellion. Rebellion in itself is moderation, and it
demands, defends, and re-creates it throughout history and its
eternal disturbances. The very origin of this value guarantees us
that it can only be partially destroyed. Moderation, born of rebellion, can only live by rebellion. It is a perpetual conflict, continually created and mastered by the intelligence. It does not triumph
either in the impossible or in the abyss. It finds its equilibrium
through them. Whatever we may do, excess will always keep its
place in the heart of man, in the place where solitude is found.
We all carry within us our places of exile, our crimes and our
ravages. But our task is not to unleash them on the world: it is
to fight them in ourselves and in others.'[2]

Camus is writing of rebellion in its social or political context, but
his words are equally true in a cultural context. Here, too, we are
in the presence of a paradox: the necessity, in order to establish
an equilibrium, of constant revolt. But as Camus indicates, the
problem is essentially one for the individual. We should not expose
our private paranoia to the world, but seek to master it in art and
through art. The alternative is an unrestrained exposure of mental
conflicts or mental confusion that in terms of visual or poetic form
is aesthetic nihilism.

[2] *The Rebel*, translation by Anthony Bower, London (Hamish Hamilton),
1953, p. 268.

I have already, in a book entitled *The Origins of Form in Art*,[3] dealt with the disintegration of form in modern art, but I would now like to be a little more specific, both in relation to literature and to the visual arts. Accepting perceptual coherence as the universal requirement in a work of art, at what point in the history of modern art and literature do we find this requirement set aside?

I will begin with literature and will briefly examine the later work of James Joyce, Samuel Beckett and Ezra Pound.

Joyce claimed that both *Ulysses* and *Finnegans Wake* were composed on a structural principle: *Ulysses* has strict correspondences with Homer's *Odyssey*: each incident is a reflection of a similar incident in Homer's epic poem. Ezra Pound, writing in French for the *Mercure de France* when *Ulysses* was first published, asserted that as a book it was more formal than the carefully wrought novels of Flaubert: 'Not a line, not half-a-line, that does not have an intellectual intensity unparalleled in a book of such length.' It has never seemed to me that Ulysses needed this kind of justification, and I suspect that Joyce used the *Odyssey*, not so much as a source of inspiration but rather as a structural prop for the images that welled up from his unconscious – a clothes-horse for his unwashed linen. At the same time a painter such as Giorgio di Chirico was using the classical structures of academic painting as a prop for the incoherent visual images that welled up from his unconscious. Any writer or painter knows that inspiration flows more freely if a ready-made channel is available.

At this point I should perhaps ask you to distinguish between the aesthetic and the social aspects of permissiveness in literature. *Ulysses* is a decisive document in this great debate, and as you know in 1934 an American court allowed the plea of aesthetic merit to prevail over the charge of obscenity. That such a distinction can be sustained is obvious to anyone with sufficient knowledge of the history of literature: literature, in this respect, is simply a faithful reflection of the behaviour of 'the naked ape', as it is now fashionable to call man. If we want our literature to be decent, we must clothe the ape, that is to say, falsify the reality. What we are discussing now is not the nature of the reality reflected by art, but the manner in which the mirror distorts reflected images.

If Joyce's *Ulysses* had not been succeeded by *Finnegans Wake* we might exempt Joyce from the charge of formal incoherence, of lack of *measure*. But in Joyce's own view, *Finnegans Wake* is a 'logical' sequence to *Ulysses*. *Finnegans Wake*, too, has its prototype – *La Scienza Nuova* of Giambattista Vico, with its cynical theory of history and its new conception of the relationship between

[3] *The Origins of Form in Art*, London and New York, 1965, pp. 174-87.

history and imagination. Joyce, we are told, read this book in Trieste and 'used it centrally in *Finnegans Wake*'.[4] But the structural parallel between these two works is not so close as it is in the case of *Ulysses* and the *Odyssey*. Joyce was inspired by Vico's structural ideas in relation to history, not in relation to the structure of the book he was writing. He took over a cyclical theory of history and applied it very loosely to the art of fiction.

Joyce's brother, Stanislaus, was a fearless and perceptive critic of both *Ulysses* and *Finnegans Wake*. James owed a lot to his brother – perhaps the very notion of using structural prototypes (Stanislaus had pointed out to him the resemblance between the 'Bachanals' of Euripides and Ibsen's 'Ghosts').[5] Stanislaus was critical of many aspects of *Ulysses*, but accepted it for its realism, its stylistic energy and beauty. He took the talent for granted: 'Dublin lies stretched out before the reader, the minute living incidents start out of the pages. Anybody who reads can hear the people talk and feel himself among them.' But he went on to complain that at every turn of this, the longest day on record, there are things to give him pause. 'There is many a laugh, but hardly one happy impression. Everything is undeniably as it is represented, yet the "cumulative effect" as Grant Richards would say, makes him (the reader) doubt truth to be a liar. You try to shift the burden of your melancholy to the reader's shoulders without being yourself relieved. To me you seem to have escaped from the toils of the priest and the king only to fall under the oppression of a monstrous vision of life itself. There is no serenity or happiness anywhere in the whole book.'[6]

These are shrewd thrusts, but for the most part they belong to the moralistic criticism I have put on one side. It is far otherwise, however, with Stanislaus' criticism of *Finnegans Wake*. The first instalment he read seemed to him to be 'drivelling rigmarole', 'or perhaps – a sadder supposition – it is the beginning of softening of the brain'. He found it all 'unspeakably wearisome', 'the witless wandering of literature before its final extinction'. These expressions are found in a letter to his brother, and there is no reason to suppose that they were inspired by jealousy; as he was later to show in an autobiographical work *My Brother's Keeper*, Stanislaus was, in spite of latent antagonisms natural in the family situation, full of affection and admiration for James, and for this very reason he criticized his brother with 'a startling lucidity of vision'.[7]

---

[4] Richard Ellman. *Letters of James Joyce* (1966), Vol. III, p. 118.
[5] Ellman, Ibid., p. 104.
[6] Ibid., p. 104.
[7] Ibid., p. 105.

At any rate, the witless wandering of literature before its final extinction is the phenomenon we are investigating. Though the wandering in *Finnegans Wake* may not be witless, it is certainly 'inconsequent, desultory, heterogeneous' – words Stanislaus used to describe *Ulysses*. Thought, he added, 'might be anything you like; but it must never be obscure to the thinker ... Bloom's wool-gatherings as often as not leave the reader guessing.'[8] But if this can be said 'as often as not' about *Ulysses*, it must be said without qualification about *Finnegans Wake*. The whole work is designed on the principle of the Anglo-Saxon riddle, the more difficult to guess the meaning the better it is. I do not altogether discount the continuous musical phrasing of the writing, the humour, the latent fire of the embedded images. *Finnegans Wake* will survive as a curiosity of literature, the obsessive spinning of a wordmaster. It should rest at that. It is its influence that has been disastrous.

What in Joyce was a masterpiece of sick humour became in his imitators a simple failure to communicate any meaning but the meaninglessness of all forms of communication, and therefore the meaninglessness of social existence, indeed, the meaninglessness of life itself, individual, or communal. Samuel Beckett has been the chief instigator in this permissive process – again a process with its moments of tragic or comic vision, but from a stylistic point of view leading to an apotheosis of futility. As one of his characters says: 'At no moment do I know what I am talking about, nor of whom, nor of where, nor how, nor why, but I could employ fifty wretches for this sinister operation and still be short of a fifty-first, to close the circuit, that I know, without knowing what it means. The essential is never to arrive anywhere, neither where Manhood is, nor where Worm is, nor where I am, it little matters to what dispensation. The essential is to go on squirming forever at the end of the line, as long as there are water and banks and ravening in heaven or sporting God to plague his creature ... I've swallowed three hooks and am still hungry. Hence the howls. What a joy to know where one is, and where one will stay, without being there. Nothing to do but stretch out comfortably on the rack, in the blissful knowledge you are nobody for all eternity.'

This comes from page 341 of the Molloy trilogy,[9] but it might have come from any of the 418 pages of this book, or any other book of the same author. Again I am teetering on the edge of a moral judgement, but a moral judgement is not my intention. A writer may express a philosophy of futility and still be a great writer: what I criticize in Beckett is a permissive logorrhoea that compels

[8] Ibid., p. 105.
[9] Calder, London, 1959.

the reader to plunge into a sea of words with so little aesthetic reward. The trouble with works like *Finnegans Wake* and the Molloy trilogy (*Molloy, Malone Dies, The Unnamable*) is that they are superficially exciting but fundamentally boring. The underlying reason is a simple one: literature, from Homer to Henry James, has been essentially a dialogue, a dialogue between the author and the 'dear reader'. With the invention of the 'interior monologue', literature became an undirected stream of consciousness, uncontrolled by any intention or desire to communicate to an auditor. Now the undirected stream of consciousness, whether in the related dream or in simulated narrative, is inevitably boring, simply because it lacks dialogic structure, which is a device evolved by the tradition of art for the effective exchange of meaning. Without this dialogic structure, the reader's attention wanders: he becomes indifferent to what is being said.

A distinction must be made here between the interior monologue as developed by Joyce and Beckett, and those various methods of representing the inner consciousness of characters in fiction which are common devices in the literature of the past. Erich Auerbach, in the last chapter of *Mimesis*, distinguishes between the unipersonal and the multipersonal representation of consciousness, and he shows how both methods, separated or combined, have been used by authors such as James Joyce and Virginia Woolf to create an illusion of realism. Auerbach does not discuss Joyce at length, but he suggests that the technique of 'a multiple reflection of consciousness and of multiple time strata would seem to be employed (in *Ulysses*) more radically than anywhere else, and yet the book unmistakably aims at a symbolic synthesis of the theme of "Everyman"'. Auerbach admits that the book can produce a very strong immediate impression on sensitive readers, but really to understand it, he suggests, is not an easy matter, 'for it makes severe demands on the reader's patience and learning by its dizzying whirl of motifs, wealth of words and concepts, perpetual playing upon their countless associations, and the ever rearoused but never satisfied doubt as to what is ultimately hidden behind so much apparent arbitrariness'.[10]

If so much doubt can be expressed about the method of representing consciousness in Joyce's *Ulysses* we may legitimately suppose that Auerbach would have found the technique as it developed to its extreme disintegration of external realities in *Finnegans Wake* totally unacceptable. It may be argued that we have no right to assume that 'the representation of reality' is the exclusive aim

[10] *Mimesis: the Representatives of Reality in Western Literature*, Trans. Willard Task, New York, Doubleday Anchor Books (1957), p. 481.

of literature and art, and indeed I have already admitted, at the beginning of this lecture, that the representation of a superreality may be the legitimate aim of the artist. It is not the nature or extent of reality that is the question, but the method of communicating reality of any kind to an audience. Both Joyce and Beckett are obviously concerned with the nature of reality – concerned to the point of desperation and paranoia – but they dissolve the action, the continuum of events, until the medium they use, words, no longer communicates a meaning, symbolic or objective.

I would like to suggest that from this point of view an interesting comparison may be made between the style and structure of Beckett's prose and those linear designs which decorate the great Celtic illuminated manuscripts and jewellery of the seventh to ninth centuries in Ireland – the Book of Kells, for example, or the Gospel at St Gall. The same phenomenon is found in early Nordic art generally. Here is a description of it by a German art historian (Lamprecht):

> There are certain simple motives whose interweaving and commingling determines the character of this ornament. At first there is only the dot, the line, the ribbon; later the curve, the circle, the spiral, the zigzag, and an S-shaped decoration are employed. Truly, no great wealth of motives! But what variety is attained by the manner of their employment! Here they run parallel, then entwined, now latticed, now knotted, now plaited, then again brought through one another in a symmetrical checker of knotting and plaiting. Fantastically confused patterns are thus evolved, whose puzzle asks to be unravelled, whose convolutions seem alternately to seek and avoid each other, whose component parts, endowed as it were with sensibility, captivate sight and sense in passionately vital movement.

Wilhelm Worringer, who quotes this passage in his *Form in Gothic*,[11] notes that Lamprecht's words expressly bear witness to the impression of passionate movement and vitality, a questing, restless tumult in this confused medley of lines. 'Since line is lacking in all organic timbre, its expression of life must, as an expression, be divorced from organic life ... The pathos of movement which lies in this vitalized geometry ... forces our sensibility to an effort unnatural to it. When once the natural barriers of organic movement have been overthrown, there is no more holding back; again and again the line is broken, again and again checked in the natural direction of its movement, again and again it is forcibly prevented from peacefully ending its course, again and again

[11] English translation, London, 1927, p. 41.

diverted into fresh complications of expression, so that, tempered
by all these restraints, it exerts its energy of expression to the utter-
most until at last, bereft of all possibilities of natural pacification,
it ends in confused, spasmodic movements, breaks off unappeased
into the void or flows senselessly back upon itself.[12]

These sentences, which eloquently and exactly describe the
character of early northern ornament, seem to me to serve as an
equally eloquent and exact description of Beckett's prose style
in *Molloy* and later works – and both Joyce and Beckett are Celtic
writers. But while we can follow this linear movement with pleasure
and even excitement when the medium is visual, the same method
used verbally demands a concentration and tolerance to which we
are not accustomed in literature, and in my opinion never can
become accustomed. Celtic ornament was used to decorate the
Gospels – a very simple narrative. In *Finnegans Wake, Molloy,
How it is* and other works of this kind, the ornament invades the
narrative, and the line of this fused expression 'breaks off unappeased into the void or flows senselessly back upon itself'.

I should perhaps at this point say something about 'the new
French school' of novelists that acknowledges the decisive influence
of Beckett – the anti-novel of Alain Robbe-Grillet, Nathalie Sar-
raute and Marguerite Duras – but I shall refrain, partly because
I have always found it difficult to read their works, but mainly
because the criticisms I have made of Joyce and Beckett apply to
them equally. Always a vital word-play, a glimmering imagery, a
sense of despair or loneliness or futility, but no forward movement,
no organic growth, no dramatic tension, no resolution of a tragic
destiny such as we find in the great literature of the past. The
creative imagination of the poet sinks in a sea of words.

I shall not deal with other examples of logorrhoea that have
followed Joyce and Beckett as inevitably as the little fishes follow
a receding tide, but instead say a few words about Ezra Pound in
this same connection. Again I would not like to be misunderstood.
Pound is a great poet, perhaps the greatest of our time. But his
work, as Yeats already perceived in his Introduction to the *Oxford
Book of Modern Verse*, in spite of its nobility – 'at moments more
style, more deliberate nobility and the means to convey it than in
any contemporary poet known to me ... is constantly interrupted,
broken, twisted into nothing by its direct opposite, nervous obsession, nightmare, stammering confusion...' The words were
written by Yeats in September 1936, at which time only the first
41 Cantos of Pound's major work had been published. Since that

[12] Op. cit., p. 42.

year the stammering confusion has grown worse with every successive batch of cantos, until in the latest cantos the incoherence is
absolute.

Stanislaus Joyce's 'sadder supposition', a softening of the brain,
is almost inescapable in Pound's as in Joyce's case, and one can
only contemplate the spectacle with awe and compassion. But this
stammering confusion is the characteristic of Pound's work that is
now imitated by young poets who wish to be considered of his
school. Of Pound's great qualities – his acute sense of musical
cadence, his vivid imagery, his poetic vision and skill, these later
poets show no trace. They mirror a great confusion and call it the
modern style.

I must now turn all too late in this lecture to the visual arts,
for the process of progressive disintegration is even more evident
in painting and sculpture than in literature. Again we have a
number of artists whose greatness cannot be questioned – at least,
not by me. But their greatness lies in the past: either they are
dead or they have reached an advanced age in which their work
has become repetitive. The great creative period lasted from about
1905 to about 1955. In those fifty years all the major painters and
sculptors of the modern movement had completed their characteristic work. I do not imply that the work done by artists such as
Picasso, Miró or Henry Moore since 1955 is in any sense necessarily
inferior to their earlier work: I am merely asserting that the peak
of their creative achievement had been reached before mid-
century and that what follows is an expansion or necessary development of their established styles.

The artists who have come to maturity since the end of the
Second World War (1945) are desperately striving to escape from
the influence of the masters of the modern movement, but the
more original they try to be, the more they are compelled to deviate
arbitrarily from the prototypes. There is no stylistic element in
action-painting, in pop-art or in op-art, that was not present in
some phase of cubism, dadaism, surrealism or expressionism. I
must emphasize the word 'stylistic', for it is easy to be original if
one abandons the sensibility and discipline that constitute the
essence of art. Art, in any meaningful sense of the word, must have
three essential qualities: a formal correspondence to emotion or
feeling, clarity (what that great contemporary critic Wilson Knight
calls 'a swift forward-flowing transparency'),[13] and a vital imagination, which Coleridge defined as the struggle 'to idealize and to
unify'. The visual arts especially must exemplify this last quality,

[13] In describing Swift's prose style: *Poets of Action*, London (Methuen),
1967, p. 164.

but it is the quality singularly lacking in the fragmented painting and sculpture of recent years.

Again we must discriminate. Kandinsky, who occupies in relation to modern painting an initiatory influence comparable to Joyce's in modern writing, has been grossly misunderstood. His principle that the work of art is an abstract expression of internal necessity has been applied without its corollary, which is, that what is necessary must also be significant to the spectator, must therefore be *composed* in a form that can be assimilated by the spectator. Kandinsky's final insistence is on composition – *melodic* composition and *symphonic* composition. Composition is defined as 'an expression of a slowly formed inner feeling, tested and worked over repeatedly and almost pedantically', and he looks forward, in the final paragraph of his pioneer work, *Concerning the Spiritual in Art,* to 'a time of reasoned and conscious composition, in which the painter will be proud to declare his work constructional – this in contrast to the claim of the impressionists that they could explain nothing, that their art came by inspiration'.[14]

No convincing classification of the painting and sculpture that has proliferated in Western Europe, the United States and Japan since the end of the Second World War is possible. Terms such as abstract impressionism or abstract expressionism are not distinctive enough; terms such as 'pop-art' or 'op-art' are inexact and unhistorical. It is a confused situation in which one is conscious of new sources of imagery and content, and of an almost desperate attempt to be tough or ambiguous. An English critic whom I greatly respect, David Thompson, writing in 1964 of the 'new generation' of British painters, uses these two words to explain the aesthetic aims and style of these artists, and defines toughness as 'a desire to play it cool, be objective, unsentimental, detached and at the same time to pull no punches, be firm, decisive, hard'. Ambiguity is defined as 'a common enough element in all modern art, though not with the new value set on puns, puzzles, and double meanings ... The ambiguity goes beyond the sort of vision that anthropomorphized landscapes. It is not the metaphor that equates two known images, so much as a central uncertainty that leaves interpretation open. And beyond that, it suggests wit, or a puzzle, or a game, as the only terms on which interpretation can rest.'[15]

[14] *Concerning the Spiritual in Art.* New York (Wittenborn), 1967, p. 77.
[15] David Thompson in the catalogue of 'The New Generation' Exhibition. London, Whitechapel Gallery, March-May, 1964, p. 8.

The parallel with the confused, spasmodic character of early Nordic art to which I have already compared the later writings of Joyce and Beckett will again be obvious. The same ambiguity prevails in both kinds of contemporary art. One of the English artists in the New Generation exhibition to which I have just referred, Paul Huxley, is quoted as saying that 'Paintings today should be about question-making, not story-telling ("it happened like this"), or recording ("I was there and it looked like this"). The sermon and the conducted tour have been dealt with and painting can only be enlightened by posing questions and making reconnaissance trips rather than supplying answers. We become more wise by not knowing.'

As a paradoxical, even a mystical saying, this is very interesting, but the alternatives implied – question-making or story-telling – evade the central issue in art, which is the creation of a symbolic form, the ability 'to idealize and to unify' the confusion of the world. Clarity, which I suggested as another essential quality in the work of art, is deliberately sacrificed. Again it is not a question of upholding traditional values against revolutionary values: it is a question of communication, of a dialogue between artist and spectator. If instead of a symbol of feeling the spectator is offered a gesture of nescience, of 'not Knowing', then he can only turn away in indifference.

In conclusion I return to my beginning, to Camus' plea for 'measure' or moderation, for the moderation created throughout history by rebellion. 'Moderation, born of rebellion, can only live by rebellion.' The artist, like any other citizen, must protest when political liberty is threatened or a censorship imposed on the freedom of thought. His moral behaviour is determined by the ancient precept: beauty is truth, truth beauty, though for 'beauty' we might now substitute another concept, such as unity. Beauty is not necessarily the aim of the contemporary artist. But if he substitutes another principle, such as vitality, he must still accept this other necessity, which I have called unity, the community that makes dialogue possible. Contemporary nihilism in art is simply a denial of art itself, a rejection of its social function. The refusal to recognize the limits of art is the reason why as critics we must withhold our approval from all those manifestations of permissiveness characterized by incoherence, insensibility, brutality and ironic detachment. The exercise of such judgement calls for the utmost critical rectitude – for the maintenance of the supremacy of aesthetic criteria – if we are not to fall into the old errors of judging art according to values that belong to another sphere of life – religious, moral, hedonistic or technological. What we seek is 'a renaissance beyond the limits of nihilism'. We cannot yet determine the outlines of such a renaissance, but we know that they must remain within the limits of art as I have defined them.

3 Paper Tygers

or, the circus animals' desertion in the
new pop poetry

IAN ROBINSON

'Surely,' remarked *The Times* (5 January 1969) 'all things considered, the situation is healthier now for modern poetry than it has
been for many years? A sickly, precious, minority art has been transformed into something robust and vigorous. The maker of verses
again has fire in his belly.' I have only one observation to make in
this essay, and it isn't very abstruse or difficult to establish. The
popular English verse of recent years has not transformed the
situation of English poetry except by replacing poetry with something that is not poetry; the new pop-poetry is moreover itself
academic, ill-written and lifeless; and *The Times*'s accolade (representative of the reaction of the establishment to pop poetry) is the
recognition of the success of a gang-movement. I shall go on to
explain why I choose to say such obvious things in public; but I
must first show that my opinion is true.[1]

Love, Love, Love never offers anything that lives up to the
title. It is, perhaps more surprisingly, also devoid of sexuality, as
I demonstrate in a related essay in my *Survival of English*.[2] Instead
of both, these verses all offer a nostalgic charmingness and pretti-
ness which would not have been out of place in pre-Victorian
Keepsakes and is as far from 'fire' or poetry as can be.

---

[1] I shall confine my discussion to: *Love, Love, Love*, ed. Pete Roche,
Corgi 1967; *Children of Albion, Poetry of the Underground in Britain*, edited
and extradicted [*sic*] by Michael Horovitz, Penguin 1969 (from which I quote
verses by Alan Jackson, Pete Roche, Ted Milton, Carole Senior, Geoff Hill,
Paul Evans, Heather Holden, Raymond Salter; John Arden, Pete Brown,
David Chaloner, Michael Horovitz, Mark Hyatt, Tom McGrath, Neil Oram,
Paul Potts and Nicholas Snowden Willey); and *The Mersey Sound*, Penguin
Modern Poets 10, Adrian Henri, Roger McGough, Brian Patten 1967, because
these are pre-eminently the texts which for present-day students are turning
'underground' into establishment.

[2] Cambridge University Press.

> They tell me you are wandering now
> With your eyes downcast and looking pale –
>   pale as a lily, someone said.

The someone who said so was surely the ghost of one of the lesser, more anaemic pre-Raphaelites. But even in later Victorian days verse could be the medium of something really recognizable as love, witness Christina Rossetti. I can't imagine love being created in any verse in any way connected with things like this:

You ask me for descriptions: hear this music.

> She is like the sorrow bird, taking
> All tomorrow's rain
> That I might see through windows to
> A starfall of tranquillity. She inhabits fawndreams,
> Speaks with birds for comfort. Like the walking wind etc. etc.

She inhabits, that is, the conventional Victorian dreamworld, and converses with anything but the real. It is all nice, sad, nostalgic.

> Really there is nothing to say.
> I have seen all that there is
> To be seen of you.

That first line rings true; but nothing will come of nothing: if the others are true as well, so much for love poetry. I stand by 'lifeless'.

Making love in these poems is somehow pre-human; it seems to leave the poets quite untouched. Sometimes it seems even pre-animal, taking us back to something more like Erasmus Darwin's *Loves of the Plants*:

> I will bring you flowers
> every morning for your breakfast
> and you will kiss me
> with flowers in your mouth
> and you will bring me flowers
> every morning when you wake
> and look at me with flowers in your eyes

How they thrive on the diet of flowers is not recorded. How nice, how vague it is – and utterly sexless. The daydreaming imagination seems not to have altered in a hundred years, except to have become more attenuated and feeble.

What the writers of *Love, Love, Love* never do is create their love there on the page. And if it isn't there for us to read, what happens in these writers' bellies is of no consequence except to them. I know,

for instance, that Shakespeare's feeling for the beautiful young
man was love (and love not of a person but of a young man's beauty
in his 'golden time', generalized into a love of beauty) just because
it is unmistakably there in the sonnets. Sonnet XXXII is deeply
witty, its humility about 'these poor rude lines' following on with
a certain arrogant irony from the splendid assertions in XVIII
and XIX of the poet's power to immortalize love, yet the closing
couplet is quite right to say that the reason for reading this poet is
'for his love' not his style:

> But since he died, and poets better prove,
> Theirs for their style I'll read, his for his love.

Though it's equally true that we only know his love through the
power of his style to create it, there in the reading, in the movement of the lines. And, obviously enough, it is this presence of
love in poetry that makes love poetry.

But if there ever was any fire in the bellies of the writers of
Love, Love, Love it evaporated *en route* to the printed page.

Perhaps *The Times* meant the Children of Albion. *The Times*
has certainly done its bit in recent years, anyway, towards turning
their 'underground' into an academic establishment, and recognizes *Oz* and all that genus as 'the alternative press'. All well and
good if *The Times* is right about the quality of the new poets'
work.

Actually what strikes one (if that is the word) about almost every
set of verses in the collection is its absolute lack of a *raison d'être*.
A couple of the editor's pieces may show what I mean, for he is,
quite rightly, more than a match for any of his contributors in this
essential quality of the collection, which is, simply, inanity. The
understanding of his more complicated poems is the peeling off of
layers of inanity to reveal an inane core. Here is one of his complete poems:

> World's End – Happening –
>
> ...Dancing   upstairs
> 'thinking' about   'my' penguin
> – nearly trod
>   on – the cats!

I offer to the compilers of future school editions the note that
his penguin is *Children of Albion*, the World's End is a pub in
Chelsea and the cats, presumably, a pop group. I don't think this
academic or allusive level makes the poem less inane than the
surface level. At least the first set of inverted commas is convincing.
Elsewhere the inanity is, so far as I can see, pure and simple:

Memo

(from Wm Blake
to sundry psychedelinquent whizz kids
assuming his name in vain):

Stop bleating
about the bush
little lambs
Get wean'd
Or get   stufft

(in some body
else's   pram – –

The moral seems to be that only the editor or his licentiates are
permitted to take Blake's name in vain and bleat about the bush.

Here's another complete poem by another poet:

Road

They tore up the old road
and buried it under a new one.
I didn't mind

Fair enough, dear boy, why should you? But was it really enough
to set the keyboard a-tapping, the postman knocking, Mr Horovitz
'thinking', Penguins approving, compositors setting, and printers
running off forty thousand copies? These poets are quite without
the sense that some things might be better worth saying than
others. But they will say their inane informal nothings nonetheless.

I meant literally my assertion that whatever they may be, the
products of the Children of Albion are not poetry; for poetry as
we know it in English is something we read. The new poetry is
quite explicitly not something to be read. Mr Horovitz is able to
quote the approval of the *Times Literary Supplement* for what
amounts to an abandonment of literature. 'There is a nucleus of
poets,' said the *TLS*, 'who are starting to treat the writing and the
delivery of a poem as two stages in a single process ... The actual
presence of an audience, provided it is alert and responsive, forces
the poet-reader to take greater care about the meaning of his words,
while a reasonably strong formal pattern is almost essential.' But
in the absence of an audience, just reading the book, it is painfully
clear that the idea of *verse* is almost lost in the Children of Albion.
It doesn't follow, as they seem to assume, that if a poet intends his
work to be read aloud he leaves all the work of shaping and stressing
to the performer. Shakespeare, after all, wrote verse for public
performance, but the good actor gets out of the verse what is
demonstrably written into it – the demonstration being the con-

vincing performance which isn't simply the actor's invention. Or, to mention the yet plainer case, Mozart too wrote for performance, but not for whatever the performer chose to make of the work. In the Children of Albion performance is an escape from the demand that they express themselves in writing, as I must show.

The poets are printed in alphabetical order and so the first is John Arden (who also is amongst the oldest,[3] being now over forty). The difference between Mr Arden's work and what follows is the difference between a writer, whose meaning comes out of the reading of his lines, and what in Bergman credits they call a skript-girl, someone providing performance-fodder.

> John paddles up and down the long brown street
> On two brown boats which are his two flat feet
> And London houses blink at him and whisper:
> 'Whose are those spectacles, whose is that thin whisker?
> Is he to be one who sees us as we are,
> Stock-brick and concrete, mortar and tar,
> Sees how we squat above an old green field
> To choke its life? We are the iron shield
> Screwed tight upon the buried face below:
> John Arden sees us: we see him: we know.'

It would be an elementary exercise to show how the strength of that writing comes out in diction, rhythm, imagery – to show, that is, that the writer commands the medium. But it is almost literally true to say that the other Children of Albion, almost to a child, can't write. What would it mean to speak of *reading* this? – and if not read it what are we supposed to do with it in a book?

> days
> > long with fern shoots
>
> > we embrace by
> > streams
> whose secrets educate
> > > the
> > pebbles
> > > banks necklaced
> with hanging roots
> > rinsed by waters
> flow
> > in this tranquillity
> > We hold allegiance
> to no one

[3] Paul Potts is listed as *b.* 1911 and links the youngsters with the Georgians they so much resemble: '... When I saw a lark fly through the air, I thought of a rainbow playing on your hair. For you walk the way an angel plays a lyre.' etc.

> our ears ripe
> for the streams
> wisdom

What could that lay-out do? What happens in fact is that in
order to read we translate it into a sort of flabbily rhythmic prose
(which raises some difficulties that the poet, performing, need not
face – where to put the stops and apostrophes, for instance). If
one transcribes the second section of that poem, its real nature as
'prose-poem' of the most traditional and vacuous kind is revealed:

> Don't misunderstand me. It's not your beautiful, pear-shaped breasts,
> or thighs soft as moss, pale as a winter moon, or lips red and moist
> like wild berries, or belly scented with roses, or hands mobile as a
> flight of doves, or the dark chamber of your sex. I hardly notice. Let's
> be friends.

I can't help noticing again that the failure of expression fits the
lack of emotion. But if we hardly notice anything, why bother (of
all things) to write about it?

The writing out as prose also shows another not accidental
affinity – with the language of one sort of advertising, the style used
to sell, for instance, soft feminine soaps and virility-inducing
cigarettes. But again I am imagining performance on the television: advertising-copy for a magazine would be less sloppy and
would be readable:

> Eyes that smile and dance...
> Eyes that cry and sigh...
> Eyes that tell, and eyes that never do...
> Newborn eyes, worldly eyes,
>   wicked eyes, winsome eyes...
>
> *—Max Factor*

Mr Factor's poem is much better than most of the Children of
Albion's: the underground mirrors the establishment but is
deprived of the tautening effects of market discipline. (It makes
its money otherwise.) This is a sort of explanation, but to offer a
raison d'être for my next quotation were beyond antiquarism:

> ineffectual posters revealing
> sunny southsea , brighton , eastbourne ,
> or where ever , a guise
> I never witnessed:
> beauties smiling down
>   onto the perfunctory
> soullness , platform:
>   here I waited an hour
>   eating cheese

So what? The sheer inanity of the results of this abandonment of expression has to be seen (not heard) to be credited:

> maybe if Johnson had Sukarno's
>   women ... maybe that is
> the Asian threat ... the South
> all over again ... the Indonesian
> will take our women ... the evidence
> the evidence,
> hear it out there,
> the African birds are squawking,
> climate changing, the wind etc.

In a preface the writer explains how his words came to be so inconsequential, but I don't understand why he thinks that a sufficient apology for publishing them:

This poem was set in motion by a strange mixture of informations: there was the revulsion I felt at the Vietnam war scene and the admiration I felt for Sukarno's concept of the New Emerging Forces. Mal Caldwell, a learned, hairy Scotsman, had just returned from Indonesia. He said that there was an air of expectancy, an idea of future, about that country, despite its faults, which was terribly absent in England. Just at that time, though, Sukarno was denouncing jazz and the Beatles. I didn't go for that much. [etc., as he says, etc.]

The preface ends: '*This poem was first read at the Albert Hall reading, June 1965. At this point you begin to listen.*' Not, that is, to read.

It follows that if writers are to 'meet the people' (paid for, of course, by you and me through the Arts Council) they must do so in person, not by writing books.

Informality is the main thing: there are no set speeches, no written questions, just thoughts and ideas tossed back and forth, with a glass of wine or cup of coffee introduced at the right moment to restore dry throats. The rows of books could not have formed a more fitting backcloth.[4]

What this has to do with art is anybody's guess, also why the books were there even in the background, for this sort of event aims to supersede the book. I really believe the Arts Council would do more for British culture by subsidizing real circuses, which are at least entertaining and depend upon rare skills; and I make another obvious but not uncalled-for remark: the great poets even

4 *The Times*, 6 May 1971.

of our century have generally published books not gramophone records.

Now it may be that, as in the case of the pop groups, any possible life in the work of the Children of Albion comes out in the performance, not in reading the text, and that the publication of these verses is as odd as it would be for pop groups to publish scores instead of discs. I concede the possibility that the performance at the Albert Hall did express a kind of poetic life, though I'm bound also to say that on the evidence of the two happenings I went to I think it unlikely. But if the poetry is in the performance, that only confirms my observation that any life is extraneous to the text, that these people are not like a playwright giving an actor something to perform, but are themselves performers improvising from something more like programme notes. Perhaps something interesting occasionally happens during the improvisations, but whatever it is it can't be poetry as that word is understood in the light of the English poets.

So it is not really surprising that, in the absence of art and poetry, what gets expressed by the Children of Albion is a sentimentality just the same as *Love, Love, Love*'s even when the contributors are different.

Beautiful

Shes beautiful I suppose
I see her every evening
we pass each other on the cliff
she says nothing
and I say nothing
and she does not come from the Sea
She comes from Bristol

That must surely be inanity aiming at emotion and, having missed, satisfying itself with the sentiment of feeble humour? But this one is sentiment *tout court* except that it's at considerable length:

Bright High Lay

It is autumn in the garden. The leaves are falling. My hand grows old. My heart is wind-swept snow. O! ! ! I enter. Alone. Listen... snow falling? I am here again. Listen ... singing? It is always beginning. The wound of awakening dissolves in the violet kiss of eternity. The clouds are far below, all is still within the flower. What is night like from above? Lying in a jewel of light. The stars are fierce. The earth is listening to the endless dancing snow. The earth dissolves in the listening. The snow is light. The perfume heart. The celestial ache. The burning liquid-fire, called flesh, is the loom. The only thread is love, is love.

Is it really? *L'amor che muove il sole e l'altre stelle*, for instance? In his next effort the poet claims to have found the 'LIVING TRUTH that's veiled by literature'. It turns out to be 'WE ARE and all IS'. One doubts both: isn't LIVING TRUTH in letter-spaced small capitals as effective a veil as literature? Isn't it in fact the same one, minus whatever gives literature the chance to live and remove veils?

And so to Mr Adrian Henri. He seems to be the pop-poetry movement's attempt to throw up a great poet. And he does stand out of the ruck in that the tone I have mentioned as characteristic of the whole group, a wistful nostalgic charmingness, has become explicit and insistent in his work, full blown into an aggressive sentimentality.

> And somewhere
> it will always be Whitsun and summer
> with sandals to keep the rain from your sunburnt feet
> And you will have just given me a bunch of artificial flowers
> lilies-of-the-valley made of cloth with stiff glossy leaves
> And turn and wave goodbye smiling
> hair over your eyes caught in sunlight by the windowframe
> ... Remember?

Much have I travelled in the realms of gold, and on first looking into Mr Henri's verses, 'Surely,' I thought, 'he is pulling our legs and this is all malevolently ironical.' He has a joky style which he mixes up with the sentiment:

> A year ago
> You planted lilies in the valley of my mind
> There were lilies at the bottom of my garden
> And ferrys at the bottom of my street.

He even sometimes prints the jokes on their own, as if on match-boxes:

> *Song for a Beautiful Girl Petrol-Pump Attendant on the Motorway*
>
> I wanted your soft verges
> But you gave me the hard shoulder.

But the centre is straight sentimentality. And a very soft centre it is.

Mr Henri's work is also as formless as anyone else's we have considered. 'Tonight at Noon' is a list of marvellous and impossible happenings (leading up to the miracle of her telling him she loves

him) which reads like jottings from a notebook. Some are entertaining, but there is absolutely no reason why there shouldn't be
five times as many, or a fifth. *Ditto* 'Without You'.

As for 'academic', Mr Henri and the Children of Albion have
a different store of common allusion but are as literary as the
writers of *New Lines*. Adrian Henri lists his heroes in 'Me': they
are a sort of heterogeneous mass, yoked senselessly together, the
characteristic lumber of an academic poet's mind. The Children of
Albion often people their *musée imaginaire* from the jazz world
('*I don't suppose I need to explain who Bird Parker was*') or from
books they read in different states of childhood (Adrian Mitchell
has a rather nice pastiche of Villon in which the vanished kings
are replaced by boys' comics) or adolescence (St-Exupéry crops up –
he was a set-text for my 'A' level French, too); but it's not less an
academic universe for that. They use words like 'eleemosynary',
'leucotomized' and 'paraplegic' and play word games of an irritatingly academic kind. Mr Henri is one of the worst in the last
category: one piece is described in a note as 'Cut-up of John Milton
Sonnet XV [the name of which he gets wrong]/*TV Times*/CND
leaflet' which makes less sense than any of the components
individually.

The Children of Albion have a certain importance in history,
though not the history of English poetry, in their deliberate attempt
to take over English literature and assimilate it to pop performance.
This is explicit, as far as anything can be called explicit, in the
editor's 'afterwords' politely called by the blurb 'a Blakean cornu-
copia'. What is to do the taking over also becomes clear.

> Several of the younger poets are clearer spokesmen than the groups
> (& stay ahead – beyond numbers) for the mixed multitudes who are
> presently animating, intermingling and loosening the perimeter
> divisions between poetry – jazz – blues – raga & modern classical
> music in the new solar sound-systems of beat caverns, pop charts and
> psychedelic 'trips'. Their poems, with the more worthwhile hits, are
> truly popular songs . . .

So they took over, as a first step, the Albert Hall and, as *The
Times* said, 'at that point poetry again became one of the popular
arts'. 'What did happen [says Mr Horovitz] – for whoever suspended disbelief – is that poem after poem resonated mind-expand-
ing ripples of empathy – uncut and precious stones in a translucent
pool.' The relation of the uncut stones to English literature is
exemplified by a poem 'instead of programme notes' which ten
of the children improvised the night before, 'prefaced by six lines
from "Jerusalem" (for the initial moving spirit of our cooperative

was the transmission, through Ginsberg, of the heritance of Blake)'.
It is stylistically, I am afraid, rather apparent where Blake leaves
off and the Children of Albion begin:

> And now the time returns again:
>   Our souls exult, & London's towers
> Receive the Lamb of God to dwell
>   In England's green and pleasant bowers.

> World declaration hot peace shower! Earth's grass is
> free! Cosmic poetry Visitation accidentally happening
> carnally! Spontaneous plant-chant Carnival! Mental
> Cosmonaut poet-epiphany, immaculate supranational
> Poesy insemination!

And so on for an indefinite number of lines or until you run out
of breath. I think the word for it is 'logorrhoea'. The flood ceases
to pour with the lines

>   You are not alone!
> Miraculous assumption! O sacred heart invisible
> insurrection! Albion! awake! awake! awake! O
> shameless bandwagon! [sic!] Self-evident for real naked
> come the Words! Global synthesis habitual for this
> Eternity! Nobody's Crazy Immortals Forever!

The first four lines were Blake, the rest, presumably, the transmission through Ginsberg. The editor comments: 'Amazingly –
and amazed – I felt we lived up to this high-sounding prologue,
with a sacramental jubilee that uncovered an ideal america –
united states of being'. Indeed, indeed they did: but I can't see
that they wrote any poetry. Poetry? Fire in the Belly? Noise as of
a successful pop group, more like. O/shameless bandwagon indeed!

All art, said Pater, aspires to the condition of music. Modern
pop poetry does, anyway; it aspires to the condition of the pop
music which spearheaded the advance of the new pop culture in
the sixties. Ginsberg, Mr Horovitz's presiding influence, went on
record during the period as believing that 'Liverpool is at the
present moment the centre of the consciousness of the human
universe'.

Now English poetry has been a law unto itself for a long time,
and it is not encouraging to find it taking its standards from a sister
art. But when the sister art reaches its apotheosis in the songs of the
Beatles, what is one to say?

Actually what influenced the Children of Albion wasn't the
Beatles, who did in their way produce some genuine popular
music, but something simpler. The real development in the pop

music of the sixties was, suitably enough, technical: in the early
years of the decade it suddenly became fashionable for popular
music to be played, with electronic help, louder than any previous
music in the history of mankind, with the possible exception of
Edwardian steam-organs. (And nobody thought of playing the latter
indoors.) Pop groups' decibel-level has to be heard to be believed.
And this, simply *noise*, the fact that you can attract attention if you
are loud enough, is the great fact behind the robust and vigorous
new verse. But the attention attracted cannot be the attention in
which music or poetry lives. The din of the pop groups drives out
the inner re-creation which *is* music, by a sheer assault on the
sense of hearing. It is a rape of the musical sense. Just so are the
Albert Hall and other happenings an assault on the possibility of
poetry.

> When the place couldn't hold no more the duke he quit tending
> door and went around the back way and come onto the stage and
> stood up before the curtain and made a little speech, and praised
> up this tragedy, and said it was the most thrilling one that ever was;
> and so he went on a-bragging about the tragedy, and about Edmund
> Kean the Elder, which was to play the main principal part in it;
> and at last when he'd got everybody's expectations up high enough,
> he rolled up the curtain, and the next minute the king come a-pranc-
> ing out on all fours, naked; and he was painted all over, ring-streaked-
> and-striped, all sorts of colours, as splendid as a rainbow. And – but
> never mind the rest of his outfit; it was just wild, but it was awful
> funny. The people most killed themselves laughing; and when the
> king got done capering and capered off behind the scenes, they roared
> and clapped and stormed and haw-hawed till he come back and done
> it over again, and after that they made him do it another time. Well,
> it would make a cow laugh to see the shines that old idiot cut.

The main difference from the Children of Albion in the Albert
Hall is that the audience in *Huckleberry Finn* knew first that the
performance was funny and secondly that they had been sold. The
king and the duke knew what they were doing, too, though they
made less by it than our sincere modern circus-artists. *The Times's*
'fire in the belly' is therefore sentimentality plus noise.
      The only defence against this takeover of English poetry by pop
performance is criticism, the possibility of seeing things as they
really are. That, in the end, is why I found it worth saying that the
Children of Albion are not poets. It is necessary to defend the idea
of poetry in our common language.
      It is not unknown for cliques to seize the rather small world of
English letters. F. R. Leavis was indignant with Eliot's *Criterion*

in the thirties for capitulating to the gang of young writers round Auden who came up from Oxford to take over the metropolitan literary world and make it safe for Marxism. But they were at least men of some not altogether negligible talent, and literate. Mr Horovitz's horde has no talent except for organization, which I do grant them.[5] Mr Horovitz is very insistent on his status as underground leader, but his underground is at least as much as Auden's itching to become the establishment, and well-equipped (with the encouragement of the Arts Council, the *Guardian*, *The Times*, the *TLS* and so on) to achieve its end quickly and smoothly. How long will it be before this tosh is examined at 'A' level as if it were English poetry? That sort of possibility indicates the need to recognize the Children of Albion for what they are; for after a certain point the momentum of the shameless bandwagon becomes irreversible.[6]

The 'transmission' of Blake has created verses without feeling, discipline, or the possibility of criticizing life. Unless that is firmly recognized there will be no chance, in the language of the most wonderful literature in the world, either of new poetry or of possessing the poetry we have. If the Children of Albion do succeed in abolishing the critical petty fogs and imposing themselves comfortably as the radiant new dawn, if they succeed in becoming contemporary English literature (though the term will presumably fall into disuse) that will be the end of our poetry past and present, and of the guarantee it has offered to so many generations of English people that passion and imaginative thought are possible in the life of our language. For they are not possible in the language of Mr Horovitz.

[5] I saw one of Mr Horovitz's well-drafted press-releases, in which, after describing his recent achievements as 'transfusions lighting the island climate's emergence from critical petty fogs to a radiant new Jerusalem dawn for poesy' he lists his recent publications, 'plus 4 new books out in 1971 ... please contact for bookings ...'

[6] Cf. for instance these recent words of an influential 'underground' figure: 'Who would think 10 years ago that the very rebellious Mike Horovitz would be let loose by Penguin inside a 400 page anthology. Perhaps *Children of Albion* ... and numerous others prove that the content of the little mags is not insignificant.' (Peter Finch in the *Arlis* Newsletter, very influential in the genesis of librarians' buying-orders.) Yes, that's the logic.

4 Ted Hughes's 'Crow' and the Longing for Non-Being[1]

DAVID HOLBROOK

A friend writes, 'the only way to overcome nihilism is by creativity'. I wonder. Wherever one turns, there is grossness and coarseness, gnawing away at the very texture of our life-lines.

Ted Hughes's *Crow* takes this nihilism into the heart of 'minority' poetic taste. The first thing we notice is the coarse brutality of the language: 'Do not chop his winkle off', 'you murderous little sod', 'the sphinx will bite your bollocks off', 'you'd treat me like a turd'. There is a raucous anecdotal tone throughout, as of the commercial traveller's tale: 'There was this man', 'There was a boy', 'There was this terrific battle', 'There was this hidden grin', 'There was a man', 'so finally there was nothing'. There is a related casualness, as of a cosmic shaggy dog story, which yet asserts its own 'profundity': 'beat the hell out of it and ate it', 'like somebody the police have come for', 'luckily his camera worked OK', 'they got so far into each other they forgot/Each other completely that was OK'.

Then there is the fashionable Sunday newspaper preoccupation with the Ecocatastrophe. I don't say there are no problems of the environment, population and pollution. But today there is a Borrioboola-Ghanian charity by which we concern ourselves with such things as the 'population explosion' and the 'biological time bomb' if these are far away enough – while continuing to enjoy the trendy barbarities and pollutions of the psychic atmosphere at home which are more menacing. This kind of fashion in causes belongs more to the Sunday colour supplements rather than science or serious biology of ultimate concern. In *Fragment of an Ancient Tablet* the woman's face displays 'many a painful frown' – her belly is the 'ticking bomb of the future'. The future, that is, is menacing and this is linked by the same sensational language to

[1] The author and the editor would like the reader to know that the above essay has been severely cut against their wishes.

the fashion for preoccupation not only with genitals, blood and penetration, but with these as a desperate manifestation of fear of the future: a desperation which seems to justify, rather than condemn, today's sensual nihilisms. It would seem to be the female element itself as the embodiment of creativity that becomes a particular target: 'beard between thighs', 'belly with its blood-knot', 'gouts of blood and babies'.

'Unspeakable guts', 'messy blood', 'dragged under by the weight of his guts', 'smashed into the rubbish of the ground', 'brains incinerating', 'loop of his blood like a garotte' – after so many words thrusting on us guts, blood, impossible pain, distortion, dismemberment, and vile images of the inside of the body, nothing is left but a mental rage, that is encapsulated within itself. Max Stirner, the German nihilist, declared that the world was nothing, and he was nothing – so, the only posture towards the world was that 'the other' and the world were – 'my food'. There is nothing in *Crow* for which to have respect or for which to feel care or concern: it belongs to the 'racking moment' of smashing everything to pieces: in one's head, at least. There is no one to whom to render account: there is no respect for 'community'. Today our culture is nihilistic in this Stirnerean way – with no social or personal goals in view.

But then the mental rage becomes boring. At first perhaps stunned, shocked, dismayed, upset, we quickly sink to a state of apathy and spiritlessness – which is, in fact, the effect today at large of so much sensational culture. The political consequences are disastrous. We cease to care: and this means we cease to care either for human beings, for 'community' – or for poetry. We become disgusted, and what we are disgusted with is not only the humanness that is being attacked – but poetry, the theatre, film, the novel, themselves. For we go to the arts, in trust, expecting that we will be given something to take into our inner dynamics to our benefit – to help us find meaning. Instead, we are raped.

The problem over *Crow* is the more grave because this poet is a serious and responsible writer. Writing in *Children's Literature in Education* on 'Myth and Education' in March 1970 Ted Hughes said:

We can't ignore that when we read a story, and enter it in a com-pletely imaginative way, the story works on all parts of our nature, and it's impossible to know finally what the influences are.

.... If you are to think of imaginative literature as an educational tool you are finally up against the fact that imaginative literature is therapeutic and does have a magical effect on people's minds and their ultimate behaviour. This is the appeal of great works of imaginative literature to us as adults, that they are hospitals where we heal, where our imaginations are healed, that when they are evil works they are also battlefields where we get injured....

Hughes believes, evidently, that literature has an effect on attitudes to life and behaviour at the deepest level. And he believes that there can be a damaging effect, from literature, on our souls. What is the effect of his own *Crow*?

The first point to make is that *Crow* places a crude barrier between ourselves and the creative poetry of Ted Hughes. It erodes the fastidiousness of genuine art. Fastidiousness is the mark of some of Ted Hughes's early work. In *Wodwo*, for instance, he ends still searching for the humanness he cannot find in himself, and he is comically modest about the hope of ever finding it:

> What am I? Nosing here, turning leaves over....
> ...again very queer but I'll go on looking ....

But he is still content to be modest in a delicate quest for answers to the question, 'What is it to be human?' In *Full Moon and Little Frieda* our attention is riveted by the exactness of the words to small, delicate moments in experience:

> A cool small evening shrunk to a dog bark and the
> clank of a bucket –
>
> And you listening.
> A spider's web, tense for the dew's touch.
> A pail lifted, still and brimming – mirror
> To tempt a first star to a tremor.

Here the mirror of the bucket's surface is a commonplace object which is yet touched by meaning. A version of the reflecting mother in domesticity, it is a symbol of female element capacities *to be* – still and brimming – and *seductive*. The seductiveness has the gentle quality of tenderness that can 'tempt a first star to a tremor'. In the farmyard, near the river of blood of the cows (which are 'balancing unspilled milk') the girl child is reflected upon as a female creature. She has within her the capacities to reflect, and so, like the surface of the shivering water in the bucket, as it is lifted, she can call out a 'first star' by 'tempting'. She *creates* a new moment in existence. The new star is the first one to appear in the evening, and it is a symbol of the first lover to be called shyly out by the little girl's capacities for 'encounter'. To call out stars by the power of 'encounter' is also to call out meaning – and here, in this delicate poem of understatement, the universe has meaning *because a child is looking at it.* There, in the heavens, is the moon-mother, which is so humanized as to be looking back at the child which the universe has created:

> 'Moon!' you cry suddenly, 'Moon! Moon!'

The *word* here is not malevolent (as words are at times in *Crow*) but creative: it intends the perceived moon, and creates it, placing it in the heavens:

> The moon has stepped back like an artist
>   gazing amazed at a work
> That points at him amazed ...

In such a poem we have great strength – the strength of true creativity. The creativity is rooted in love, and the recognition of love: words and perceptions go out like a 'shaft of attention' (Husserl) to *make* reality and truth.

Such fastidious attention to the true nature of human existence would, however, seem 'pallid and artificial' beside the falsifications and exaggerations of *Crow.*

In the volume *Wodwo* we catch a glimpse of the pseudo-male protagonist of *Crow* – the imposture of 'masculine protest': the horseman whose mount is shod with 'vaginas of iron'. He gallops on towards the harsh treatment of the rows of vaginas in *The Battle of Osfrontalis*, in *Crow.* To him femininity must be suppressed or merely used: as to Stirner, the 'other' is merely for use, functions and organs. But this black figure is also galloping away in terror from the 'female element' so creatively perceived in *Full Moon and Little Frieda.* So we cross a gulf from one book to the other, from a perception of the creativity of a child's human vision, to a coarse hysteria, which offers us a vilification of human 'meeting' in the language of the gutter press:

> Horrors – hairy and slobbery, glossy and raw ...

How did Ted Hughes cross this gulf between his earlier works and *Crow*? It is possible that the influence of critics like Alvarez had something to do with it. Alvarez had a clear idea of how poetry *must* develop – towards more nihilism, imbalance and hate:

> The movement of the modern arts has been to press deeper and
> deeper into the subterranean world of psychic isolation, to live out
> in the arts the personal extremism of breakdown, paranoia, and
> depression ... The modern artist seems to create his sickness in his
> work giving himself over to it for the sake of the range and intensity

of his art. He cultivates not his own garden, but his psychosis, or
at the very least his psychopathic tendencies.

Encounter, 1965

When it comes to Ted Hughes, what Alvarez applauded was the
powerful violence he 'unleashed' in himself:

> Even an Englishman like Ted Hughes, who starts out as a nature
> poet and whose work contains more animals than the London zoo,
> lavishes all that loving, sharp detail on his menagerie only for what-
> ever corresponding sense of unpredictable violence he finds in him-
> self. He writes as a nature poet gone blind....

There is an underlying and pessimistic model of human nature,
by which man is a victim, a thing, a product of natural laws, and,
in a universe which will pass away and is anyway subject to
universal entropy, he is only a futile organism:

> little boneless little skinless
> Ploughing with a linnet's carcase
> Reaping the wind and threshing the stones...

All effort is futile and puny, bringing no harvest, because of death
and the ultimate running down of the world. Our futile pulsing
is at one with all life in the animals:

> drumming in a cow's skull,
> Dancing with a gnat's feet
> With an elephant's nose with a crocodile's tail.

All these shapes are but version of the random trials of evolution:
the picture of life in the universe behind *Littleblood* is a deter-
ministic, pessimistic one, belonging to biology before neo-
Darwinism. It takes no account of later thinking or even of
Lamarck. It has certainly not advanced to the philosophical biology
of Adolf Portmann and Helmut Plessner – which recognizes levels
of being, and in human being the emergence of consciousness as a
manifestation of a complexity that seems to be seeking to develop
itself.

Consciousness is merely a burden:

> Grown so wise grown so terrible
> Sucking death's mouldy tits.

It is 'wounded by stars' because the universe seems so indifferent
and meaningless: it is menaced by the 'leaking shadow/eating the
medical earth' – by universal entropy, darkness seems to be eating
the earth, as if it were a medical case bleeding to death.

The universe is nothing but a herding of meaningless nothings:

Crow saw the herded mountains, steaming in the morning.
And he saw the sea,
Dark-spined, with the whole earth in its coils...

The stars are 'mushrooms of the nothing forest' – little pulses that spring up in a vast emptiness, 'the virus of God'.

And he shivered with the horror of Creation...

But this phrase the 'horror of Creation' coarsely begs the questions behind the particular gesture Ted Hughes adopts. We may I believe refer, in deploring this crude phrase, to a philosophical position from which to reject the nihilism of *Crow*. *Crow* may be said to originate in a pessimistic passivity – a state of 'letting the world shove its meaning down on us' as Roger Poole puts it. It is possible (as Poole shows in *Towards Deep Subjectivity*) to believe that the cosmos invites from us an impulse to confront it, in order to discover and embrace the truth of its nature and origins, from the consciousness (like Little Frieda's) that can give it meaning from the mind which emerged from it. Thus it can be seen as a reality which gains its significance (as Lewis Mumford says) from our capacity to *see* the universe and comprehend it even if we do not understand it. The universe is only of significance because man perceives it, and seeks to give it meaning. Without that light, it is nothing:

> For man to feel belittled, as so many do now, by the vastness of the universe or the interminable corridors of time is precisely like his being frightened by his own shadow. It is only through the light of consciousness that the universe becomes visible, and should that light disappear, only nothingness would remain. Except on the lighted stage of human consciousness the mighty cosmos is but a mindless nonentity. Only through human words and symbols register- ing human thought, can the universe disclosed by astronomy be rescued from its everlasting vacuity. Without that lighted stage, without the human drama played upon it, the whole theatre of the heavens, which so deeply moves the human soul, exalting and dis- maying it, would dissolve again into its own existential nothingness, like Prospero's dreamworld.[2]

And so, too, with time and mortality, which are so triumphant in *Crow*. They too can enhance our freedom. As Frankl says:

> Temporality is ... not only an essential characteristic of human life, but also a real fact in its meaningfulness. The meaning of human life is based upon its irreversible quality. An individual's responsi- bility in life must therefore be understood in terms of temporality and singularity...

The Doctor and the Soul

[2] *The Myth of the Machine*, Lewis Mumford p. 33

We are on the threshold of a new view which both finds the complexity and the mystery – but also finds man at home in the universe. From a combination of the new perspectives of philosophical biology and the new existentialism, we need to develop today a more creative sense of the relation of man to this vastness he perceives – creative in the sense that it is both more responsible and has intentionality. In Husserl's conception of how we perceive by that 'shaft of attention', we can find the capacity to see a meaningful world which transcends the limitation of 'objectivity', that has failed to take into account the subjective realities of the being who *sees*.

The creative writer can only find his freedom if he finds this view, that gives point to his creative effort. This is not to demand anthropocentricity – but to demand a greater awe, that is capable of tasting the immense responsibilities loaded upon man by his role as the seer of what otherwise would be unseen, and his capacity, through consciousness, to search for some understanding of the potentiality in matter that he represents. This, again, raises immense problems of the nature of knowledge itself, as Leavis has pointed out, discussing Blake:

> His compellingly presented conception of an ultimate human responsibility ... recommends itself peculiarly to our needs at this crisis of human history...

Any corruption of our attitudes here jeopardizes survival. As Leavis goes on:

> ...what human creativity *has* created and continually recreates in response to change, in the human world, and it entails of its very nature the recognition that (in Collingwood's words) it 'must ultimately depend for its existence on something other than itself.'[3]

Crow renounces this creativity, and concomitant responsibility. His Creation is not only a reality to be regarded with horror; it is a hallucination:

> In the hallucination of the horror
> He saw this shoe, with no sole, rain-sodden,
> Lying on a moor.
> And there was this garbage can, bottom rusted away,
> A playing place for the wind, in a waste of puddles...

This is man, as seen in the opening sketch of the American *Oh Calcutta!* – by Samuel Beckett – a Nothing lying among garbage. What Crow sees is all there is: there is no denying it.

[3] *The Human World*, no 7. p. 63.

Crow blinked. He blinked. Nothing faded.
He stared at the evidence.
Nothing escaped him. (Nothing could escape.)

While posturing as 'the contender', Hughes also tries to lock us
in the reductionist vision of man, as seen by the ironical (and
'realistic') Crow. No one can escape from their state in existence:
nothing *must* escape our objective view of this. Crow lets none of
this reality escape his ironical penetration. Blink as Crow will, the
truth will not be dispersed. Nothing can escape the prison of the
'objective' view – or must be allowed to.

The world only 'is' – there are no levels of being; there is no
transcendence of the weight of one's guts – there is no meaning and
there are no values. The message of Samuel Beckett's cult of
inanition has sunk dismally home – so that Ted Hughes himself
is 'seen' by 'God's nightmare', Crow – in *Crow Alights* – as a
nothing.

Any attempt to recover from trash is caricatured:

> When God, disgusted with man,
> Turned towards heaven.
> And man, disgusted with God,
> Turned towards Eve,
> Things looked like falling apart.

> But Crow   Crow
> Crow nailed them together,

>   heaven and earth creaked at the joint
> Which became gangrenous and stank ...

> Crow
> grinned
> Crying: 'This is my Creation',
> Flying the black flag of himself.

Crow is the only alternative – the embodiment of egoistical
nihilism. At the Crucifixion, Crow 'starts in on the two thieves':
when there is a battle, Crow 'has to start looking for something to
eat'. He may weep, but in spite of himself he must stab at living
substance and eat it: out of this ingestion

>   Came the eye's
>   roundness
>   the ear's
>   deafness.

Not only, as in *Littlesoul*, is Hughes's Crow living and breathing in spite of himself. He must endure the anguish of being aware of the way in which living things must consume others – while at the same time being aware of his own consuming need for others (his dependence) and his need for meaning. Yet he has from time to time a dreadful apprehension of the eye that must and does see – and yet sees no meaning: the ear that hears, and yet is deaf: 'life without feeling alive', as Laing puts it.

So, in *Crow*, the breakdown of poetic language is at one with the failure of perception, and this in turn is due to a loss of confidence in the delicate web of 'encounter' between human beings, and also in all the female elements of being that belong to 'encounter'.

In *Crow*, for instance, sexual relationships are reduced to grotesque acts of meaningless violence, in which every word is exploited for the juice of repulsiveness, or hate, which it can yield ('sniff ... fasten ...'). Primitive schizoid fears of mutual incorporation are exploited, so that (as often) under the 'excuse' of a reference to the nuclear bomb, there can be an 'acting out' indulgence in a primitive vision of the Primal Scene (i.e. sadistic parental intercourse).

> They sniff towards each other in the emptiness.
>
> They fasten together. They seem to be eating each other.
>
> But they are not eating each other.

This is a regression to the infant's primitive fears that sex is a mutual eating that brings threats of annihilation. There is no reference to love – the humanizing force that ameliorates such fears in all of us:

> They have begun to dance a strange dance ...

This meaningless act, taking place between two ghastly creatures, done 'without guest or God', is the only gesture in *Crow* towards survival. If man is to survive, he can only do so as a monstrous mutation who has no consciousness of his own sexuality, no capacity for choice, but is simply at the mercy of uneducable and blind instinctual drives. This survival is one which is only to be seen, cynically, as the futile but determined proliferation of monstrosities. Hughes is bitterly ironic:

> And this is the marriage of these simple creatures –
> Celebrated here, in the darkness of the sun....

The 'human form divine' in *Crow* is utterly without redeeming

features. In *Full Moon and Little Frieda* we have intentionality
and love making the universe – and making it love her. In
Fragment of an Ancient Tablet the emphasis is on the animal
below-waist reality that undercuts human meaning in the body.
The human form is ('above') 'well known lips', 'her brow, the
notable casket of gems', a 'word and a sigh' – but ('below' – that is,
'*really*') 'the belly with its blood-knot', 'gouts of blood and babies'.
The reality is guts and biological forces, not consciousness or meaning.

> Above – the face, shaped like a perfect heart.
> Below – the heart's torn face ...
>
> *Fragment of an Ancient Tablet*

The 'ticking bomb of the future' is her womb with its creative
urge, that can only lead to catastrophe. The woman's vagina looks
like a brutal wound.

So

> Burning
>
>   burning
>
>   burning

(in *Crow's Last Stand*) becomes not a compassionate incantation
over the sterility of a civilization (as in Eliot's *Fire Sermon*), but
a statement that *all creation is doomed to entropy* (and the sooner
the better). All that is left is a passive eye recording – and unwilling
staring at the meaninglessness of nothingness:

> there was finally something
> The sun could not burn ...
> – a final obstacle...
> Crow's eye-pupil, in the tower of its
>   scorched fort.
>
>   (p. 81)

The seeing eye in *Crow* does not give meaning to the universe:
this eye can only doggedly view the malignancy of everything.
Yet this eye knows that love – and the universe – will persist, even
despite the most intense dynamics of the nihilism that hates them.

In this brutal universe Crow is both *that-in-the-self-which-
endures*: and also a knot in the dynamics of the self that *can* endure.
He is split-off knot of 'masculine protest'. This split-off indestructible self is a paranoid-schizoid phantasy – like the self we invent in
a disaster that can survive by magic even if the body and self are
annihilated. The invention of Crow then is a form of magical
'bad thinking'.

This creature is even outside God and God's power: outside natural law. Ted Hughes, talking to George Macbeth on the radio about Crow, called him 'a childish hanger-on to the events of Creation'. We could interpret this to mean that he is the kind of nightmare creature a child might imagine who plays tricks of a malicious kind and is not always under control. He was 'created by God's nightmare' – so, he is not the product of dream and vision, but like a nightmare that comes unbidden. He 'tried to become a man' and is 'ready to turn into I don't know what': he will evade all human realities by lying himself into any shape.

It is significant that Crow bears human male genitals on the cover of Ted Hughes's book. He is 'indestructible' said Hughes in his radio talk, 'like Horatio'. In this we may glimpse the self-curative element in *Crow*. Surely nothing in fact could be further from Horatio's balanced and sane embodiment of values than Crow? But to Ted Hughes he seems to represent some intellectual concept, or structure, or posture to the universe, by which one could endure – or rather, avoid existential dread. So long as this spurious identity can sustain the sense of being a horseman, 'shod with vaginas of iron', it can fend off paranoid dangers. Crow is a defence against 'unthinkable' fears. But if he were to be seen as a mere black jacket hiding an inner emptiness, the self would collapse into nothingness.

So, having landed himself with Crow, Ted Hughes moves further and further away from the more complex and true problems of being human, such as he touched on in *The Full Moon and Little Frieda*. Development of the relationship between 'encounter' and creative perception becomes more and more remote. So, caught in nihilistic circuits, Hughes becomes less and less free, even as he protests his negative claim for freedom, as happens to many present-day writers.

For Crow, despite his capacities for survival, is everywhere a passive victim, without *potentia*, without any power of finding meaning in his world. He can find no authenticity except that of merely continuing to exist, and no freedom except that of merely surviving, the alternative being reduced to nothing.

> 'It was a naked powerline, 2000 volts –
> He stood aside, watching his body go blue
> As he held and held it...
> The earth, shrunk to the size of a hand grenade
> And he held it he held it and held it and
> BANG!
> He was blasted to nothing.

This is from *Truth Kills Everybody*. Truth is Proteus ('steaming ... stinking'). The real truth is 'bulging Achilles', the oesophagus of a shark, a 'wreath of lashing mambas, a screeching woman, Christ's hot pounding Heart'. It is, we might say, an infinite variety of forms of objectivity, existence reduced to nothing but the matter and functions of which it is composed, with Christ's divinity reduced to a pulsing organ, and, in the end, the earth reduced to the final moment of entropy.

Once we unravel the trick of inverting every value and every positive, from a philosophical formula based on a coarse 'objective' nihilism, *Crow* appears rather as foolish *blague à thèse*. The poet simply turns birth on its head and calls it *A Kill*. Instead of being 'equipped with nimble limbs', Crow is

> flogged lame with legs ...

He is not born into consciousness but

> Shot through the head with balled brains –

that is, his brains are in his head like a lump of lead or 'balled' in the sense that they simply follow his testicles, or are 'ballsed up'.

> Shot blind with eyes
> Nailed down by his own ribs ...
> Clubbed unconscious by his own heart ...

The body is not only a burden, as it is to Hamlet: it has been thrust on one by violence: life itself is a malicious stab, only seen in a flash as one drowns in one's own blood:

> Seeing his life stab through him, a dream flash
> As he drowned in his own blood ...

To be born is to be split open and dashed on to the earth, as if jettisoned by an air disaster:

> letting the cry up through him at a distance
> And smashed into rubble of the ground ...

But at the moment of birth, it is not that the neonate comes into the light, but

> ... everything went black

Everything is given up to blackness:

> Black was the without eye ...
> a black rainbow
> Bent in emptiness
> over emptiness ...

and agony –

> In the beginning was Scream ...

It is true that fleetingly Crow is begotten, born and flies – but as a mere survivor or victim

> but flying ...
> Trembling featherless elbows in the nest's filth ...

The message of the poems is that 'one is' merely.

If we adopt this pessimistic determinism, man is a victim and can never gain his freedom. Our deepest objection to *Crow*, then, is that as a depressing picture of existence as victimization it merely twists even stronger chains round the sensibility – so that any attempt to find and exert the dynamics of love, meaning responsibility and freedom seems futile. One simply opts for egoistical survival. One of the poems added to the 1971 edition of *Crow* is *The Contender*:

> There was this man and he was the strongest ...

He is hanging to a cliff. The expression of his plight is forcible: but it is a desperate forcibleness – the brittle language of the colour supplement: of advertising, and technological media ('Deep, surge, thrust, plunge').

> There he nailed himself with nails of nothing ...

Here is poetry of the 'taboo on tenderness':

> All the women in the world could not move him ...

> They came and their tears salted his nail-holes
> Only adding their embitterment
> To his effort ...

Like Christ he lies crucified

> Grinning towards the sun ...

> And towards the moon ...

> Grinning into the black
> Into the ringing nothing
> Through the bones of his teeth

> Sometimes with eyes closed

> In his senseless trial of strength

Man in *Crow* is a 'bag of bones', a skull, whose endurance of cosmic infringement is absurd ('senseless').

By contrast, we may compare the view of the philosophical biologist:

> The whole biological development of a typical mammal has been re-written in our case in a new key: the whole structure of the embryo, the whole rhythm of growth, is directed, from first to last, to the emergence of a culture-dwelling animal – an animal not bound within a pre-determined ontological niche like the tern or the stag or the dragonfly or even the chimpanzee, but, in its very tissues and organs and aptitudes, *born to be open to its world*, to be able to accept responsibility, to make its own the traditions of a historical past and to remake them into a foreseeable future.[4]

This is a view of man as a creature, who, in his anatomical struc-ture, and in his unique capacity for consciousness, stands erect and develops a creative 'positionality' to his world. This is the creature seen and cherished by positive existentialism, who defines himself by his free choices, and whose primary impulse is to fulfil his *potentia*.

By contrast Ted Hughes's man and woman in *Crow* are the victims of God, a 'cruel bastard' who either jokes or is indifferent. God sleeps on the problem of human bodies lying 'without souls'

> Dully gaping, foolishly staring, inert
> On the flowers of Eden ...

Crow acts – bites the Worm in half: 'God's only son.'

The Worm is God's only son, because the only thing God begat directly in Creation was death. So, it is Death that is bitten

> Into two writhing halves...

Here, we have the death instinct with a vengeance, lying behind the id-instinctual drives of sex.

> He stuffed into man the tail half
> With the wounded end hanging out.
>
> He stuffed the head half headfirst into woman
> and it crept in deeper and up
> To peer out through her eyes
> Calling its tail-half to join up quickly, quickly
> Because O it was painful ...
>
> *A Childish Prank*

Here the face of woman in love is the face of death which has

---

[4] Marjorie Grene, *Approaches to a Philosophical Biology*, p. 48.

eaten its way up her genitals, after being bitten in half by Crow, so that what looks out of her eyes is the face of death. The man in desire is possessed by penis-death, seeking to join with the death-worm in the woman. Their coupling is a brutality, half-worm, outside themselves and their volition:

> Man awoke being dragged across the grass.
> Woman awoke to see him coming.
> Neither knew what had happened.
>
> God went on sleeping.
>
> Crow went on laughing.
>
> (p. 19)

God is indifferent to the creation of our most creative acts: that in which we find our deepest source of meaning, if it is an act of love. Sex was a practical joke thrust on us by God's nightmare, as a prank of his deathly voraciousness.

This again, is the schizoid view of 'encounter': because of the hungry mouth of the regressed libidinal ego, love is too dangerous. The poem *Lovesong* gives a clue to the obsession in *Crow* with eating and the guilt and anguish bound up with it. *Lovesong* is a statement of a primitive fear of the harmful consequences of love, as being a kind of cannibalistic mutual identification. It is a poem that does not really belong to *Crow*, because it is human and real. The fears expressed are those of 'implosion' such as R. D. Laing discusses in *The Divided Self* that the hunger in love will prove so demanding that it destroys the identity and even the existence of the other. (It is also, of course, an expression of the sucking, biting, and incorporative-sadistic impulses lurking beneath any sexual relationship, not least in phantasy.)

> He loved her and she loved him
> His kisses sucked out her whole past and future or tried to
> He had no other appetite
> She bit him she gnawed him she sucked
> She wanted him complete inside her
> Safe and sure forever and ever
> Their little cries fluttered into the curtains...

The last line makes the sucking a sexual act. In the end, after this mutual eating (such as the child imagines the parents' sexual act to be):

> In the morning they wore each other's face...

Hughes sees the world as being full of incorporation which makes it seem too terrible:

The swift's body fled past
Pulsating
With insects
And their anguish, all it had eaten.

The cat's body writhed
Gagging
A tunnel
Of incoming death-struggles, sorrow on sorrow.

And the dog was a bulging filterbag
Of all the deaths it had gulped for the flesh and the bones.
It could not digest their screeching finales.
Its shapelessness cry was a blort of all those voices ...

Even man he was a walking
Abattoir
Of innocents—

This is both an expression of the truth of animal existence: that everything, to live, must prey. But at the same time it is reductionist in that it makes the cat *nothing more* than a tunnel of guts: the dog's cry here is only 'shapeless' – yet this is not so, for a dog (to the new biology) has many voices, in its capacity to give tongue, its signal-gestures, its encounter rituals: and its positionality in the world.

Crow wants to try to live better:

Crow thought 'Alas
Alas ought I
To stop eating
And try to become the light?

But his eye saw a grub ...

So, despite his idealism, here, Crow becomes a victim of his drives of his savage nature. He weeps, but he cannot escape – so, 'came the eye's roundness', of voracious predatory vision, and the ear's deafness to screams of the dying: yet everything begins with 'Scream'.

By adopting a pseudo-biology Hughes vindicates his picture of human sexuality as a disgusting form of impulse, unwillingly experienced and mutually destructive:

'A final try', said God. 'Now, LOVE.'
Crow convulsed, gaped, retched and
Man's bodiless prodigious head
Bulbed out onto the earth, with swivelling eyes,
Jabbering protest—

And Crow retched again, before God could stop him.

And woman's vulva dropped over man's neck and tightened,
The two struggled together on the grass.
God struggled to part them, cursed, wept—

Crow flew guiltily off

Human birth and human love are the creation of a mistake of
'God's nightmare' – which God would have prevented if he could –
the product of a retching attempt to pronounce an unspeakable
concept! As he seeks to justify his nihilism by absurd references
to 'science', Hughes's 'vitalism' has become a devitalization.

A poem like *Examination at the Womb Door* rests on the view
that death and entropy swallow everything and so this makes
everything a nullity. Yet it could be rewritten entirely from
another point of view:

> What created this face that has expressions,
> signs, looks out to perceive the world?
> —Life.
> What developed this pattern of
>   positionality, that
> keeps upright and flies?
> —Life.
> What gave this creature a trial in the
> evolutionary process?
> —Life.
> In what can we find a sense of
> meaning that makes death
> and entropy irrelevant, in
> terms of the need to exert
> a quest for authenticity in
> the face of temporality?
> —Love

I do not claim that this is poetry. But it does indicate that to make
a successful poem in the positive quest for meaning in such a
vein, would require something more serious than *Crow*.

For *Crow* is a serious attack on our seriousness. It is at times
like an 'adult comix' parody of philosophical poetry, and so we
don't know how seriously to take it, as in *Conjuring in Heaven*:

> So finally there was nothing.
> It was put inside nothing...
>
> Chopped up with a nothing ...
>
> nothing more could be done with it

And so it was dropped. Prolonged applause in Heaven.

It hit the ground and broke open—

There lay Crow, cataleptic.

If we are not to take it seriously, then how do we justify the offensiveness and obscenity? There *is* a serious problem behind *Crow* – which is that of the female element. The protagonist is recognizably the creature of *Gog* and *Wodwo*:

> ....tongue still moving
> To find mother, among the stars and the blood spittle
> Trying to cry...
>
> (p. 79)

And here, as in *Littleblood*, among all the pseudo-male 'bad thinking' props there is a recognition of the needs of the unborn creature, the Regressed Ego, Littlesoul, who needs to be reflected. This is a problem of finding the 'significant other' in woman, while eliminating the burden of 'mother':

> There was a person
> Could not get rid of his mother....
>
> (p. 70)

In the welter of words one can detect in *Crow* the record of a desperate struggle to relate, and to find the woman. But since love is so dangerous, the pursuit of love gets out of hand, and becomes an outrage. Woman, because of the substitution of hate for love, is found to be at the heart of the failure of meaning in the universe – while any quest for love and meaning must inevitably turn out to be a bloody catastrophe. Here the poems which enact this are *Crow's Account of St. George* (pp. 31-2) and *Criminal Ballad* (pp. 38-9) whose subjects are similar.

The first poem links the desperate quest for meaning in relationship to the feeling (taken in from science) that the universe is meaningless.

> He sees everything in the Universe
> Is a track of numbers racing towards an answer...
>
> He refrigerates an emptiness
> Decreates all to enter space
> Then unpicks numbers.

In Whitehead's terms, the science of this scientist-protagonist is 'a mystic chant over an unintelligible universe'. Although the scientist delights in his quest for truth, by rational processes, he is haunted by the spectre of a demon:

With tweezers of number
he picks the gluey heart out of an inaudibly speaking cell—
He hears something. He turns—
A demon, dripping ordure, is grinning in the doorway....

                                                    (p. 31)

The scientist tries to exorcise the demons which challenge his
rationalism by concentration. But, we may say that the scientist
could very well be haunted by a number of demons. First, his
'numbers', despite his passion, 'answer no serious questions at all'
(Husserl). Secondly 'cutting the heart in two' with a 'knife-edge
of numbers' is a schizoid activity that separates 'objectivity' in an
unreal way from the realities of the subjective. Moreover, the
apparent rationality of his science thus denies the irrational
questions – or, we could say, all those aspects of being-in-the-
universe which (as Roger Poole argues) science since Galileo has
merely thrust aside and denied, and which can only be found
by subjectivity.

Ted Hughes's Scientist, however, is not challenged by a Blakean
vision of subjectivity – but only by a Devil who is a paranoid
split-off, representing Hate, and the *malignancy* of the universe:
it is Crow, in another guise. Thus, creative freedom is negated
throughout. The Devil is one which Hughes employs to project
over everything in his Grand Guignol way and to negate all the
positive dynamics of the universe:

                            A bird-head,
    Bald, lizard-eyed, the size of a football, on two staggering bird-legs
    Gapes at him ...

The scientist smashes it, and it displays the shark-face of the
demons of Hieronymous Bosch and Breughel:

            The shark-face is screaming in the doorway
            Opening its fangs...

The scientist can be so tempted, just like a St Anthony, because
his own incantations are really a form of mysticism. But the awful-
ness of the Devil here is a psychotic vision:

            A belly-ball of hair, with crab-legs, eyeless,
            Jabs its pincers into his face...

– and when destroyed it turns out to have been 'his wife and
children'. So, it is female-element-being, and the creativity of
Life itself, that has menaced him. In fact it is love that is the
demon – and we have reached the schizoid moral inversion, 'good,

be thou my evil!' The scientist has been haunted, in fact, by his own capacity to embrace the 'subjective' and to find irrationality.

But when irrationality appears it is not a manifestation of creative subjectivity: all faith in that has been abandoned. Instead we have the cultivation of psychosis as the only alternative – another of today's fashions. What is the message? 'However much the scientist concentrates on his rational interpretation of the truth of the world, another truth will confront him – the truth of that Hate which is embodied in the shark, and embodies the malignancy of universal entropy. If he tried to exercise this threat to his sanity he may well find himself attacking and destroying the significant other, the object of his own love and their children. For their mortality, and their mystery, and their very existence, as forces of life, are a manifestation of those malignant forces in the universe, which belong to all that rationality excludes – and all that rationality excluded is hideous and evil.' This is a strange message for a poet, whom one could expect to side with Blake rather than Newton and D. H. Lawrence rather than De Sade.

Some poems in *Crow* read like records of psychotic episodes, in which we may see the desperation, and the quest for meaning, survival, purity – such as the water makes in the Eskimo song, by desperate attrition:

> It came weeping back it wanted to die...
>
> Till it had no weeping left...
>
> Utterly worn out   utterly clear ...

Hughes identifies with the water. But to this desperate quest Woman must be sacrificed:

> Then, lying among the bones on the cemetary earth
> He saw a woman singing, out of her belly.
>
> He gave her eyes and a mouth, in exchange for song.
> She wept blood, she cried pain...
>
> The pain and the blood were life. But the man laughed—
>
> The woman felt cheated.

(pp. 92-3)

Winnicott speaks of how the fear of phantom woman in our conscious life, the castrating mother (who is also the mother in ourself, and our female element) has caused infinite suffering throughout history and the world. Hatred of woman is today a predominant theme of our culture – she is exposed, raped, purged, tormented, killed, humiliated – for the sake of man's quest for reality. In her blood is our triumph – we laugh at her humiliation.

In this mood of hatred of the feminine, sex is a cruel joke:

> Words came in the likeness of vaginas in a row—
> He called in his friends.

The complement is the male abandonment to violence:

> the racking moments
> Of the man smashing everything
> He could reach...

Strength and inviolability lie in giving oneself up to the joys of hating – and to death, to a longing for non-being: 'I have made nothing my cause.'

> The grin
> Sank back, temporarily nonplussed,
> Into the Skull...

In *Crow's Theology* philosophies which declare that one exists because God loved one are cynically denied:

> He realized that God spoke Crow—
> Just existing was His revelation.

An indifferent universe of unresponsive dead matter cannot reflect (and here there is no sense that a child could give meaning to the Moon). Universal entropy swallows all:

> But what
> Loved the stones and spoke stone?
>
> And what spoke that strange silence?
> After his clamour of caws faded?
>
> (p. 35)

The only things that are real are meaningless, nothingness, and Death.

> What spoke the silence of lead?
>
> Crow realized there were two Gods—
>
> One of them much bigger than the other
> Loving his enemies
> And having all the weapons

Why then write poetry? At the hard core of *Crow* is a longing for that non-being which alone (like the lead and the rocks and the silence) seems real. Yet even to set out to shock us denies the nihilism. So, the nihilistic energy of the poems implicitly gives the lie to the denial of meaning. The 'other God' here, of death and entropy, does not really have all the weapons. Indeed, if there is such a drift of mere matter, it is a nothing, compared with us who are aware of it. We are not nothing despite the death that overwhelms us personally, or shall overwhelm our species when the Earth dies. None of our ultimate nothingness expunges the marvellous moments such as that when, like Little Frieda looking at the Moon, we are conscious of the universe, of our own creation, and thus 'make it' by our intentionality, by our creative perception. Our ultimate nothingness merely imposes on us an urgency of being responsible, aware, and fastidious – in our search for authentic choice and action. This is a responsibility, too, to the future, and to the survival of what can endure and survive. This is our freedom.

In *Crow* the unconditional mystery of man is denied, together with the poetic which expresses his unique higher level of being in consciousness. With this denial, Hughes forfeits freedom, by denying intentionality.

This hardly seems the most promising path for poetry in our time. *Song for a Phallus* represents the extreme of pseudo-male doing, or 'masculine protest' in *Crow*.

The poem belongs to the present outburst of fanatical immoralism which expresses a distrust of all forms of normal being. Saul Bellow makes Mr Sammler say:

As long as there is no ethical life and everything is poured so barbarously and recklessly into personal gesture this must be endured ... there is a peculiar longing for non-being ... why should they be human? ... The individual ... (seems to want) a divorce from all the states he knows ...

Mr. Sammler's Planet (Penguin, p. 164)

The fear of the regressed libidinal ego, unborn, becomes rationalized in a final turning against the possibility of ever being born:

He split his Mammy like a melon
He was drenched with gore
He found himself curled up inside
As if he had never been bore ...

Such a coarse and destructive poem is an index of a catastrophic descent into nullity, a plunge towards nothingness – in a culture which has at last lost confidence, not only in being, but also in the capacity to symbolize, and in the worth of creativity.

But, in truth, there is no inescapable reason in science or philosophy to see the world as an unintelligible and alien cosmos, in which man is not at home, and which is but designed to torment him with his nothingness. On the contrary, the life-sciences and philosophical anthropology are saying the opposite. Whether or not there is a God for us, it is absurd to attribute catastrophes in life to the work of a 'cruel bastard'. The wonder is not that we are 'abandonné', but that we came into existence at all. Indeed, it is absurd for the most conscious and complex creature in creation, he who makes the cosmos by his being conscious of it, the one product of that universe to be able to perceive its nature, to declare that everything simply *is* and is simply nothingness, at the mercy of hostile forces, and his own dismay.

5 Precarious Complacency

A Note on the Contemporary Novel

S. W. DAWSON

> We feel it not to be the paradox it may at the first blush seem that
> the state of the novel in England at the present time is virtually
> very much the state of criticism itself; and this moreover, at the risk
> perhaps of some added appearance of perverse remark, by the very
> reason that we see criticism so much in abeyance. So far as we miss
> it altogether how and why does its 'state' matter, and why and how
> can it or should it, as an absent force, enjoy a relation to that con-
> stant renewal of our supply of fiction which is a present one so far
> as a force at all? The relation is this, in the fewest words: that
> no equal outpouring of matter into the mould of literature, or
> what roughly passes for such, has been noted to live its life and
> maintain its flood, its level at least of quantity and mass, in such
> free and easy independence of critical attention. It constitutes a
> condition and a perversity on the part of this element to remain
> irresponsive before an appeal so vociferous at least and so incessant;
> therefore how can such a neglect of occasions, so careless a habit in
> spite of marked openings, be better described than as responsibility
> declined in the face of disorder?
>
> HENRY JAMES[1]

The trouble with modern fiction is that, to borrow a phrase from
my doctor, there's a lot of it about. It is necessary to distinguish,
and the most obvious distinction is that between popular and
fashionable fiction. Popular fiction is not normally reviewed in the
'serious' papers, and covers an enormous range from mild pornography through 'romance' and 'adventure' to science-fiction,
thrillers and the detective story. It is produced for solely commercial reasons, and like all popular entertainment today it is
parasitic on the fashionable novel, just as commercial art and music
are parasitic on their fashionable equivalents. The time-lag between
the fashionable and the popular is continually decreasing: that,
and the great volume of production, are the striking characteristics
of popular fiction today. Its only interest is symptomatic, but

[1] *The New Novel*, 1914.

because it *is* parasitic, it is less significant, even symptomatically, than the fashionable novel.

The fashionable novel is reviewed in the 'serious' papers, though one has to add at once that the position as regards criticism is, partly as a result of the increased volume of production, worse than it was when Henry James wrote the passage quoted above. Novel-reviewing today is in a state of critical somnambulism, and it is not easy to suggest how, in face of such a mass, criticism could possibly cope, and to whom it would in any case address itself. The reviewer is, willy-nilly, part of a commercial machine on the publicity side. However good his intentions he has neither the time nor the space to do much more than go through the motions. Often, like the advertising man, he is corrupted by the necessity of a kind of self-respect into believing that there is some value in keeping the game going (that is, preserving the distinction between the popular and the fashionable) and having a handful of names of 'distinguished' modern novelists. This at least saves us all from the humiliating consciousness of gulping down without discrimination everything the machine feeds to us, nuts, bolts and all. The 'Arts' pages of the weeklies have become intellectual fashion pages, reminding us, like the 'posh Sundays', that we are a nation of consumers, and that it is the newest, the latest, that really matters. The *Guardian* follows suit. It is worth reflecting, however, that while there is a sizeable number of middle-class subscribers avid to be told which electric toaster, family car or private school offers the best value for money, there is little enough support for any attempt to inject some healthy sales-resistance into the book-market.

I write as a teacher of English who has made the attempt, over the last twenty years, out of a possibly misplaced sense of responsibility, to keep in touch with fashionable fiction. This attempt I have now largely abandoned. Again and again a novel by a new author seemed rather better than the common run, sang a little tune, as it were, that bit more catchy than the others. Then, as novel followed novel, it was still the same little tune, either in a different key or with an increasingly portentous orchestration. Finally, as one realized that this particular talent was never going to amount to anything, one discovered that the author was now 'established', 'important' or 'distinguished'. The system has its own momentum.

It should be said, too, that this whole business goes on with hardly a hint of recognition that the English novel has a great past; for reviewers the classics of the past might as well not exist. The notion (essential to criticism) that the classics are alive insofar as they offer to the present the challenge of comparison is no longer with us. The classics are dead – that is what is clearly implied, and too often the academic world, avid for thesis or examination fodder, is enthusiastically on hand with the embalming fluid. There is even, I suspect, the unspoken idea around that to make such comparisons would be somehow unfair, as if any novel that could not be judged by such standards was worth judging at all. (Which doesn't mean that what doesn't 'come up to' those standards is worthless.)

The translation of Solzhenitsyn's *August 1914* provided a piquant illustration of my point. Its appearance set reviewers writing about its significant relation to the great nineteenth-century Russian writers, indeed going so far as to ask whether it challenges comparison with Tolstoy. They didn't make a very good job of it, by and large, but the point is that neither to them nor to us do such discussions seem absurd, as they would if what were in question were (say) Angus Wilson's relation to Dickens. No one actually *says* that to be confronted thus with a great writer is to be made sharply aware of what a small matter the English novel has become. Apart from attempts to turn Solzhenitsyn into a political talking-point, and leaving aside the customary inanities of Mr Toynbee in the *Observer*, the main escape-route seems to be a stress on his Russian-ness. As if his greatness did not consist chiefly, not in telling us what contemporary Russia is like, but in speaking to us of our human experience, and doing this with such force because of his essential Russian-ness! That Solzhenitsyn strikes more to the centre of *our* humanity by being more Russian than our own novelists are English does not occur to them.

Of course, one is often told not to take such a situation too much *au sérieux*. There have been many periods in history (like the later eighteenth century in our own) when the lack of the first-rate has tempted men to praise the third-rate. It is only human nature. But what of value has ever been achieved by mere human nature in that sense? Blake was tormented by normal, decent, cultivated men who could see that he was gifted, but couldn't see that his gifts were in a different category from those of writers they had allowed themselves to admire. In art the 'intelligent' and the 'accomplished', not to mention the clever, are the enemy of the truly significant, not its auxiliaries.

I have made the assumption that contemporary English fiction is a very small thing, and that anyone with more than an inkling of what standards are will agree with me. What *is* wrong? Geoffrey Grigson told us not long ago that it was a matter of luck.

.... the lucky thing is to have enough mature or maturing authors whose loyalty, let those authors be various as they may, is evidently and always to the best; and whose reputation and influence are such as to compel that powerful club, which can't be eradicated, to something of an identical sense of worth.[2]

I think there are serious confusions here, but the most basic response is surely recoil from a resort to the merely fortuitous in such a connection. Certainly when we question the simplicity of this account we run into certain dangers, attendant on all attempts at cultural and social diagnosis. The air is thick just now with political, sociological, psycho-analytical and moral analyses of our 'spiritual sickness', most of them vexation and vanity of spirit. (The recent pornography *brouhaha* is a case in point.) The only positive satisfaction most of this stuff affords is to its practitioners; like the popular ecologists, whose doomsday syndrome they share, they want to make our flesh creep *and* give themselves a warm glow of self-satisfaction. Nevertheless we *know*, don't we? that if the fashionable literature of the age is trivial, heartless, repellent even, something is wrong far beyond what can be described as 'luck'. If the 'life' we find in novels seems so thin, is not that lack of substance a lack of meaning and value, which no writer can merely spin out of his own entrails? Is there not a decay of language, so that the deepest things cannot be spoken of, or must be encased in defensive irony? Ask yourself what the phrase 'make love' has meant in all its various richness, and what it means in the average modern novel.

In reply to Mr Grigson, Basil Davidson had this to say:

.... there won't be and there can't be any good writing stuff in England until there are writers, again, who stand on social reality and speak for it, who stop tucking themselves away and practising between mirrors, who get hold of what happens in the streets and matters in the population, and make it live in poetry....[3]

Mr Davidson clearly writes from the left, and a great deal depends on what you mean by social reality. Reality is inescapably social, just as it is inescapably individual. But to keep it as simple as possible, would it not be agreed that there is 'more to' life than what the contemporary novelists can show us? If I were to pick out one word in Mr Davidson's letter as crucial (whether he meant it so or not) it would be 'poetry'. There are times when one wonders whether the language of our cultivated middle-class – and a great deal is implied in that word 'language' – is any longer capable of poetry, the power to create in words a sense of life. (This, of

[2] *The Times Literary Supplement*, 24 August 1972, p. 994.
[3] *The Times Literary Supplement*, 15 September 1972, p. 1060.

course, leaves us with the word 'life' on our hands, but as F. R. Leavis has remarked, we can't do without it. Life, one might say, is precisely what is left out of the discussions of sex, love and marriage in 99 per cent of the weeklies and paperbacks.)

What the modern novel substitutes for life is a determined and often hysterical cleverness. An obvious example is Muriel Spark. What does her cleverness amount to, even in such comparative successes as *Memento Mori*? Her characters are all what the reviewers call 'sharply observed'; that is, they exhibit clichés of language and behaviour which we, and Miss Spark of course, recognize as such and are superior to. They are all more or less absurd – the tone and most of the action are farcical. The other shot in Miss Spark's locker is fantasy. In *Memento Mori* there are the mysterious telephone calls enunciating the inevitability of death. However seriously they may be intended (and there is a kind of seriousness there) the effect is of a clever idea, of the sort that is sparked off by 'wouldn't it be funny/interesting if ...?' The characters, or most of them, are disturbed, but we aren't, and neither is Miss Spark. We can judge that by the faint (ever so faint, because Miss Spark *is* clever) touches of sentimentality which go into the manufacture of the characters who are not disturbed.

Miss Spark has her own individual flavour, but her work is fairly representative of contemporary fiction in a number of respects; the characteristics I want to focus attention on are farce and fantasy. Most fashionable modern novelists are more or less farceurs. The farcical set-piece is a great stand-by of Iris Murdoch, and Anthony Powell's *Music of Time* sequence is little more than a series of farcical incidents loosely strung together. His only interesting creation is Widmerpool, whose successive humiliations express a rather snobbish combination of fear, hatred and contempt. Farce is essentially a reductive mode; at its most extreme it reduces persons to machines in a violent celebration of triumphant meaninglessness. It consorts easily with fantasy, which in itself is rarely compatible with the highest imaginative powers. The fantasy of the great English satirical poets, Jonson at his richest and Pope in *The Dunciad*, has a paradoxical creativity in that its very solidity implies the positive sense of life which appears elsewhere in their celebratory poetry. Their characters are not diminished – they remain menacing even when seen to be absurd. Their nearest contemporary equivalent is to be found in the best parts of Joseph Heller's *Catch—22*, which derives from the rather different Central European tradition, to which belong Kafka and Schweik. (Were there not signs of an attempt to draw on this tradition in early Iris

Murdoch, an attempt which quickly softened into nursery whimsy?)[4]

It is remarkable how many novels are described in their publishers' advertisements as 'funny'; sometimes, revealingly, as 'desperately funny'. Being 'funny' like this usually conveys the sense of a half recognition and a final evasion of something which is feared, like troops helpless under fire. (American 'funny' novels, on the other hand, are often genuinely terrifying – the sense of dissolution, of imminent meaninglessness, is so much sharper.) The paradoxical phrase which occurs to me is 'precarious complacency'. This has nothing to do with comedy – it is precisely that, the great liberating and humane comedy of the English tradition, which is missing. It seems to have died with Lawrence. As a friend remarked to me recently, it is precisely this comic power which announces the presence of a great novelist in Solzhenitsyn, particularly in *The First Circle*. Comedy is courage, the trusting of the human spirit to life (and art); the farce and fantasy of the contemporary English novel is a recoil from life which would be desperate if it dared.

There are other kinds of cleverness, of course, like Angus Wilson's. If those early stories, 'sharply observed' little darts directed at the liberal intelligentsia, like the anti-Jewish stories one is assured are so popular among Jews, were a very small matter, could anyone seriously claim that Mr Wilson, by stretching his small talent thinner and thinner over longer and longer volumes, has added weight to his achievement? In *No Laughing Matter* the cleverness has become merely the boring elaboration of mechanical technique, and the accumulation of a mass of material, like the *bric à brac* period recreation of the opening paragraph. The impression is irresistible that he dislikes all his characters, and it is no coincidence that his most powerful book (and also his most unpleasant) was also his most fantastic. In *The Old Men at the Zoo* the hatred and disgust reach a disturbing pitch.

William Golding, too, is surely an example of a small talent blown up out of all proportion by the reviewers; his quasi-allegorical significances are painfully excogitated. When one has worked out what he is up to, in *Pincher Martin* or *Free Fall*, one can, perhaps, admire the cleverness of it, but the sixth-form conception of evil which underlies his work, and the utter unspontaneity of it all, are finally wearisome and distasteful.

[4] And talking of nurseries, what are we to make of the cult of fairy-tale fantasy associated with the name of Tolkien? Not to mention the great volume of so-called 'science-fiction' which it so oddly resembles.

It would be tedious to make a roll-call of all the established reputations. I am not concerned to make Mr Grigson's point – it seems self-evident so far as it goes. What I want to suggest is that there is, about the relation between the novel and criticism, or rather the lack of it, something more than merely praising the second-rate. Consider, for instance, the career of Edna O'Brien. Her early work showed a genuine if minor talent, but in her later novels the comic *esprit* has been submerged by sour resentment at her own femaleness (she's not alone in this) and a desperate desire to find vital significance in peasant brutality and ignorance. The decline of Miss O'Brien, like the equivalent though very different decline of Miss Murdoch, is the effect of self-indulgence.[5] This self-indulgence has been connived at, if not positively encouraged, by a basic irresponsibility in our whole intellectual climate. The novelist's fancy meets no resistance – he has a 'reading public' but no audience, and hence no sense of life. This is not a unique situation, and one could point to the later writings of Blake, Henry James and Lawrence, all indubitably men of genius, as evidence of the same lack: *Lady Chatterley's Lover*, for instance, is a clear case of self-indulgence.

It is customary to say that there are novelists who deserve our respect, like (in their different ways) Doris Lessing and Stanley Middleton, whose concern is palpably to tell the truth. But their truthfulness is not the truthfulness of art, and their interest is not the interest of art. They strike no poetry from life. To do that is no doubt a rare gift, a gift possessed by few writers at any time. Perhaps David Storey has been granted it more fully than any of his contemporaries, though whether he will make anything of it is another matter. *Radcliffe*, his most ambitious work, is as a whole a failure, with its sexual violence, its over-insistence, and its incoherent 'Gothicism'. Whether they indicated the decay of a talent, or merely the lurch into falsity of a serious artist who has lost his way, is a question the answer to which must be postponed. His novels are, to give a slight slant to Eliot's phrase, raids on the inarticulate – they are about inarticulateness, and the way it explodes into violence when hemmed in by meaningless ugliness. Mr Storey is trying to *see*, and in certain of his scenes he makes us see, with disturbing clarity – I am thinking of the erection of the marquees, and Tolson on his motor-bike. The very vitality of the writing points beyond the ugliness of the material; though

[5] Exigencies of space leave one open to misinterpretation. What I am *not* suggesting is (a) that there is any deliberate cynicism on the part of these writers, a conviction that they can get away with anything, as it were, or (b) that there can be any simple quasi-legislative rôle for the critic *vis-à-vis* the novelist.

perhaps 'points' is the wrong word, since Mr Storey doesn't appear to have any clear idea of what he is 'up to'. In the situation of the novel today a remarkable force of character and intelligence is called for – the writer is too much on his own.

There is a significant irony in the fact that the novelist who increasingly strikes one as most powerfully contemporary, Solzhenitsyn, is an exile within his own society. And a certain melancholy amusement may be derived from the fact that our reviewers find him 'old-fashioned'. It is odd, to say the least, that it should be a Russian novelist to whom one finds oneself turning for the significant contrast. It is obvious, the novels themselves providing the evidence, that the moral can hardly be, in the ordinary sense, a political one. Why can a Russian writer draw strength from the past as no English writer can? May one entertain for a moment the possibility that the malign influence of a stupid and inhuman tyranny has been in some respects less destructive than the alliance of commerce, technology and the values of Bloomsbury?[6] That philistinism is a less dangerous enemy than enlightenment? These are, I am aware, perilous speculations, susceptible of no simple answers. That they even suggest themselves is an indication that the English novel is in a bad way, and that, though we may join Mr Grigson in praying for writers of genius, we may feel that the omens are not propitious.

---

[6] Can anyone reading the recent crop of Bloomsbury biographies doubt what a dire *portent* these people were? Lawrence's explosive reaction seems progressively less exaggerated as their legacy becomes clearer.

6 Suicide: The Condition of Consciousness

An essay on Albert Camus'
The Outsider and *The Fall*

MASUD KHAN

Introduction

... at a certain moment in its history the moral life of Europe
added to itself a new element, the state or quality of self which
we call sincerity.

LIONEL TRILLING

There are only two traditions of reading a book: to distract ourselves from the chores of daily existence or to commit ourselves to
the sensibility of a book. Here we are concerned with the
second tradition. Every reader in this tradition brings an expectancy to his commitment. I shall go as far as to say that every such
reader has a theory that guides his expectancy, be he overtly aware
of it or not. This is why in the vast literature available to each of
us we commit ourselves seriously to only a few authors and their
creations and not even all the creations of one author. The nature
of my expectancy from a book is that it will gradually teach me the
secret of its own becoming and the necessity for it to come into
being. I believe that each book is a riddle that contains its own
specific clues to its true understanding. The true success of a book
lies in direct ratio to its achieving an autonomous wholeness of its
own, independent of the subjectivity of its creator, the author. That
in achieving this autonomy it also subsumes the most private and
subjective elements of the author's life-experiences constitutes the
true paradox of artistic creation. All this has been said better and
more vividly by Camus in his 1943 article, 'Intelligence and the
Scaffold', an article he wrote for a special number of the periodical

Confluences entitled 'Problèmes du roman'. It is an essential humility every reader has to cultivate, namely to accept that all his insights are always reactive to the givens of an author. That article of Camus' appeared a year after the publication of *The Outsider* in 1942 and for me it is a most authentic statement of Camus' artistic aims. *The Myth of Sisyphus* which had appeared hot on the trail of *The Outsider*, in my judgement, in many respects distorted the expectancy of readers for decades: readers who were uncomfortable with the reality of the novel anyway, and who grabbed at the philosophy of the absurd to distract their attention from the complex and anguished affectivity of the book. I am almost inclined to believe that a reader nurtured in the Christian traditions of European cultures is hard put to empathize with the paradoxical sensibility of *The Outsider* and *The Fall* and their style of achieving fruition.

The Outsider

THE FOUR AWAKENINGS OF MEURSAULT

Argument

My argument (as the title indicates) is that in *The Outsider* Camus attempts to imagistically portray four distinct types of *awakenings* through the presence and narrative of Meursault in his socio-physical environment. I have deliberately eschewed the use of the cliché term 'character of Meursault' because Meursault achieves the unity of being a character only in the last paragraph of the novel. The four awakenings I would categorize as:

1. Awakening from the stasis of 'condamné à mort'.
2. Awakening from a state of innocence.
3. Awakening from a state of *méconnaissance* into recognition of Self and others (from corporeality into affectivity).
4. Awakening into mind: becoming personalized intelligence.

These categories are arranged here in an arbitrary schema. In the imagery of the novel they are transparently superimposed and confluent. It is this multiple super-imposition of themes that constitutes the book's unique style, its distinctive and enigmatic virtue and its status in modern literature as 'The Outsider' in its own right, as Sartre (1943) has pointed out. Camus has stated that the modern writer 'has given up telling "stories" and creates his universe'. And has explained the necessity of the use of images as deriving from the modern writer's conviction 'of the uselessness of any principle of explanation', and his certainty of 'the educative message of perceptible appearances'.

1. *Awakening from the statis of 'condamné à mort'*

Meursault has become one of the most extravagantly interpreted characters of modern fiction. He has been variously treated as 'un demi-raté intellectuel' (P. H. Simon), as a pagan god-figure (Champigny, Brée), as an anti-hero (Cruickshank), as hero of the absurd, and as 'the only christ whom we deserve' (by Camus himself in his preface to the American edition in 1955). But about one issue most critics are agreed: he is a man condemned to death and we owe his narrative to that inescapable fatality and fact.

What constitutes the nature of this identity of being a man condemned to death is more often than not interpreted in terms of society's hostile vindictive action against a man who has murdered one of its own citizens. I do not agree that this is the essential definition of the status of 'a man condemned to death'. My argument is that the death he is condemned to is an internal reality that he objectivates into an external fact through the gratuitous instrumentality of murder. It is the stasis of condemned to death from within that I shall study now from the images of the first half of the novel.

We encounter Meursault in a mood reminiscent of Prince Hamlet: he has been made aware of something but has neither the certainty nor the comprehension of it. The telegram tells him 'mère décédée ('your Mother passed away'). His first statement is 'aujourd'hui, maman est morte. Ou peut-être hier. Je ne sais pas,' ('Mother died today or, maybe, yesterday; I can't be sure'). He is benignly confused and refuses to examine it, though we see him afflicted with Prince Hamlet's royal ailment: 'meet it sire I write it down'. He will notate and imprint each sensation and impression diligently but take no responsibility towards it himself. In his case it is not his mother's ghost but the public prosecutor who convicts him of a tardy unfilial disposition. Of that later.

The next reaction he notates in himself is that of embarrassment *vis à vis* his employer and is conscious of its absurdity. When he asks for leave to attend the funeral he finds himself saying: 'ce n'est pas de ma faute.' ('It is not my fault.') Then he travels in a tired sleepy unresponsive state. The quiet deadness of the exact imagery makes us feel we are in the presence of an *organism* rather than a person. His reactions endorse this tone of deadness. He is well-behaved like his creator and registers all the impingements and records them. He has no hunger. He is in a state of static grief and it is not only about his mother's death. One begins to suspect a death has silently taken place much earlier: and only gradually we learn when. It is characteristic of Camus's use of imagery at this point that not only is it multivalent in terms of theme but also in terms of time. It reflects past and future simultaneously in the present. The absoluteness of the present is this two-dimensionality of time. His response to Marie's proposal further indicates his deadness towards his human environment; his negative response to his employer's suggestion of promotion not only shows his deadness towards himself but also where it derives from: when his educational life had stopped. But even more essentially we discover during his brief conversation with Salamano that deadness had entered his relations with his mother before she was put in the Home. So Meursault has been in a stasis of death for a long long while and lives it with an unprotesting authenticity of habits where experience has no meaning, only a perceptual-cum-sensation impact. It is this stasis he has to awaken from. His first intimation of the need to awaken is registered in his reactions when he hears Salamano crying for his lost dog and he 'began thinking of mother'. (Je ne sais pas pourquoi j'ai pensé à maman.) Soon after Meursault uses a patently Camusian prescription for awakening from the stasis of the inner death of grief: murder! We have seen this vehicle of action used by Camus in *Caligula* already and shall see it again in a story 'The Renegade'. The hyper-sensitive physical reactivity in Meursault is the same on the day of the murder as it was on the funeral day. And with murder he awakens himself out of this organismic torpor and becomes conscious of the meaning of hate in others and himself and with these of the meaning of love in life.

Murder and suicide in Camus are two sides of the same penny. They happen at the actualization of the limits of consciousness, that is, self-awareness. Camus states in *The Myth of Sisyphus*: '... killing yourself amounts to confessing. It is confessing that life is too much for you or that you do not understand it.' And in *The Rebel* Camus had postulated: 'In every act of rebellion, every man concerned experiences not only a feeling of revulsion at the impingements of his rights but also a "spontaneous loyalty to certain aspects of himself",' and Camus concludes with a typically cartesian rhetoric: 'I *rebel* – therefore we *exist*', and in Camusian narrative rebellion leads to death as inevitably as self-awareness does to suicide.

2. *Awakening from a state of innocence*

Meursault's stance of innocence before the murder is imaged in terms of: (a) direct immediacy of physical response to all sense-data (b) lack of malice (c) lack of reading meaning or motivation in human actions. Everything has a unilateral validity with Meursault and the human environment is basically confluent: only nature is the aggressor: sun, heat, light and noise. But this nature is not malevolent. It just is: equally resplendent in its gifts and its brutalities. All is accepted and accommodated to. Similarly, instinctual needs are facts of life and not compelling and complex wish-systems. Meursault eats when hungry, laconically talks when talked to, makes love without emotive elaborations, and serves when called upon. In a world where everything is striven for and arranged, fought for and argued about, he moves with a placid awareness without heeding its implications and meanings. He acts exactly but rarely in terms of a future. He lives, is tired, excited, fulfilled, hungry, even confused but does nothing to co-ordinate his experiences into a logic of life. He is happy and does not know he is happy. He is anguished without awareness. We see him as such but not he himself. And this world is being questioned by others all the time: the porter at the Home, Marie, Raymond and Salamano. But he drifts on blissfully transparent and immediate. Until the murder! Then he awakens and feels the concern, the hate and the love of others and for others! The second awakening! Henceforth his own life has meaning but not innocence. The characteristic virtue of this state of innocence is its generosity towards others. Meursault in the first half, before the murder, rarely refuses anyone anything. Everyone has equal rights on his attention. This generosity in him has been often misinterpreted as indifference (Y. C. Treil 1971). But it is the opposite of indifference. It is only through this generosity of innocence that he empathizes with the other's needs: with his employer's, Marie's, Raymond's. Even the arab's when he dissuades Raymond from shooting him uncautioned. It is precisely this generosity in him that will be most picked upon by the public prosecutor and used against him as a stance of complicity. He never questions the motives: if he can, he accommodates to their wishes. It has a child-like quality as Champigny has pointed out. It is natural and hence valid. It has no awareness of values. Another feature of this innocence is an *hauteur* of honour. Meursault always behaves honourably: that to him means authentically, and sincerely. He never lets his mind distort his experience or his response. He has a simple dignity that is convincing to everyone. His word is accepted in

favour of Raymond at the Police Station. It is this dignity of innocence that makes Marie call him 'a queer fellow' and warn him
she might hate him for it one day. As he shall hate himself and
others will hate him after the murder. He has to awaken himself
out of this innocence because it estranges him at root. The essence
of this innocence is that it is physical. Camus explains it in *The
Myth of Sisyphus*: 'The body's judgement is as good as the mind's
and the body shrinks from annihilation.' Hence Meursault cannot be convinced he has killed another living body. For him it
was an accident that traumatizes him to awaken to that which he
cannot psychically assimilate: murderous hate of *the other*. He
refuses to lose innocence, even when knowing it is no longer
possible.

3. *Awakening from a state of* méconnaissance *into a recognition of self and others (from corporeality into affectivity)*

Closely related to and subtly interwoven into the experience of
innocence is the stance of *méconnaissance*. We have met this
theme in the essay 'Between Yes & No' and also in Camus's
account of his first visit to Prague in the essay 'Irony in the Soul'.
After finishing *The Outsider* Camus was to devote a whole play
to this theme (*Cross Purpose*), and the same theme is anticipated
and reported in the piece of newspaper that Meursault reads in
the prison. What constitutes this stance of *méconnaissance* and
how do we encounter it in the book? I would like to offer the
hypothesis that the experience of *méconnaissance* crystallizes in a
world where Meursault feels himself at one with his environment,
especially the human environment. What has been often characterized as his feeling of absurdity is in truth little more than a lack
of recognition of the separateness of others from his own Self.
Méconnaissance consists in the perpetuity of a rapport which has
no differentiating awareness of the Self from the other. Hence a
feature of it is a repetitive experience of being ill at ease in the
company of others and dealing with it through withdrawal in the
service of adaptiveness. It is further characterized by heightening
the perception of the physical natural environment (sun, heat,
noises) as the only differentiating grade of experience. Camus uses
the maximum of his art and artifice to delineate the experience of
méconnaissance in the narrative of Meursault. For example when
during Marie's first visit to Meursault in prison after the murder,
where according to my argument the process of awakening into

recognition has already started, while the physicality of Marie and the room and others is registered in great detail, alongside Camus puts a youngster and his mother enveloped in an oasis of silence. And the matrix of *méconnaissance* is this sense of oceanic oneness with an object who cannot be communicated with. In this area of *méconnaissance* communication is irrelevant and impossible and it is misinterpreted, not only by the other characters in the novel, but by almost all the critics of the book as well, as a stance of estrangement and as an experience of absurdity in Meursault. That I regard as a misreading of the true experience in Meursault. In the novel until the point where he begins to gradually awaken into recognition of himself and the environment Meursault has no self-conscious awareness of estrangement from others. On the contrary he is convinced that he 'was just like everybody else; quite an ordinary person'. He is aware of this while talking to his lawyer the first time but sees that it will serve no purpose to communicate. Therefore one has to postulate a psychic and mental state in Meursault in which he can be aware of the difference between him and other people and him and his environment without having any motivation to harmonize this difference. It is the validity of this state in him, especially in the first half of the book and throughout the trial that creates the maximum tension between his experience and that of the other characters of the book, as well as between him and the reader. But to explicate this stance in terms of the theory of the absurd, and/or in terms of *Le Sentiment D'Etrangeté* as Fitch would like to call it, is to introduce value systems that are in fact foreign to Meursault's authentic experience. In this world of *méconnaissance* everybody impinges on each other, they hurt each other, even to the point of murder but there is no conflict or contradiction involved. And certainly no need for explanation. The factativeness and corporeality of the experience is its only validity. Neither mind nor imagination nor affectivity play a discriminating role in the arrangement or elaboration of this experience of *méconnaissance*. That it is not feasible in life is quite clear from the beginning and Camus sees to it that Meursault is aware of a certain discrepancy from the very start. The first time he owns up to recognizing others and himself as distinct objects about whom others can have a value judgement is in his conversation with Salamano where he is surprised to hear that the neighbours thought poorly of him about his sending his mother away to the Home. One of the basic functions of the trial episode is to transform *méconnaissance* into recognition and Camus with a terrible lucidity adumbrates the dawn of recognition in Meursault of himself as a distinct separate entity in a world of other human beings. It is in fact the most pitiless account of a man awakening towards himself and others and his fight against this awakening into recognition. This awakening into recognition had once again been started by the act of murder.

One fundamental characteristic of the state of *méconnaissance* is its capacity to sustain a febrile state of confusion throughout the book. Until Meursault's outburst with the Priest he is in a state of confusion. It is a theme that occupies a central position in Camus' sensibility and artistic endeavour. In his story 'The Renegade' he makes a maximal and terrifying delineation of such a state. That story was originally titled 'L'Esprit Confus'. The state of confusion changed into a state of conflict and muddle only with the dawn of recognition. Up till that moment it can sustain in it the most heterogenous incompatibles. One of the traits in Meursault's sensibility which makes him like *The Outsider* to most of the Western readers is that for two-thirds of the novel he lives by this balance of unambivalence and non-conflictuality in circumstances where the Western reader would expect a great deal of soul-searching and tormented Self-examination of conflict. In many ways the genius of Camus' art in this novel lies in his being able to depict in the life space of one character the complex process of acculturation and differentiation that it has taken some 2,000 or more years to crystallize in the cultural consciousness and sensibility of the Western man.

One further function of this stance of *méconnaissance* is that there is neither a YES nor a NO necessary to it. All relations are of a vegetative attachment and adaptive rapport. Thus love and hate are undifferentiated affects. Superficially viewed it is this which gives Meursault's behaviour its tone of sullenness, reticence and callousness. To him these are but the natural attributes of his confluent distance or physical intimacy in moral values as much as a man living in a stance of pre-ambivalent undifferentiated affectivity. Only the act of murder is going to compel him once more to take stock of his love and hate and become aware of a freedom that his own action looses for him. Up till now he has lived in a world where freedom was a synonym for existence itself: it involved neither choice nor decision. To this theme of *méconnaissance* Camus brings his most bitter and lucid irony. Like when the magistrate promises Meursault that if he repents he would 'become like a child, with a simple trustful heart, open to conviction', little realizing that that was precisely what Meursault had lost, and Meursault was in himself in his own awareness even now. In the state of *méconnaissance* everything was possible. Once it changes into recognition a *fatality* enters which allows for a lucidity but without hope or respite. Throughout *L'Envers et L'Endroit* we hear Camus say that in his brightest sunlit moments there was the presence of a *threat*. This *threat*, this everpresent suspicion of an X-factor which would intrude and compel decision and choice in the hour of maximal freedom and natural abandon was what was to *make* Camus one of the great writers in the French tradition of moralists.

4. *Awakening into mind: becoming personalized intelligence*

This awakening constitutes that aspect of Meursault's sensibility which binds him closest to Camus the writer and thus gives him the added function of becoming the narrator of his own experience. It is for this reason that to discuss this aspect of Meursault is tantamount to discussing the whole style and method of creation in Camus. To Camus, *intelligence* means something at once sacred and potentially nihilistic. It entails the end of beauty and innocence, but also the very means that make living in the human world a responsible act from choice and freedom. Many critics have been puzzled by the rather sudden change of a naïve laconic physical Meursault into an intensely intelligent mind, assessing itself and pitting itself starkly and violently against all the traditional Christian lore of his people. This way of evaluating what happens in the novel is not only untrue to what Meursault experiences, but also disregards the means Camus uses to establish the inescapable human responsibility of becoming mind at all cost. In 1945, he was to make a very passionate plea, 'that we must save intelligence'. In his essay, 'Intelligence and the Scaffold' (1943), Camus gives us an explicit statement of his aims as a novelist, a French novelist:

You need to be two men in order to write. In French literature, the great problem is thus the translation of what we feel into what we want to make other people feel. What we call a bad writer is one who expresses himself by reference to an inner context that the reader cannot know. This leads the mediocre writer to say everything he pleases.

The great rule of the artist, on the contrary, is to forget half of himself in favour of communicable expression. This inevitably involves sacrifices. And this quest for an intelligible language whose function is to mask the immensity of his fate, leads him to say, not what he pleases but only what he must. A great part of the genius of the French novel lies in this conscious effort to give the order of a pure language to the crises of passion. In short, what triumphs in the works I am discussing is a certain preconceived idea, by which I mean intelligence.

And later, he says explicitly:

The novel uses intelligence to create its universe in the same way that the theatre makes use of action.

The awakening of mind in Meursault creates one of the most enigmatic twists in the creation of this novel. I had said at the start that Meursault suffers from Prince Hamlet's compulsion: to note and record his impressions rather than to experience them or give them meaning. He is also the narrator in first person, and yet through at least two-thirds of the novel he remains innocent of the meaning of his experiences or their implications. This has been often explained away by the theory of the absurd and Meursault being its spokesman. To me, this is a rather forced judgement and the irony of it is that Camus himself foisted this bias on his readers by all the dogma of *Myth of Sisyphus*. One must not be misguided by Camus's *préjugées*, as he calls them in his 1958 introduction to *Envers et Endroit*. *L'Etranger* has its roots in the pre-Sisyphus Camus.

To say that is, of course, to over-state my case. *The Myth of Sisyphus* does give us many essential clues to a true understanding of Meursault's whole way of experiencing, cognizing and negating reality at its three levels: the affective, the psychic and the spiritual. Camus explicitly states: 'At the end of the awakening comes, in time, the consequence: suicide or recovery.' In *The Outsider* we have neither suicide nor recovery. But murder. And yet, as we shall see, here murder and suicide become mutual and reciprocal. An examination of Meursault's awakening to what he is and what he has lived, through his mind's awareness and interpretation of it, would make that clear. Camus states in *The Myth of Sisyphus*: '... in reality there is no experience of death. Properly speaking, nothing has been experienced but what has been lived and made conscious.' We have already examined Meursault's somewhat bemused and bored response to the magistrate's attempts to awaken human affective responses in him. When the magistrate had asked him: 'Why did you pause between the first and the second shot,' all Meursault can recall are the actual sensations he had experienced at the time: 'I seemed to see it hovering again before my eyes, the red glow of the beach, and to feel that fiery breath on my cheeks – and, this time, I made no answer.' Sensation was his absolute of experience. It is only in the last two sections of the book (4 and 5) that Meursault feels like communicating and attempts something near to what one would call introspection. Up till then Camus's narrative is so guilefully written that we do not become aware that all the 'story' as it goes through Meursault's consciousness is little more than a verbalized transcript of sensations: perceptual and physical. There is no comment or interpretation involved or implied. For example when Meursault does feel like cutting short the rigmarole that his lawyer and the prosecuting counsel had talked about him, he ends up with: 'However, on second thoughts, I found I had nothing to say.' The prosecutor insists, 'the prisoner is an educated man ... he knows the value of words'. And the only response it evokes in Meursault is: 'I noticed that he laid stress on my *intelligence*. It puzzled me rather why what would count as a good point in an ordinary person should be used against an accused man as an overwhelming proof of his guilt.' A little later he negates the whole issue by stating: '... I'd have liked to have a chance of explaining to him (the prosecutor), in a quite friendly, almost affectionate way, that I have never been able really to regret anything in all my life. I've always been far too much absorbed in the present moment, or the immediate future, to think back.' Here Camus uses irony in its most lethal and effective aspect of negating human responsibility by the very human responses: friendliness and affection! The prosecutor had found his soul 'a blank'. Once again in his recall of the prosecution Meursault loses 'the thread and was conscious only of the steadily increasing heat'.

Throughout these two sections Camus exploits with exquisite mastery and cunning the juxtapositions of mental states and physical sensations in Meursault. One deters and cancels the other, henceforth: '... I found that my mind had gone blurred; everything was dissolving into a greyish, watery haze.' And the ultimate private triumph of Meursault over his prosecutor and all the proceedings narrated in Section 4 is:

> Only one incident stands out; towards the end, while my counsel rambled on, I heard the tin trumpet of an ice-cream vendor in the street, a small, shrill sound cutting across the flow of words. And then a rush of memories went through my mind – memories of a life which was mine no longer and had once provided me with the surest, humblest pleasures: warm smells of summer, my favourite streets, the sky at evening, Marie's dresses and her laugh. The futility of what was happening here seemed to take me by the throat, I felt like vomiting, and I had only one idea: to get it over, to go back to my cell, and sleep ... and sleep.

In a most factual impersonal abrupt statement he tells the conclusion: 'I was to be decapitated in some public place.' I say *tells* because one cannot identify it as a communication: Meursault is alone with himself now; he has no audience, witnesses, persecutors, defendants or accomplices. Only from this state of absolute and total aloneness will he begin to introspect, or rather what would be his equivalent for such a psychic activity *vis à vis* one's life.

The last section of the book, section 5, makes us impersonal and uninvolved, and certainly unsolicited, witnesses to this new psychic experience in Meursault, trying to shift from innocent corporeality into the awareness that comes with becoming a mind and a human person. Meursault focuses now on a concrete detail: 'The only thing that interests me now *is* the problem of circumventing the machine, learning if the inevitable admits a loophole.' I have deliberately italicized the *is* in that statement, because very subtly Camus shifts the locus of time here. Meursault henceforth *is in his present with an awakened consciousness of it.* Up till now there has always been an ambiguity in the narrative of Meursault between what was happening and what was being reported. Now the happening is in his *mind.*

The first function of becoming mind in Meursault is the release of the capacity to remember:

> When such thoughts crossed my mind, I remembered a story Mother used to tell me about my father. I never set eyes on him. Perhaps the only things I really knew about him were what Mother had told me. One of these was that he'd gone to see a murderer executed. The mere thought of it turned his stomach. But he'd seen it through and, on coming home, was violently sick. At the time I found my father's conduct rather disgusting. But now I understood; it was so natural. How had I failed to recognize that nothing was more important than an execution; that, viewed from one angle, it's the only thing that can genuinely interest a man? And I decided that, if ever I got out of gaol, I'd attend every execution that took place.

Immediately after this Camus introduces the most astonishing and unexpected complexity in his characterization of Meursault. We have encountered and known Meursault so far only as a phenomenological entity whose cerebrations merely notate into a verbal narrative his physical sensations and experiences. Camus gives him a new identity now: a psychological one. Meursault is thinking about how one could escape 'the rat-trap' of the guillotine and muses:

> Still, obviously, one can't be sensible all the time. Another equally ridiculous fancy of mine was to frame new laws, altering the penalties. What was wanted, to my mind, was to give the criminal a chance, if only a dog's chance; say, one chance in a thousand. There might be some drug, or combination of drugs, which would kill the patient

(I thought of him as 'the patient') nine hundred and ninety times in a thousand.

Camus's narrative leaves one in no doubt that he intends the reader to note and register this new identity of Meursault not as a prisoner but as *a patient*. The prisoner can be innocent; the patient is inevitably responsible for his condition and sustains it from will and choice. The prisoner can be an innocent victim of impersonal laws and prejudices and hence can make himself indifferent to them. As Meursault had done so far. But a patient *suffers* from what he is and cannot be impersonal towards it. Camus gives his narrative a brusque and abrupt turn and leaves it at that. He does not explicate it in terms of Meursault's subjectivity. In fact Meursault accepts the new status of being 'a patient' by thinking about the apparatus of execution: 'the man under sentence was obliged to collaborate mentally, it was in his interest that all should go off without a hitch'. He also reassures himself for his lack of introspection: 'Imagination has never been one of my strong points.' And regresses to consoling himself with what his 'Mother used to say that however miserable one is, there's always something to be thankful for.' And further tries to sustain himself with memories of Marie but nothing works for him in this psychic domain:

> Then I did something I hadn't done for quite a while; I fell to thinking about Marie. She hadn't written for ages; probably, I surmised, she had grown tired of being the mistress of a man sentenced to death. Or she might be ill, or dead. After all, such things happen. How could I have known about it, since, apart from our two bodies, separated now, there was no link between us, nothing to remind us of each other? Supposing she were dead, her memory would mean nothing; I couldn't feel an interest in a dead girl. This seemed to me quite normal; just as I realised people would soon forget me once I was dead. I couldn't even say that this was hard to stomach; really, there's no idea to which one doesn't get acclimatized in time.

Just at this point Camus introduces yet another dimension. The corollary to the psychological man (patient) is the spiritual being! He introduces the chaplain:

> My thoughts had reached the point when the chaplain walked in, unannounced. I couldn't help giving a start on seeing him. He noticed this evidently, as he promptly told me not to be alarmed.

This is Camus's only concession to the Christian ethos in this novel. And here we have the acutest presentation of *méconnaissance*. The chaplain talks of despair and guilt, while Meursault can experience and identify only fear in his present situation. And the whole psychic structure of Meursault breaks down finally:

> Then, I don't know how it was, but something seemed to break inside me, and I started yelling at the top of my voice. I hurled insults at him, I told him not to waste his rotten prayers on me; it was better to burn than to disappear. I'd taken him by the neckband of his cassock, and, in a sort of ecstasy of joy and rage, I poured out on him all the thoughts that had been simmering in my brain. He seemed so cocksure, you see. And yet none of his certainties was worth one strand of a woman's hair. Living as he did, like a corpse, he couldn't even be sure of being alive. It might look as if my hands were empty. Actually, I was sure of myself, sure about everything, far surer than he; sure of my present life and of the death that was coming. That, no doubt, was all I had; but at least that certainty was something I could get my teeth into – just as it had got its teeth into me. I'd been right, I was still right, I was always right.

After his *excitement*, as he calls it, Meursault falls asleep, only to awaken with the certitude that death was freedom:

> Almost for the first time in many months I thought of my mother. And now, it seemed to me, I understood why at her life's end she had taken on a 'fiancé'; why she'd played at making a fresh start. There, too, in that Home where lives were flickering out, the dusk came as a mournful solace. With death so near, Mother must have felt like someone on the brink of freedom, ready to start life all over again. No one, no one in the world had any right to weep for her. And I, too, felt ready to start life over again. It was as if that great rush of anger had washed me clean, emptied me of hope, and, gazing up at the dark sky spangled with its signs and stars, for the first time, the first, I laid my heart open to the benign indifference of the universe. To feel it so like myself, indeed so brotherly, made me realize that I'd been happy, and that I was happy still. For all to be accomplished, for me to feel less lonely, all that remained was to hope that on the day of my execution there should be a huge crowd of spectators and that they should greet me with howls of execration.

Thus, Meursault evades both the psychic and the spiritual to accept the finality of death as freedom and the necessity to experience the hatred of those he had not included in his existence. He had returned to his corporeal being as the ultimate reality: here life and death are equally sentient in experience! This paradox is what the four awakenings of Meursault had led him to. It constitutes the triumph of his affirmation of life as much as it encompasses his negation of intelligence and spirituality. For Meursault living is its own true sentient reality and death is its absurd and concrete fruition. By his affirmation of death by guillotine Meursault transmutes murder, through social justice, into suicide through choice; suicide thus becomes the condition of consciousness. In this context suicide and sincerity are one and the same in the human experience.

The Outsider was published in 1942, but a brief entry in the Carnets in May 1940 states: 'The Outsider is finished.' Few books have drawn so much attention and such diverse appraisals as Camus's The Outsider. Perhaps one reason why this short brusque limpid and flatly articulate novel has had such momentous impact is that in the character of Meursault Camus most vividly and economically captured and epitomized the central crisis of sensibility in European cultures in mid-century, namely the death of humanism. With almost a prophetic vision Camus created a character in Meursault who was to be the archetype of the generation of here-and-now instant people of the post-war period. The hippies, 'the beautiful people' and a host of others who have opted out of the continuity of tradition and are imprisoned in their immediate subjectivity and corporeality, with a militant negation of all intellectual and moral values, are all reflected in Meursault's transparent and fragmented sensibility. Meursault is the first character in European literatures in whom self-awareness never achieves either the intensity or comprehension or continuity of true self-reflective introspection. He cerebrates at the lowest level of awareness, outside pure physicality. The four awakenings of Meursault merely indicate a human potential in him which never coheres or personalizes into a deep affective consciousness of self or others. Hence the four awakenings of Meursault are symbolically as futile as the four shots he fires into the Arab, already dead from the first shot.

A singular virtue of Camus's literary creation of Meursault is that he is presented to us in no other context or frame of values than himself. In the Carnets, just after the start of the war, Camus had noted:

Rule: Start by looking for what is valid in every man.

What is valid in Meursault is the negation of mind, time, continuity and affectivity. He is not against anyone, only non-mutual. And his whole experience across the Camusian narrative never grows or changes in character. He lives to meet his death with the same two-dimensional fervour and exaltation as he had existed in all the happenings of his day to day life. The two-dimensionality of Meursault consists of personal corporeality and external space. It is the inter-action between these two that constitutes his true experience of himself and reality. To say this is not to belittle his experience of life. It is this element in Meursault which makes him paradoxical in the context of sophisticated European Christian industrial cultures. One must not forget that in Camus's conception and creation Meursault is a man who is happy and right. This is why I said earlier that Meursault belongs to the Camus of the pre-Sisyphus period, to the Algerian Camus. And perhaps the most graphic description that Camus has given us of the world and ambience of humans from which he abstracted the character of Meursault is in *Nuptials*. I quote one significant passage:

> But after all what denies me in this life is first of all what kills me. Everything that exalts life at the same time increases its absurdity. In the Algerian summer I learn that only one thing is more tragic than suffering, and that is the life of a happy man. But this can also be the path to a greater life, since it can teach us not to cheat.

> Many people, in fact affect a love of life in order to avoid love itself. They try to enjoy themselves and 'to experiment'. But this is an intellectual attitude. It takes a rare vocation to become a sensualist. A man lives out his life without the help of his mind, with its triumphs and defeats, its simultaneous loneliness and companionship. Seeing those men from Belcourt who work, take care of their wives and children, often without a word of complaint, I think that one can feel a certain shame. I certainly have no illusions. There is not much love in the lives I am describing. I should say rather that there is no longer very much. But at least they have eluded nothing. There are some words that I have never really understood such as sin. Yet I think I know that these men have never sinned against life. For if there is a sin against life, it lies perhaps less in despairing of it than in hoping for another life and evading the implacable grandeur of the one we have. These men have not cheated. They were gods of the summer at twenty in their thirst for life, and they are still gods today, stripped of all hope. I have seen two of them die. They were full of horror, but silent. It is better that way. From the mass of human evils swarming in Pandora's box, the Greeks brought out hope at the very last, as the most terrible of all. I don't know any symbol more moving. For hope, contrary to popular belief, is tantamount to resignation. And to live is not to be resigned.

It was from this physical ambience of lush summer and its gay humans that Camus had created the sensibility of Meursault. A sensibility that accepted the exalted authenticity of corporeal experience and made it omnipresent to the exclusion of mind and all its machinery of complicated duplicities. The body never cheats: that is Meursault's basic faith. The paradox that Camus presents us in *The Outsider* is the authenticity of corporeality which negates in turn both mind and culture and which equally paradoxically makes the choice of happy life synonymous with choice of death. In other words suicide becomes the condition of consciousness.

That was the young Algerian Camus giving us his first serious schema of human existence in *The Outsider*. Some sixteen years later the Europeanized Camus was to give us his disillusioned version of the murderousness of the omnipresence of mind, as against corporeality, in his last novel *The Fall*, published in 1956, some four years before his own absurd death in a motor accident in 1960.

The Fall or The Mind as Murderer

Clamence is the obverse of Meursault. Yet they are two sides of the same penny. Or to use a title of Camus's early writings, they are 'L'Envers et L'Endroit', which has been translated into English as 'The Wrong Side and The Right Side'. Only anyone, no matter how canny and erudite, would be hard put to decide who of them is the right side and who is the wrong one. Be that as it may, the dramatic contrast is explicitly actualized by Camus in his narrative, both in its technique of address and its sensibility. Clamence talks to *someone* all the time. He has an explicit relation with his interlocutor, even though the interlocutor remains anonymous and muted all through the narrative. Meursault on the contrary had merely verbalized his awareness. We can listen in but it is not explicitly addressed to us. Meursault was sheer corporeality; Clamence is total mentation. Meursault does *something* (the murder) and it changes his whole experience of life. Clamence is inert during the narrative. It has all happened and he is merely mentally reactive to it: that is his existence as we know and experience it from Camus's narrative. Meursault was innocent and stays so unto death; Clamence is haunted by guilt and remorse. Time was concrete and instant with Meursault; with Clamence it is absent. Clamence is a continuity of mentation; he cannot escape from it. He cannot sleep to rest, like Meursault. Meursault is vital; Clamence is hyper-mentated inertia. All this is explicitly stated by Camus through the verbiage of Clamence. Another important difference: Meursault is laconic, abrupt, episodic in his speech-consciousness; Clamence is interminable verbiage by way

of *free-association* (to use a Freudian concept). And three statements of Clamence establish this fact.

> We lack the energy required for evil as well as that required for
> good.

> My idea is both simple and fertile. How to get everyone involved
> in order to have the right to sit calmly on the outside myself?

> I adapt my words to my listener and lead him to go me one
> better.

It is my contention that we can comprehend the true intent of
Camus's narrative in *The Fall* only through a detailed examination of Clamence's relation to his interlocutor, who disappears
through that very function in the end, just as Clamence does. The
omnipotence of the mind murders both! The novel opens in a
bar in Amsterdam. Clamence sees a stranger whom he is going
to address as 'cher monsieur' and/or 'mon cher compatriote'
throughout the novel. Monsieur never utters a word throughout
the novel and we gather his reality and reactions from Clamence's
interjections towards him. Clamence solicits him to accept his help
towards ordering a drink. The tone of the novel is set at this point
by a nuance of avid derision towards the proprietor of the bar
whom Clamence designates as 'the worthy gorilla'. This is in
the first section. There are six sections of this novel, which is a very
cunning piece of miscalculation, because in fact the novel consists of five interviews or *entretiens* between Clamence and his
interlocutor. Just as *The Outsider* has five parts.

FIRST ENTRETIEN

In this first section, the whole relationship between Clamence
and his interlocutor is one of provoking hope in the interlocutor,
to get Monsieur interested in Clamence under the pretext that
it is Clamence who is interested in him. The technique that
Clamence uses to establish this intrigue with Monsieur is very
simple. Everything which normally a person would suspect in the
service of self-protection when they meet a stranger Clamence
immediately verbalizes to Monsieur. For example, he says, 'I
am talkative, alas, and make friends easily.' A little later he adds,
'Style like sheer silk too often hides eczema.' He now shows interest
in Monsieur, and asks him, 'Are you staying long in Amsterdam?'
and then immediately establishes a first oblique note of complicity
by a remark that is as innocent and beguiling as this: 'The heart

has its own memory.' And in case Monsieur should become wary
of all this, Clamence adds that touch of self-deprecatory cynicism,
which is to disembarrass one's needfulness of others by a vulgarity
of candour: 'It always seems to me that our fellow citizens have
two passions. Ideas and fornication.' By this time he has set the
outlines of four walls round Monsieur. If I may anticipate Clamence himself in his narrative, he has put Monsieur in the world of
'the little-ease'. There is already at this point in the narrative
another insinuation, thrown in very obliquely: namely, the reference to an empty rectangle marking the place where a picture has
been taken down. We shall see the significance of it later. Very
soon Clamence further flabbergasts Monsieur by declaring he is a
judge-penitent and introduces himself as 'Jean-Baptiste Clamence
at your service.' And continues, 'Pleased to know you. You are in
business, no doubt? In a way? Excellent reply! Judicious too: in
all things we are merely "in a way".' Already you see a certain
banter here, where familiarity and *méconnaissance* will criss-cross
with each other into a sort of spider's web. You can almost say
in Hamlet's words that Clamence's confessional is the play in which
he shall catch the conscience of the king (here Monsieur). Then
he declares his profession which is that he is a lawyer and he
announces that the profession is double. And he introduces by this
time yet another dimension and that is his *nudity*. I deliberately
want to use the word nudity, because he declares, 'Only one thing is
simple in my case. I possess nothing.' Because he is going really to
rob the consciousness of Monsieur of all its protective devices,
should Monsieur think that this man has somewhere a hidden
intention regarding him. Clamence clears the slate. Then Clamence
turns to self-conscious confessional to insinuate rapport: 'My
profession is double, like the human being.' What I mean is that
Clamence has a sudden apprehension that Monsieur may think
that Clamence is doing a confidence trick, so he cancels that too by
yet another of his witty statements: 'When one has no character,
one has to apply a method.' Still a suspicion lingers in him that
Monsieur has every reason to be on guard. So what does Clamence
do? He robs him of this particular natural self-protective attitude
also by declaring about himself, 'Even when the attraction is
strongest, I am on my guard.' He continues and then he realizes
one thing more. The last objection that a man could have to a
garrulous stranger is that of soliciting, so he says, 'You are most
courteous, but it is my overflow. As soon as I open my mouth,
sentences pour out.' And then he goes on about Holland and other
things. Quite suddenly, here he introduces the second theme, and
by this time the first act of complicity is established. He is just

going to take leave of Monsieur when he says to him, 'Till
tomorrow then, mon cher compatriot.' But before the parting, he
insists on the basic theme: 'Suppose after all that someone should
jump in the water.' Thus the first entretien ends. What is significant in the first section is the tone of the relationship which I will
characterize as ingratiating Monsieur, evoking hope in him, and
disarming all his possible doubts, and at the same time, insinuating
a concern about something important that *had* happened to
Clamence. What starts off by seeking to be a relationship has already
changed a little bit towards complicity, and towards the end of the
chapter the person who was addressed as 'cher Monsieur' has
changed to 'Monsieur et cher compatriote'. By establishing these
subtle fractional identifications, he dislocates Monsieur from his
separate identity. Hence the need for an atmosphere of ambiguity
and undecidedness: *vis à vis* himself and Monsieur. Clamence is
already beginning to *perform* in front of Monsieur. He uses wit
platitudinously, at this stage, to provide a décor: 'We are at the
heart of things here ... The middle-class hell, peopled with bad
dreams.' Soon he will be using wit as a weapon.

SECOND ENTRETIEN

We find Clamence with Monsieur, in the same bar, slightly gloating
over the fact that he had got Monsieur's attention with his use of
the phrase 'judge-penitent'. What follows is a very subtle sort of
a lampoon on himself. The fact that he has established rapport with
Monsieur, that is, has got him involved, compels Clamence to
introduce one of his diabolical ruses: 'I earned my living by carrying on dialogues with people I scorned.' So Monsieur has not much
of a future with Clamence. This is followed by further devaluation
of himself as a lawyer, to sustain the balance. He had complimented
Monsieur on his courteousness and now he debunks courtesy in
himself. He lets it be known to Monsieur how he really has never
been with anybody. He has always been operating from heights.
'I was talking, it so happens, of those supreme summits, the only
places I can really live,' and therefore we already notice how he is
beginning to distance Monsieur from himself. Everything that had
been worthwhile in his life, that he had done well or enjoyed, he
devalues. His profession, his body, and even, in fact, his present
seeking, because he makes it quite clear that he is seeking someone
to spite himself. As he says, 'I see that this declaration amazes you.
Have you never suddenly needed understanding, help, friendship?
Yes, of course,' and in the very next sentence he debunks what he is

seeking, or rather the value of what he is seeking, because he says,
'I have learned to be satisfied with understanding. It is found
more readily and besides, it's not binding.' And now, somewhere,
the second thing that he had insinuated in the first entretien turns
up. Monsieur is curious about that evening that he had referred to.
And so Clamence says, 'What? What evening? I'll get to it, be
patient with me.' So he asserts his omnipresence. What had started
off in an appeal for sympathy, understanding, and dialogue, is now
taking on the shape and form of a mechanism to control the object.
And at this point Clamence deposits his personal, private weakness
as an aside: 'Maybe we don't love life enough? Have you noticed
that death alone awakens our feelings?' But both he and Monsieur
can't take this, so Clamence has got to undo it immediately, undo
it in the mind of Monsieur and for himself as well. That is the
important point I am trying to make at this stage of the narrative.
That every success that Clamence achieves by way of a rapport, he
has to undo. Therefore, we hear him saying a little later, 'That's
the way man is, cher Monsieur. He has two faces: he can't love
without self-love.' And then we have a great deal more of evasive
chatter, which is very significant towards an understanding of
Clamence, but not in the context in which I am talking at the
present moment. He edges nearer to telling about that evening.
He makes it absolutely clear that what happened to him happened
when he was riding 'on the crest of a wave'. And now he tells of
laughter at the Pont des Arts. How after a very well-fed good evening he had heard this *laughter* in a mood where he felt he was
dominating his environment, where he had a feeling of power,
almost of completion. He heard the laughter behind himself and
he was dazed. At this point the second entretien ends, but before
it ends he points to someone in the bar and repeats the theme of the
theft, which is now identified as the theft of the painting. Here we
are near to the climax of the novel, because we have heard of the
laughter, we have heard of the theft, but at the same time, everything is so ambiguous, and what was in the first entretien an
appeal to create a relationship with Monsieur, is now already
changing into a subtle form of discouragement, as if Clamence was
giving him a chance. The vehicle of this discouragement is insinuating that he would like to be sharing the fate that Clamence has
come through. So the slight nuances of self-pity hold a touch of
insolent pride to them now. But the situation is open at this
moment. We see a stance of need and a gesture from helplessness,
or rather from an area of helplessness, which after all is what loneliness is, already beginning to transmute itself into an abyss of
grandiloquent self-consciousness, in which Monsieur is gradually

losing more and more of his own initiative as reverberated in the omnivorous consciousness of Clamence. We get at this point an uncanny sensation that it is Monsieur who is falling.

THIRD ENTRETIEN

Clamence starts in a stance of deliberate politeness and thanks Monsieur about his curiosity about the laugh, and he protests that he is not feeling quite up to the mark. He makes a nostalgic reference to Sicily and the sunlight, and suddenly he interjects, 'Commanding is breathing – you will agree with me?' Thus he already establishes himself in the omnipotence of his own dismay to relate to anybody. He adds a little later, 'Somebody has to have the last word,' and then he really lets it be known to Monsieur that for all practical purposes the game is over between them: though he puts it in the abstract impersonal, 'We have become lucid. For the dialogue we have substituted communiqué.' So Clamence has given up the hope of a dialogue and henceforth the whole thing is going to spiral down towards a communiqué. Then, with a virulent objectivity, he describes and defines his double-face, and how he is a play actor, and in the very way which he debunks himself, he literally, through words, decomposes Monsieur's presence and sentience as acid does. He announces, 'Fundamentally, nothing mattered.' Then suddenly he recovers himself. He really has not quite got his victim yet. So he says, 'Let's be fair to myself.' This is the first time in the narrative that Clamence has used the word 'us' to include Monsieur and himself as one unit, yet talking about himself as a different entity altogether. A little later we hear him dictating to Monsieur, 'I lived consequently without any other continuity than that, from day to day, of I, I, I.' And culminates it in his statement, 'I never remembered anything but myself.' But now that Monsieur has been put in his place and is no longer a person with autonomy, style, or presence, but merely a mechanism that Clamence can use, Clamence's fatedness begins to express itself, and the metaphor that Camus chooses to describe can hardly be matched anywhere else. It takes a very simple form. A yarn about a motor-cyclist who had offended Clamence, and whom Clamence had failed to put down, to dominate, and this is where we hear for the first time the words 'Code of honour' and 'shame' turn up, but it is important to remember in this context that by now Clamence to all practical purposes is talking *in his own head* to himself. Monsieur is an inert vegetable, but still it is significant for us to note here how much helplessness, shame, and lack of completion, are at the root of it all. It is for the first time also that in this context Clamence notices not Monsieur but his environment. He says, 'Why, it's raining again. Let's stop, shall we, under this portico?' So now the hell of Amsterdam has swallowed up Monsieur. And now Clamence can exercise the techniques by which he re-established himself from the state of humiliation, helplessness, and non-completion. Even more pertinently we see him use his technique of becoming the person who is going to be guilty, and then parcel it out to the rest of mankind. We hear also about Clamence and his sensuality; Clamence's deficiencies from his accounts of his affairs with women, etc., etc. To absolutely nail down the fact that Monsieur has no longer an autonomous presence, Clamence states, 'I'll agree with you, though you politely haven't said a word, that that adventure is not a very pretty one. But just think of your life, mon cher compatriote! Search your memory and perhaps you will find some similar story that you'll tell me later on.' And by this one simple statement, the guilt-provoking omnipotence of Clamence has swallowed up the autonomous presence of Monsieur. And then there is a lot of cynicism, but suddenly he recovers himself and lets it be known in almost an aside that perhaps it is shame that is at the root of it all. 'Isn't it shame, perhaps? Tell me, mon cher compatriote, doesn't shame sting a little? It does? Well, it's probably shame, then, or one of those silly emotions to do with honour. It seems to me in any case that that emotion has never left me since the adventure I found at the heart of my memory, which I cannot any longer put off relating ...' But we should note that before he really tells of the crucial thing on which he pins down his awakening towards himself, he has now destroyed the possibility of a relationship, sympathy or dialogue with Monsieur. So in fact he is merely chattering in his head to himself. We now read of that fateful night, three years before the laughter, when he had just left a mistress and he was passing a bridge when he saw a slim young woman, dressed in black, and then: 'I had already gone some fifty yards when I heard the sound ... of a body striking the water. I stopped short but without turning round. Almost at once I heard a cry repeated several times, which was going downstream; then it abruptly ceased ... I wanted to run and yet didn't move an inch ... I felt an irresistible weakness steal over me ... I told no-one.' There is a sort of pause where he draws attention to Zuyderzee, and as if Monsieur has made his last movement as a human being in this entretien, Clamence says absent-mindedly, 'What? That woman? Oh, I don't know. Really I don't know. The next day and the days following, I didn't read the papers.' That is how the third entretien ends.

If we follow the tone, we notice that in this third entretien, Clamence is much nearer his style when he was a lawyer in Paris: elegant, polite, uninvolved, and explicit. In his gestures he is persuasive. He is still paying lip-service to establish a dialogue, but already he is certain that it is an act of complicity that he has achieved. Hence he adumbrates the role of the communiqué. Once it is established that there can be nobody there to hear him, he comes forth and declares everything. Particularly the tragic climax which is the drowning of the woman. So from this point on it is Clamence who is going to talk in the void and abyss of his omniloquent self-consciousness which can be heard by no one, stopped by no one, assuaged by no one – hence it is too late, as we shall hear at the end of the novel. And that is the climax of Clamence's encounter with Monsieur. The next three sections are largely a way of establishing what had happened to Clamence, but in fact they are not very relevant to the relationship between Clamence and his interlocutor, or Monsieur. I shall therefore rather briefly go through these.

FOURTH ENTRETIEN

Straight off, it starts with derision: 'A dolls' village, isn't it? No shortage of quaintness here! ... A flabby hell, indeed! ... I have no more friends: I have nothing but accomplices ... To make up for this, their number has increased; they are the whole human race. And within the human race, you first of all.' Now he has absolutely made it clear that Monsieur has no personal identity left so far as Clamence is concerned. He is the first accomplice, the first victim. Then follows the talk about suicide, and it is in this context of mistrust, lack of an object, the search for an ideal state, that the theme of suicide is launched – and sandwiched with the theme of suicide is the theme of judgement. Therefore, we begin to have a suspicion for the first time that the only stance left for Clamence which would make life feasible for him in the face of the necessity of suicide, because of the impossibility of innocence, is to become a judge. But not just a judge, a judge-penitent: 'We should like, at the same time, to cease being guilty and yet not to make the effort of cleansing ourselves ... We lack the energy required for evil as well as that required for good .. I was obliged to make myself a judge-penitent.' And now he brings in everything, absolutely everything, because he is above himself also, and he flaunts his virile self-pity, his duplicity in order to conquer, his scorn, but above all, his lack of seriousness, and the whole thing reaches a sort of nadir of self-denigration. But it is no longer his denigration – it is the denigration of mankind, of which at that moment Monsieur is the sole representative, but not Clamence. And he says very clearly, 'One must accuse oneself in a certain way, which it took me considerable time to perfect.' There is just a little tinge of life still left in the vegetable Monsieur now. Therefore Clamence counsels him: 'Don't you think we should keep silent to enjoy this rather sinister moment? No, I interest you? You are very polite. Moreover, I now run the risk of really interesting you. Before explaining myself on the subject of judges-penitent, I must talk to you of debauchery and of the little-ease.' Clamence knows of course by now that it is not a dialogue. It is only him and him alone. Therefore, in the fourth entretien we see the beginning of the fall of Clamence, and how it establishes its pace and momentum. The fourth entretien is divided in the narrative into two sections: Sections IV and V.

Section V

What had started earlier in the fourth entretien now reaches its maximum crescendo in the fifth section. Here already there is 'we.' 'What should we do there, I ask you? ... *We* have a sense of decorum; scum gives us a stilted manner ...' Monsieur is no longer identifiable as separate from Clamence, and we have here perhaps the most brilliant polished rhetoric of mockery, sacrilege, blasphemy, degradation, and despair. If anywhere in Camus there is a testament of private fate rendered with a bejewelled objectivity, it is here. And everything is thrown in – Christ and everyone – because once Clamence has lost hope of relatedness, he is, to use Joyce's apocalyptic witticism of despair – H.C.E. (here comes everybody), the hero of *Finnegans Wake*. And therefore, the section ends in a bizarre parody of Christ's words, 'I am the end and the beginning, I am the law, in short, I am the judge-penitent.'

FIFTH ENTRETIEN (*Section VI*)

And gradually we reach the final stage in which Clamence is in bed ill, and the tone changes. He is now the anti-hero and the stasis of inertia has set in, and we see that this man has never experienced anything, never been anything. He is nothing but words and his only virtue is that he has been, as he puts it, permissive towards himself. And that abnegating from grace, he had established judgement as his master, of which he was the sole mechanism and of which only omniloquence was the route to that endless *fall* which is his future. This, to me, is Camus's definition of the new task of Sisyphus, not pushing a stone up but sustaining its fall for ever. Hence we hear about his fear of freedom. And at the very end he lets it be known that all his life his idea has been very simple: 'How to get everyone involved in order to have the right to sit calmly on the outside myself?' And here Camus tells us a very significant detail, because after all by this time there is no Monsieur left. There is only the reader and Clamence and the instrumentality of the presence of Camus as the writer. So we are given the secret which we must never forget when reading this book. Clamence says: 'No, I navigate skilfully, multiplying distinctions and digressions too. In short, I adapt my words to my listener and lead him to go me one better.... The prosecutor's charge is finished. But at the same time the portrait I hold out to my contemporaries becomes a mirror.... Then imperceptibly I pass from the "I" to the "we".... The more I accuse myself, the more I have a right to judge you.' But in fact, at this point there is no 'you' left, but only Clamence himself. And we watch a person getting asphyxiated. In fact, the last chapter of this book is a very subtle form of a description of a man drowning, who cannot breathe, who cannot move, and who has a last wish left: that is to be decapitated. 'I would be decapitated, for instance, and I'd have no more fear of death; I'd be saved ... I could again dominate. ... All would be consummated.'

I want to restate that what we have seen is how Clamence was seeking a dialogue from within the reality and reciprocity of a relationship to a stranger. But in fact, a diabolical mechanism of his mind (which I have interpreted to be the function of mind as murderer) can no longer allow him to be in that area of vulnerability, helplessness, and trust, from which alone conversation is possible. Hence a very genuine act changes into compelling murder on another, but unlike the murder by Meursault, this is a mental murder, a judgement. So it is limitless, bloodless, soundless, and absolute. Leaving the murderer both penitent and judge. And from here it is but natural that the end should be either suicide or involvement of another with their consequent elimination. I shall now summarize my argument about Clamence's relationship to his interlocutor and its logic. Many critics have tried to identify a parallel between Camus's use of dialogue between two people to the use made of this by others. It is in fact both at once: 'One had to overwhelm oneself to have the right to judge others.' Some have said he is very like the hero from Dostoievsky's *Notes from the Underground,* a person soliloquizing; I do not think so. Another person has said that it is very much like listening to a person talking on the telephone. I think, that, too, is not true. Furthermore, I do not think it is like the relationship between the two speakers in Diderot's novel *Rameau's Nephew.* I think the only way for us to identify the nature of this entretien that Camus establishes is to compare it to the clinical situation: where a person in need comes or seeks out to tell his story to another with the aim of seeking a cure. Let us remind ourselves that in the last entretien, Clamence takes up the stance of a *patient* very deliberately. If I were to abstract my own experience in this area, I would say that the vast varieties of clinical syndromes and psychic ailments in terms of the communicative pattern can be divided into three groups:

1. Where a patient arrives, is confused, is in distress, and has no way of speaking or communicating his distress, but is legitimately in the area of his vulnerability and pain. The instruments to print this into the communication have to be forged mutually.

2. Where a patient comes and his inner distress and conflict and pain has more or less neatly organized itself in terms of symptoms or problems. This is the most usual sort of patient, where verbal communication is the most adequate means of finding out and knowing and resolving, that is, healing.

3. Lastly, there is the patient who arrives with every intention to have a dialogue, and in fact gradually establishes a sort of sovereignty of a communiqué about his life-space and as one listens to such a patient, one finds that one's role and function are gradually eliminated by the very nature of the communication, its style and its content. I think it is precisely this third type of communication that Camus uses between Clamence and Monsieur to show how reaching out from an area of need towards another person, the process grows not towards communication but changes into issuing a long communiqué and the aim changes from relating to being understood. This craving to be understood is an autonomous state in Clamence towards which no separate person can contribute. Hence we see that by the end of the narrative, Monsieur has become a sort of inert mirror-image of Clamence: 'But of course you are not a policeman; that would be too easy ... You practise in Paris the noble profession of lawyer! I sensed we were of the same species. Are we not all alike, constantly talking and to no-one?'

The pathos as well as the absurdity of Clamence's predicament is that he is drowned in the omniloquence of his own mentation. In the end this interminable mentation destroys not only his interlocutor but himself as well. Thus through Clamence's mentated odyssey Camus shows us that the mind's expertise can be just as murderous as the body's musculature. And that in the last resort what one murders is never *the other* but only *one's self*. Therefore the condition of consciousness, corporeal or mental, is suicide. The opening sentence of *The Myth of Sisyphus* states it explicitly:

> There is but one truly serious philosophical problem and that is suicide.

Conclusion

In the characters of Meursault and Clamence Camus depicts for us two basic types of alienation and dissociation of sensibility that are prototypic of the individual as an entity in contemporary European cultures. In Meursault this alienation is through the self-sufficiency of corporeality, which though rejective of none, is equally un-mutual and non-belonging. Meursault is a physical human isolate. Camus shows us that his attempt at 'recovery' does not succeed and he chooses death as his rightful fruition. Meursault can neither relate to anyone nor be related to. He is sympathetic in an impersonal animal way. In a certain sense he is almost noble. And he is always utterly true and un-cheating. But he has neither feelings nor object-relating. He is an isolate and would much rather perish as such than yield to human mutuality with individuals or culture. Clamence is equally alienated, but in a different way. He is not so much an isolate as an autonomous entity. His mind can exploit instinct and social situations, but it stays dissociated and alienated in itself. Nothing reaches him. His attempt at recovery through confessional communication only destroys his interlocutor, and then pushes him to death by his own hyper-mentation.

That a writer nurtured in a social milieu that was only derivatively European should have so acutely and accurately diagnosed and crystallized the *sickness* of the European individual is the true measure of Camus's genius. Without apology or parody or cynicism he portrayed in the characters of Meursault and Clamence what was to actualize as the corrosive malady of the industrial European cultures: an egotistical alienation that is as lethal in the end to the future of the individual as it is nihilistic of the traditions of the cultures he is reared in. Camus did not prescribe suicide as a solution; he diagnosed it as the only logical climax and fruition of, both the corporeal and mentated pursuit of selfhood, and consciousness, in contemporary European cultures.

Bibliography

Brée, Germaine, Camus, Rutgers University press, New Jersey 1959.
Camus, Albert, 1942 The Outsider, Penguin Modern Classics 1961.
Camus, Albert, 1942 The Myth of Sisyphus, Hamish Hamilton, London 1955.
Camus, Albert, 1956 The Fall, Penguin Books 1963.
Camus, Albert, 1957 The Exile and the Kingdom, Hamish Hamilton, London 1960.
Camus, Albert, 1962, 1964 Carnets, Hamish Hamilton, London 1963, 1966.
Camus, Albert, 1951, The Rebel, Hamish Hamilton, London.
Camus, Albert, The Collected Plays of Albert Camus, Hamish Hamilton, London 1965.
Camus, Albert, 1968 Lyrical and Critical Essays, Alfred A. Knopf, New York.
Champigny, R., Sur un héros paien, Gallimard, Paris 1959.
Cruickshank, John, Albert Camus, Oxford University Press, London 1959.
Fitch, B. T., Le sentiment d'étrangeté, Minard, Lettres Modernes, Paris 1964.
Pingaud, Bernard, L' Etranger de Camus, Classiques Hachette, Paris 1972.
Quilliot, Roger, La Mort et les Prisons, Gallimard, Paris 1970.
Sartre, Jean Paul, Camus's 'The Outsider' in Literary Essays, The Wisdom Library, New York 1943.
Simon, Pierre-Henri, Présence de Camus, Editions A. G. Nizet, Paris 1962.
Treil, Claude, L'Indifférence dans l'oeuvre d'Albert Camus, Editions Cosmos, Paris 1971.
Trilling, Lionel, Sincerity and Authenticity, Oxford University Press, London 1972.

7 The Language of Enlightenment

A. C. CAPEY

He that hath light within his own clear breast,
May sit i' the centre and enjoy bright day.
But he that hides a dark soul and foul thoughts
Benighted walks under the midday sun.
Himself is his own dungeon.
JOHN MILTON, *Comus*

O dark dark dark. They all go into the dark,
The vacant interstellar spaces, the vacant into the vacant,
The captains, merchant bankers, eminent men of letters,
The generous patrons of art, the statesmen and the rulers,
Distinguished civil servants, chairmen of many committees,
Industrial lords and petty contractors, all go into the dark,
And dark the Sun and Moon, and the Almanach de Gotha
And the Stock Exchange Gazette, the Directory of Directors,
And cold the sense and lost the motive of action.
And we all go with them, into the silent funeral,
Nobody's funeral, for there is no one to bury.
T. S. ELIOT, *East Coker*

Yea, and no man dared even throw a firebrand into the darkness.
For if he did he was jeered to death by the others, who cried: 'Fool,
anti-social knave, why would you disturb us with bogeys? There *is*
no darkness. We move and live and have our being within the light,
and unto us is given the eternal light of knowledge, we comprise
and comprehend the innermost core and issue of knowledge. Fool
and knave, how dare you belittle us with the darkness?'
D. H. LAWRENCE, *The Rainbow*

Introductory: Catchwords and the Literary Critical Challenge

It is significant that the critic responsible for giving currency
to 'enlightenment' in its derogatory sense should have been des-

cribed as inhabiting an 'unaired corner' – the critic, F. R. Leavis; his detractor, Graham Hough, in a *New Statesman* review. The light and the dark are not now the generally agreed phenomena that they would be in a culture which was sure of its standards and directions, and when Mr Leavis issued *Nor Shall My Sword*, sub-titled 'Discourses on Pluralism, Compassion and Social Hope', more than one reviewer felt obliged to inform us that those terms, widely accepted as attitudes or goals deserving of support, were in fact challenged in the Discourses. Between those who question the popular orthodoxies and those who accept them there is no debate; the forces for acceptance are too strong to feel the need to do more than shrug the shoulders at the rare challenge put to them. To question compassion, or the assurance with which it is invoked, is felt to be an assault on the finest and least selfish motives of civilized man: 'Surely you want, or know that you *ought* to want, the best for other people's children as well as your own? Surely you pity, or know that you *ought* to pity, people with less material wealth than your own? Surely brotherly love, neighbourliness as exemplified by the Good Samaritan, is at the heart of the Christian Gospel?' To assert the uniqueness of Christianity, its fundamental character in its origins among 'a peculiar people' and the paternal-ist (*sic*) selection of its first ministers is to question the unquestion-able assumption that an 'open' approach to 'comparative religion' is the properly pluralistic and compassionate way ahead for a liberal and multi-racial democracy, of which equality will be the hallmark; while to suggest that the prescription of equality may be a debatable means to inadequately conceived ends (in educa-tion or in anything else outside abstract arithmetic) is to risk immediate classification as an élitist, a back-lasher or a Tory.

The difficulty of isolating the fashionable catchwords and 'deep-sleep phrases' for reflective scrutiny is not that they *do* possess some valid meaning – that they express for the intelligentsia the partial truth which maxims and proverbs have for the uneducated – but that they have infiltrated the very places which exist to challenge them: the universities, colleges and schools. There they cohabit, in increasing comfort (it seems), with genuine thought and scholarship; and an inquiry into their use in places of education and learning may be mistaken for Black Paper misgivings. The risk of instant dismissal – as tide-stemmer, crusader or Leavisite – must be taken, however, in the belief that there *is* an intellectual public willing to consider the utility of another light than that shining upon enlightenment – a light shed simply by the setting of questions.

In saying that educational institutions exist to challenge the current catchwords and the assumptions they derive from and give expression to, I am not proposing to limit the purposes of schooling. What I am emphasizing, as the *raison d'être* of English studies (English lying necessarily at the nervous centre of 'the humanities' and our national culture), is the critical spirit of the undertaking. The critical spirit is not something applied to our literature, but something provoked and sharpened by growing consciousness of it, by the critical spirit supremely alive in it. And the critical spirit, with its developing sense of the complexity and profundity of life and truth, cannot rest on the kind of assurance represented by 'liberty, equality, fraternity' or (to come up to the minute) 'participation', 'involvement', 'relevance' and 'openness'. The prejudicial assumptions behind those words as commonly employed are so deeply grounded in confidence of their indisputable rightness that 'thought' is given little room to manoeuvre; and the opposite danger for anyone trying 'thoughtfully' to resist the fashion arises in the temptation to throw in his lot with Peter Simple and the Amis-Conquest 'Educational Dictionary' of *Black Paper Three*. The critical study of literature, in requiring the free play of the mind and the sensibility, and the simultaneous subjection of them to the book in hand, inhibits the facile dependence on catchwords as expressions of truth and purpose. Two illustrations must suffice.

Consider *Anna Karenina*. Participation with the peasants and involvement with their lot is an element in Levin's dream and ideal, but Tolstoy does not succumb to the dialectic opportunities afforded by the relation of Levin to himself. The differences between master and men are not merely inequalities caused by malignant defects in the social order but differences in the rhythm of life and expertise: an important lesson for Levin is that the peasants can scythe a field without tiring themselves. A Marxist view of Oblonsky – the amiable, philandering husband of Dolly – would similarly be less comprehensive than Tolstoy allows: Oblonsky's reliance on friends in high places for his lucrative income (he has already wasted Dolly's wealth) goes no nearer 'placing' him for the reader than does his initial affair with the governess. When Anna is ostracized for breaking the rules, for being 'open' about her affair with Vronsky, something more subtle and challenging is presented than the hypocrisy of Russian high society: the marriage of Levin and Kitty, and even the pitiable state of Dolly's marriage and her threadbare wardrobe, are contrasted with the contraceptive pretence of Anna's life with Vronsky, a life which has the superficial dignity associated with 'rôle-playing' and a 'life-style'.

The study of literature, we may say with *Anna Karenina* before us, inoculates us against the tyranny of catchword and cliché; a great book compels by its complex organization and life our recognition of the inadequacy of familiar 'thought-forms', creates through its positive subtleties the standards against which we may negatively 'place' the crude shorthand of jargon and the assumptions that jargon makes. The Steeplechase chapter, without intending to do so, disposes of the doctrine of 'audience-participation', exposes the phrase as a glib simplification of the delicate and shifting relations between 'done', 'shown', 'observed' and 'shared'. The scene on the course, where Vronsky rides his horse confidently at first, then carelessly and disastrously, is observed by Anna, agitated in the stand; and Anna's exposed feelings (so much more than observations) are observed by her husband, who is implicated in the drama and yet insulated from it. No one who has read the Steeplechase chapter can again utter the catchphrase with quite the ease it requires; his sensibility has been modified too far to permit it.

'Hierarchical, élitist, establishmentarian, static, closed, anti-democratic' – the words are Albert Rowe's,[1] if words so redolent of enlightened abuse can be said to be personally his. Applied to the world of *Anna Karenina* they would intimate a failure of sensitivity towards the novel, a socio-political distortion of what Tolstoy offers us; in fact they describe Mr Rowe's view of 'our society until recently'. Whether Mr Rowe would sound his enlightened trumpet if he were writing of Chaucer we cannot be sure; but certainly the age of Chaucer is far enough removed from ours to qualify for the given description. In applying Mr Rowe's terms, however, we have to bend their intended significance to match a different picture. There was indeed a social hierarchy in Chaucer's day; it is reflected in *The Canterbury Tales*, and specifically in *The Prologue*. But the hierarchy which gives the Knight the first place and allows us to think of the Cook at the bottom of the table is not to be dismissed as a primitive or immature conception from which it has been our achievement to advance. Democracy is practised when the Host seeks approval from the company at the Tabard for his plan; but the unanimous consent expressed is a less than human response to a loud-mouthed bully, 'fit to be a marshal in a hall'. The intervention of the Knight, when the quarrel between Pardoner and Host threatens to obliterate the very notion of a pilgrimage, is felt as the proper responsibility of *primus inter pares*: the intervention, the recalling of the combatants and the company generally to the object of their journey, expresses creative

[1] See his essay in *Education for Democracy*, Penguin.

as well as corrective authority applied to turbulence. Certainly the Knight is of the élite: Chaucer does more than tell us of his qualifications; he shows him actively engaged, on behalf of the pilgrim band, asserting the authority that is rightly his – felt indisputably to be right, and so authoritative. Without the Knight, the pilgrims would be subject merely to the Host, life and soul of the party and self-appointed master of ceremonies. The freedom each pilgrim enjoys, to be himself and to tell his tale, is at the least associated with the delicate sense of hierarchy in an established order. To describe Chaucer's society as static and closed would not carry the critical import that the invocation of the words in Mr Rowe's context is designed to carry; social stability and the security of a determined purpose on earth are of some account, especially when presented – as Chaucer presents them in *The Nun's Priest's Tale* – in an ironic and qualifying manner. Chaucer's values and judgements are not the product of a static and closed mind; they are fine and dramatically tentative, and being so they point to qualities in fourteenth-century society that we are not liberally endowed with today.

'There can be no going back': I am not meaning to suggest that Chaucer's or Tolstoy's society represents something worth our diligent efforts to recover, nor even that the past deserves more respect from educationists than it commonly receives. The specific purpose of the illustrations has been to demonstrate the utility of literary studies at a time when catchwords of a peculiarly disrespectful character towards our national heritage (consider the force of the temptation to place inverted commas around that phrase) are exercising an insidious tyranny over us. The demands a great poet or novelist makes on us to be precise in our formulations about his work, and to eschew simplifications of vocabulary and attitude, are demands we need to be able to meet if we are to mount an assault on the language of enlightenment from a sure position.

'All Change!'

The language of enlightenment draws many of its words and ideas from the language and ideas of technology, industry and economics, with results that would be ridiculous if they were not menacing. The application of such terms as 'plant', 'productivity' and 'utilization' to school buildings and churches has affected the *thinking* about their nature and purpose. The Welsh mountains have mineral resources, and so (with the logic of enlightened derivation) schools acquire resources centres, theological colleges are described as resource-points, and the complimentary adjective 'resourceful' ironically disappears from the scene. The United States army speaks of its hardware, and sure enough schools acquire hardware departments and colleges advertise lectures on 'The Uses of the Hardware' and 'The Philosophy of Overhead Projection'. Does it *matter* that such language is humourless, pretentious and fundamentally thoughtless? After all, we know what it *means*; why object to the current shorthand?

The point is that the words mean rather more than they purport to mean. Their employment signifies that the speaker is of the present and looking eagerly to the future, that he is one of the enlightened. To call a theological college by its customary name might imply that young men were being prepared there for 'the office and work of priests'; and since the notion of priesthood is regarded by the enlightened as inappropriate in a participating democracy something suggestive of a supply-depôt is to be preferred. A school's resources centre is not always or only dignity language for the stock-cupboard and filing cabinets, but a sign that the *spirit* of technological revolution has been adopted. The reviewer in *The Use of English* who expects eventually 'there will thud on to [his] desk a bulging unseemly package – the first Interdisciplinary Thematic Projectile – [which] no doubt he will have to plug ... in',[2] exemplifies the kind of resistance to change which the futuristic push of the 'hardware' provokes in some of us: invocation of the word denotes eagerness to press forward to the day when the teacher shall be one teaching-aid or resource among other and mechanical ones.

The enlightened educationist feels no personal resistance to those pressures. A characteristic statement of faith is this, from the editorial of *The Dudley Educational Journal* (Vol. I, No. 1):

> It is apparent that we must change our educational ways and restructure our educational system in the light of the philosophy which informs our times.... It is also apparent that this restructuring must involve a new kind of reciprocal relationship with the schools and the acceptance of a new partnership in the teacher training process.

When *The Human World* quoted that, as representative prose in an 'unremarkable' publication, it expected the reader to make the obvious dismissive judgement and to pass on to more engaging matters. But for the student of enlightenment the feeble language provides a pertinent example of the trends in educational dis-

[2] David Ogilvie, in Vol. 22, No. 4.

course. The author is as far as it is possible to be from the unenlightened Gibbon:

> The present is a fleeting moment, the past is no more, and our
> prospect of futurity is dark and doubtful,

or from the humanly desperate Burns, momentarily envious of
the living mouse:

> Still thou art blest, compar'd wi' me!
> The present only toucheth thee:
> But, Och! I backward cast my e'e
>   On prospects drear!
> An' forward, tho' I canna see,
>   I guess an' fear!

The light that never was shines unclouded upon Dudley: 'It is
apparent ...' How, one wonders, would the author respond to the
challenge: 'Oh? I hadn't noticed....'? It is inconceivable to him
that anyone should want to put such a question. Once the prose
has got into motion (it starts with the 'tide in the affairs of men' –
Brutus at his most obtuse and platitudinous) it creates its own
ideal response; the reader is assumed to be in the swim with the
writer, borne along by the current of change to which he adapts
himself without question. Thought has fled the page before the
words begin to deliver their enlightened message; language serves
only to communicate the pre-determined idea.

   And the idea? – There isn't one, of course, unless the James
Report and the ATO reviews are to be taken as read, crouching
obscurely between the lines of assured optimism. The assurance
rests on nothing so solid as the James Report, but on the placid
iteration of key words and phrases. If these seem tired – 'involve-
[ment]', 'relationship' and 'partnership' have an especially
routine ring – they should not delude us into supposing them
the harmless patois of the Education Department. 'Partnership'
and 'relationship' are amicable smoke-screen words for the sinister
intention to prise apart the universities and their colleges of education, and to place the emphasis in the colleges on 'teaching skills'
– the skills which practising teachers may be supposed to have so
mastered as to be ready to pass on to their successors. (Ursula, thou
shouldst be living at this hour!) If 'reciprocal relationship with
the schools' means anything it means a reduction in the time and
importance at present accorded to a student's main subject (his
opportunity to read for personal pleasure and profit regardless of
his professional concerns), more 'methodology' and less educational
theory; while 'those who can't teach' are to exchange pulpits with
'those who can't do'. The intention, however confused and clouded

by the jargon, emerges with stunning clarity in the final phrase: the way forward to the Mechanical World Picture typified in the factory 'process' (see Mr Abbs' essay in this volume) is actually to be via yesteryear's despised notion of 'teacher training'; the wheel, as in *Animal Farm*, has come full circle.

Whether the enlightened educationist perceives the irony is doubtful; his enlightenment is focused on and in his vocabulary, in the creative activity of dismantling the old edifice and building a new, in the hand of reciprocal friendship extended across the deep divide between college and school to someone he *must*, willy-nilly, accept as his partner in the enterprise. 'Must' is an essential word in the enlightened man's dictionary, and in the passage under review it is supported by 'acceptance' to denote the compulsory purchase of our opinions; we are not to consider a proposition, we are simply to accept the inevitable. It is the same imposed fatalism that may be detected in the injunction to 'come to terms with' something; unless we come to terms with the trend we shall be 'left behind', 'irrelevant', 'a backwater' – and the appeal to fear in the injunction is as insidious and nasty as such appeals are in the language of advertising. There are to be no negotiations in the coming to terms; the end in view is pre-determined.

The passage is representative; if it were not so, there would be no case for dwelling at length upon it. In the following example, a little less representative, the appeal to force not only lacks argumentative vitality but slips into the hectoring tones of the bully:

> ... The changes [which the schools] will be forced into will be towards becoming democratic communities ...
> The changes are being, and will be, forced on the schools, because for the first time the majority of the members of our society are demanding a more equitable sharing of educational resources and of wealth, and a better quality of living. Those educationists who are moved by a concern for their neighbours' children equivalent to the concern for their own should help forward these changes by all the means in their power.
> ('A Headmaster's View', *The Dudley Educational Journal*, op. cit.)

The bully has the mob behind him, or so he claims. He cannot rely, as the editor of *The Dudley Educational Journal* can, on insidious support for the language of enlightenment, but stands, a Napoleon at Vienna, with overwhelming numbers at his back. 'Forced', 'demanding' and 'should' are menacing words, mixing uneasily with the appeal to selfless compassion, which in the context looks suspiciously like an invitation to jump on the bandwagon. We are not expected to challenge the reality of 'the majority', to question whether due 'concern' exists in the demand for 'equitable sharing'; we are merely to succumb to the twin appeals of enlightenment and 'power'.

The voice there is Albert Rowe's. Here, from a leading article in *The Guardian* for 4 October 1972, is Mr Short's:

> The aim will be to create a comprehensive post-school sector in which priority in the allocation of resources will be given to those institutions, autonomous or public, which are ready to offer broadened opportunities.
>
> ... The expansion to cater for [the doubling of numbers of students qualified for higher education] must take place anyhow and the pressures to find the resources which this will create will lead to widespread rationalization of resources; for example, by sharing facilities, groupings of institutions, the creation of new, more comprehensive, institutions, etc.
>
> [There] must be ... a reduction in the present unit costs in higher education. It is quite indefensible that when vast numbers of young people receive an appallingly inadequate education for want of resources, the universities should under-use their resources to the extent they do; for example, an academic year of four ten- or eleven-week terms would still leave vacations far in excess of what most people have and enable first degrees to be taken in two and a half years.

Who can resist the prospect of 'broadened opportunities', 'expansion' and 'the creation of new ... institutions'? Nor is it pie in the sky: the vision is accompanied by hard, realistic reference to 'the allocation of resources', 'the pressures to find the resources', the 'rationalization of resources' and the 'want of resources'. No one could accuse Mr Short of seeking something for nothing; he knows as well as any one that education costs money.

The combination of laudable vision and realism is not, however, so irresistibly right as the author intends it to be. The 'broadened opportunities' signify not the extension of higher education but its modification to suit the abilities of those (the majority) who are not capable of benefiting from a university. The real implications of 'allocation', 'pressures' and 'rationalization' become clear: there are to be no 'new institutions', but the universities are to change their character and their standards to accommodate students who are not qualified to benefit from them; 'comprehensive' is less a generic term for post-eighteen education than a prescription for change similar to that being applied to secondary schools. And what is to happen to the university students (earlier in the article stigmatized as an élite)? – They and their teachers have had it too good for too long: cut down their holidays to size; accelerate the production-belt. Apart from the envy and malice implicit in the proposed 'sharing' and 'groupings' (with the consequent effect upon the meaning of those words), and the idea that the greatest good of the greatest number depends not on increasing the provision of higher education but on the contraction of one part of it, we have to observe Mr Short's failure to understand what a university *is*, what it can mean to a nation to have institutions whose *raison d'être* is something more disinterested than merely vocational or utilitarian pressures would allow it to be. His ignorance of the purpose of university vacations is depressing.

There are no doubt progressive voices in education today who would wish to dissociate themselves from Mr Short, and certainly he does not represent enlightened thought at its most respectable. But as a politician and erstwhile minister of education he makes a point of reminding us of the power of the executive in an area increasingly discussed in *avant-garde* political terms; and however unpolitical the intentions of the editor of the *Dudley Educational Journal* there is a discernible trend from *his* opinions via Albert Rowe's frenetic outburst to Mr Short's – a trend further exemplified by the editors of *Education for Democracy*, the spirit of whose remarks is that of a bulldozer clearing the ground for the 'development' of democratically conceived high-rise flats:

> We want more and better education of a type appropriate to a democracy, and leading towards a much more democratic society than we have at present. Education for democracy, not for aristocracy, meritocracy, plutocracy, or any other kind of élitist system.

'The future in their bones'

Educational jargon makes menacing inroads into our language. We are continually exhorted to rethink, radically to reappraise, to create a fresh climate for this or that, and by way of workshop experience (preferably in a small group discussion situation) to develop new approaches and make innovations. If we and our work are to be relevant, we must stimulate involvement and student participation in decision-forming processes, referring unresolved conflicts back but meanwhile making as much eye-ball contact with our pupils as our resources permit. Ideally each contact-session is an unstructured shared experience: a multimedia, multi-form course with performative elements is the viable route to semantic hygiene. In such a democratic situation the rôle of the teacher is non-paternalist, open and exploratory.

The difference between that paragraph and the kind of thing

we are accustomed to reading in educational textbooks lies not so much in the quantity of jargon as in the purpose to which it is put. One would hesitate to condemn educational writing on the strength of its numbing effect on the layman. Nevertheless some of the prejudices and presumptions of enlightenment – especially its inability to stand back from itself and take a critical glance from the layman's position – may usefully be emphasized by presenting the jargon not as shorthand for thought but as gobbledygook. I may go back to my paragraph and reappraise its utility; am I bound thereby to find it useless? A new approach to a problem may help us in solving it, but without some notion of the goal the ways towards it may not matter very much. If discussion by small groups is a useful means of education, is it the only or the best means? The current fashion is 'creative talk' – but what about, on what basis, and for what ends, are not questions fashionably asked. I may wish to share an experience with my students – but some experiences are private, some become different experiences when shared, and 'sharing' anyway carries too strong an emotive aura to be serviceable in educational discourse. It belongs, one suspects, with 'groups', 'involvement', 'participation' and 'democratic' as an element in a general attitude which has been allowed to sprout unquestioned – an attitude which relies on 'paternalist' and 'authoritarian' to make the case against the unenlightened.

Words, wrote Taya Zinkin, have an unfortunate habit of imposing themselves and excluding thought. Such imposition/exclusion is to be found even in the language of English specialists, where (if my earlier account of the value of literary study holds) it is most to be deplored. Here, quoted by John Dixon in *Growth through English*, is Paul Olsen 'on the work in the US curriculum centres':

> My feeling is that in so far as we've done anything good it's been in creating a kind of intellectual community among college people and school people, working together, trying to go through the great tradition to discover what might be relevant to the question, trying to rethink these things for ourselves, trying to create curricular materials in very small groups which work intensively, trying then to elaborate the relationships between these materials, and sending people back to their own schools. When they get back to their own schools, they themselves create similar kinds of study groups; ... *they create their own curricula.*

The use of 'creating' at the head of the passage exemplifies imposition/exclusion. The word carries today enormous cachet, so that the writer can simultaneously assure us of his right attitude to education and expect from us a comprehending nod of approval. It has no more purposeful function there than that: it helps the modest 'feeling' and the workshop-man's 'done' to nudge us into accepting the 'intellectual community' as a measure of clearly defined aims and achievements. But 'community' in turn is a restful word: without thinking about it we are expected to respond alike to it, to glow in the warmth of its general implications. 'Working together' adds nothing to the sense; but again it acts as an earnest of the writer's up to the minute faith in 'very small groups', the *sine qua non* of the best modern practice. The incremental repetition of 'trying' operates rhetorically in association with 'working together' and 'work[ing] intensively'; its purpose is to assure us that the groups have their sleeves rolled up, their braces taut. The word *means* nothing, descriptively; and its emptiness spreads to the surrounding generalizations – the discoveries, the rethinkings, the relationships and the materials – which beg for acceptance as legitimate abstractions on the strength of their enlightened connotations.

That anything worth our sustained attention should be present among such windy guff is not to be expected, and by the time we reach the author's triumphant conclusion, *they create their own curricula*, we may well be stupefied beyond the capacity for thought. We would be wrong, however, so to submit to the impositions/ exclusions of the style. The deadness of 'create' at the end of the intensive-creative-elaborative process is effectually a decoy; our attention needs rather to be fixed on the sinister implications of 'their own'. Those apparently inoffensive words have not arrived by accident. They are at the heart of the inevitable conclusion to be drawn from enlightened disrespect for 'the great tradition' (uttered too easily for it to indicate ability or willingness to consider the idea of a tradition), enlightened search for relevance ('discovery' and 'question' in the context carry no sense of honest doubt or genuine openness to the unknown), and enlightened individualism: 'their own' stands at the end rhetorically supported by 'their own schools' (twice). Association of the branches stemming from the 'curriculum centre' is not to be through a commonly derived purpose and substance; instead we are promised proliferation of discrete particles, recognizing no authority beyond themselves, and resembling each other only in their style of reproduction.

'The great tradition' is of course a ready target. Misconceived respect for 'well-tried customs', our 'heritage' (national or literary) and books which have 'stood the test of time' has been partly responsible for the impatience shown in enlightened circles towards 'traditional attitudes which ... impede progress' (J. Vaizey, quoted by Mr Abbs). But a certain cocksureness seems to have overtaken and by-passed the respectful disrespect that *Scrutiny* used to show.

That there may be something worth retaining from 'the Heritage of Literature', of benefit to the present phase of civilization, is brushed imperiously aside by the characteristically enlightened thinker:

> This is literature enshrined, something to know about, like historical or geographical facts, in order to establish one's cultural *bona fides*. The key word used in this approach is 'taste', and it is promulgated by the universities in their own degree courses, and in their public examinations, with a corresponding effect upon school syllabuses. One is familiar with those who know about Shakespeare and know what poetry is – and what it is not – without actually having to experience either.[3]

One wonders which universities the authors have in mind, and whether 'taste' can be developed from merely 'knowing about' books 'without ... having to experience' them. One wonders whether the authors have ever visited a shrine, and whether they do not rather mean 'embalmed' or 'becalmed'. One wonders... but one isn't asked to wonder: one is expected simply to applaud the writers' neat dismissal of an aunt sally whose removal is required to make room for discussion of other 'approaches [to English] in our educational system'.

Of another 'approach', less cavalierly treated, the authors have this to say:

> ... The school of teaching represented by approach B [*Literature as Mores*] has been chiefly concerned to establish a canon of literary works that embody 'the best that has been thought and said' – and felt: that is, the concern has been with literary art as the embodiment of the civilisation of any given period and the affirmation of perennial values within the context of that period...
>
> But this is likely to have little relevance to the growing child, whose concerns are his immediate external and internal condition. The approach, therefore, runs into difficulties where it seeks (or is felt by the pupil) to impose patterns of values and feelings. We think it fair to say that approach B fails to take sufficient cognisance of the pupil's own individual creative needs, of his need to create his own pattern of values and feelings within his contemporary context.

It is outside my brief to take detailed issue with the writers. They have their reply in the words of Raymond O'Malley,[4] who writes

---

[3] M. Torbe and D. M. Wallerstein, 'General English in a Primary College of Education', *The Use of English*, Vol. 22, No. 1.

[4] 'I cannot think of the teaching of English otherwise than as a continuing evaluation from the beginnings of speech right through to the books written in eventual retirement; from nursery rhymes ... to *King Lear* ... The evaluation and the criticism are a never-ending process; values can't be established once for all, packaged, stored and brought out at need ... A

from within 'the school of teaching represented by approach B', and whose sense of the child and of the child's values shows nothing of the determined assurance represented by 'the growing child's ... concerns are (*sic*) his immediate external and internal condition'. That the teacher 'cannot pilot his pupils' taste towards "the good" in literature unless he has succeeded in arranging all the literary works he knows, both past and present, in a hierarchical order of value'[5] is the point between 'the affirmation of perennial values' and the question of its 'relevance to the growing child' that the writers have omitted – conveniently, for their purposes, which are to present 'approach D, ... the result of a fertilization of English by ... Institutional Linguistics', as the proper course to follow.

The matter is worth an argument, elsewhere. Here, I wish to isolate the peculiarly enlightened features of the passage – to stress, with a backward glance at Olsen's 'creation of their own curricula', the significance of 'the pupil's own individual creative needs', 'his own pattern of values', and the supposed irrelevance of 'the best that has been thought and said' to 'the growing child'. Of course, once you claim, with the necessary tautologous emphasis, that the individual belongs to himself, that his values are his own, you are no longer *aware* of 'the best that has been thought and said'; the Arnoldian dictum shrinks to idiosyncratic proportions, there is no 'best', 'values' becomes a synonym for 'personal preferences', and Tom Brangwen sitting by the sheepfold under the stars must have been sentimentally misdirected. No longer need you look over your shoulder at 'the one bright book of life' or reckon as worth contemplation the Laurentian assertion that 'the novel is the highest form of thought': it's irrelevant to the growing child.

'Revolution in Religion'

A pair of photographs in *The Guardian* for 6 July 1972 faced the reader who fell for the bait on p. 1 – 'Bishop advocates lowering the age of consent', or words to that effect. On p. 14 the eye was arrested by the naked bottom of a girl advancing on all fours (perhaps what is meant by 'the woman taking the dominant rôle'?) towards a large, bearded and clothed man reclining in bed and waiting unenthusi-

judgement is more than a whim, more than an indulgence of personal inclination. It is made in relation to standards attained through individual discipline, standards not only perceived but felt, and taken into the bloodstream. 'Received' judgements just don't work in the circumstances of English teaching.' (*The Use of English*, Vol. 23, No. 2, p. 144)
[5] F. S. Whitehead, 'Continuity in English', *The Use of English*, Vol. 22, No. 1.

astically upon the event. In heavy type across the middle of the page
was 'Sex and the law'; and a grinning Dr John Robinson, in full-
bottomed wig, lacked only a finger to point us to the sexual
liberation available under religious emancipation. The text of
his article proved to be not so different in tone from the spirit of
the pictorial titillation as one would have expected from an address
delivered originally to the Methodist Conference earlier in the
year. One crucial passage is this:

> [The criminal law] is not there to express ... 'the anger of morality',
> however 'abominable' may be the object of its disapprobation. It is
> there as far as possible to enable people to be free, mature, adult
> human beings, or what the New Testament calls 'sons'. Of course, it
> cannot make people sons. But it has a rôle, a limited rôle, in hinder-
> ing the hindrances. It is limited because the free processes of
> influence, education, example and persuasion are so much more
> productive...

And Dr Robinson's final paragraph concludes:

> ... The way is open, now more than ever, for the immense corporate
> task of helping to transform ourselves from a paternalistic society,
> through the adolescent pains and follies of a permissive society,
> *towards* a more genuinely mature society.

That there is a distinction to be made between the law and
morality may be granted; but their relation is important too, and
if the law did not reflect, however negatively and imperfectly, the
values and standards of society it would be no true law. 'The
punishment of wickedness and vice and the maintenance of ... true
religion and virtue' – a seventeenth-century version of Dr Robinson's position – are not only a personal but a social and national
responsibility. To see the 'limited rôle' of the law as excluding
'the anger of morality' is to reduce it to that of a bureaucrat, with
consequences for the anger of morality:

> 'I am not condemning you,' said the Judge. 'I am merely arranging for
> you to be detained for a few years. I do not myself rape girl guides
> to rounds of applause from my friends, but if you find fulfilment
> in doing so you are free to say so. My job is not to compare my life-
> style with yours and pass moral judgement (for who am I to judge
> you?): it is simply to present you with the bill for your exercise.
> Let me see now – that will be seven years, less discount for personal
> propriety ...'

– If that is unfair to Dr Robinson, would it also be unfair to say
that he appears himself to be incapable of the anger of morality,
that he finds the 'pains and follies of [the] permissive society'

THE LANGUAGE OF ENLIGHTENMENT

somewhat other than 'abominable' (the inverted commas indicate it is not a word he is personally ready to use), that he is less interested in expressing 'disapprobation' than in celebrating freedom, maturity and a generation come of age? Such things are positive, disapprobation is negative; above all, let us be *positive*! The negative words have only to be uttered for us to take the implication: there *is* no abomination (not, at any rate, in 'the field of sex').

Dr Robinson's positives, however, are not valid alternatives to the inadmissible negatives. 'Free', 'mature' and 'adult' make their unmistakable appeal to members of the permissive society, as if the writer were turning to them and saying: 'Look, I can use those words too: we speak the same language.' In using the words, which could equally well be employed to describe the bare-bottomed advance of the emancipated woman engaged in a mature relationship with an adult lover, Dr Robinson is in fact being disingenuous towards both the permissivists and his co-religionists. He really has no business to confuse 'the glorious liberty of the sons of God' (a liberty attainable through means not dependent on the world and the flesh) with freedom from childhood constraints and being given the key of the door. Nor should he allow 'free', which he first invests with religious qualities, to appear in a second and very different context: who, in 'the free processes', is free – the persuader or the educated, and if not both why not? In Christian terms the freedom is of the nature of the *acknowledgment* of 'sonship', realized through it; liberty to reject the Christian claim is different. A secularist might suitably object that Dr Robinson is playing to the secular gallery while really purposing to indoctrinate us. Certainly the Methodist Conference is being assured that the Conversion of England not only does not depend on the law but can be accomplished much more thoroughly without its support.

For the law has 'a limited rôle'. Dr Robinson is prepared to have the law 'protect the young and the feeble-minded', but really (as an adult) his interest lies beyond the law. He has a vision of 'a more genuinely mature society' that has passed through the adolescent present from the childhood of the past – a childhood governed by a stern Victorian father, against whom we have as adolescents rebelled (painfully and foolishly, it is true – but once the age of consent has been lowered the pains and follies will fade away). My own vision is of the Methodist Conference stirring to join the Bishop in 'the immense corporate task' of converting the nation by stealth: Don't mention *God*, get them to think of a ripe apple or the fullness of middle age.

When 'paternalistic' and 'mature' are delivered with such

assurance, 'the way is open' for 'the revolution in religion'. That phrase heads an article by Ninian Smart, published in *The Guardian* two months after Dr Robinson's piece, and beginning:

> Religion is getting to be important again. A revolution is going on in religious education as more and more teachers and educationists perceive the exciting possibilities of teaching religion in a serious, open, and emphatic way.

The reader is not to question 'serious, open and emphatic'; he is simply to catch the infection of mounting excitement and join the revolution. The language is irresponsible in that instead of challenging the mind it insists on the reader's unthinking endorsement of its presumptions, making its appeal in the hectic manner of a TV advertisement. Journalistic terms require the writer to express his 'rational and sensitive view' thus:

> In the past the subject has suffered from being seen as, and indeed often taught as, a weekday dosage of Sunday school. Early mental wounds have lingered on in the spirits of grown men in high educational places, so that it is hard to get across a rational and sensitive view of the subject: but times are happier now.

– The 'rational' element there is an appeal to the rationalists for support – the rationalists and secularists who think and write of religious instruction harming children, of it inflicting 'mental wounds' upon them; the writer is vote-catching from the opposition. His irrational appeal is enforced by the allusion to 'spiritual wickedness in high places', by the implied charge that the 'grown men' who disagree with him have not grown up (how could they, suffering from their lingering Sunday school wounds?), and by the caricature of past practice as 'a weekly dosage of Sunday school'.

That there are discriminations to be made – that men's ideas and motives may be more complex and respectable than 'mental wounds', that the history of RE is not to be so cavalierly dismissed, that Sunday schools themselves are worth a closer look than can be provided by a phrase calculated to produce a consenting giggle – such things do not concern the writer. He acknowledges a present and a future, but no past. His central image is that of the 1970 Conservative Manifesto – RE 'should stand on its own feet'. Images of ill-health, disablement and deprivation are presented in contrast to such manly independence and vitality. 'RE has been crippled by dogmatism and an arid biblicism', 'religion is too important to be propped up by special pleading', and 'teaching Christianity as though [it were] the universal faith of the land ... can create a lot of ill-will, as well as scarring some pupils' feelings'.

'The new RE', on the other hand, 'just because it transcends dogmatism, can heal sectarian wounds [viz. in Northern Ireland].' The language leaves no room for discrimination, for thoughtful evaluation of pre-revolutionary practice. Nor is it designed to do so. We are pressed into going all the way with its author, the 'rational and sensitive' way invisible to the mentally wounded – the way ahead for a multi-religious society and peace in Northern Ireland.

The writer's contention is that since the arrival in our schools of 'Jewish, agnostic, atheist, Moslem, Hindu and Sikh', the time has come to provide the children with 'options and a wider perspective through the teaching of the comparative study of religion'. That sounds liberal enough – though 'options' is an unfortunate word in the context, suggesting inappropriately that the pupils are free to take their choice (perhaps they are, in the classroom); and the 'wider perspective', a term commonly used by the enlightened, may mean only that the children are to get a 'dosage' (it could hardly be more) of many religions rather than one. The writer is optimistic:

> ... the teaching of explicitly religious phenomena and ideas should be realistic. Beliefs must be seen to gear in with practice ... beliefs must be seen in the context of the rituals – the belief in God, for example, being inseparably united to the worship of God. Bible lessons in the past have often been useless and foolish because they did not relate to the use of the Bible in church, still less to the ongoing life of Christianity.

Whether the school timetable will allow for 'experimental worship' (my phrase, with apologies), or whether school children are capable of grasping the variety of Christian forms of worship (let alone those of other cultures), seems to me the sort of question we might have been asked to consider. But the syllabus presents no apparent difficulties to the writer; as was said of C. P. Snow in another context, 'he has no hesitations'. That the 'wider perspective' may prove a prescription for wider ignorance – the magnitude of the task, the limitations of the teachers and the incapacity of the children together producing Tom Sawyer's confusion between the first two disciples and David and Goliath – is not envisaged by the writer, off whose pen roll 'the Upanishads ..., Gandhi, yoga, caste, bhakti, Vishnu and Shiva' – knowledge which the children will tap in the course of widening their perspective. (For a sixth former to widen his perspective while reading *A Passage to India* would of course be a different matter.) Only when he comes to mention

> the implicitly religious nature of many of men's thoughts and feelings – their coming to terms with death, the nature of human

> love, the sense of the awe-inspiring, the relation of men to the
> material universe, and so on

does his assurance waver:

> By encouraging reflection on these matters, so far as it is within the
> capacity and readiness of the pupil, RE can relate explicitly religious
> ideas to these areas of puzzle and wondering.

But even the reservations are muted by the progressive concept of
'readiness'; and we are still asked to accept, without specific illustration, the suitability for schoolchildren of the abstract concepts
relayed with such ease and aplomb ('and so on').

The Other Side – and the Vital Darkness

Confident abrogation of tradition, continuity or simply 'the past'
is a characteristic vice of the language of enlightenment, present
in some degree or other in the examples given. Further examples
are listed by Mr Abbs, whose illustrations of the 'informing belief
in growth' show how pervasive is the language of enlightenment –
sometimes consciously propagandist (as in advertising), sometimes
an expression of eagerness to keep abreast of the rapidly changing
times, sometimes unconscious. But perhaps the most disturbing
feature is the absence of debate, the assumption that there are no
questions to be asked, and the consequent 'failure of communication' between writer and critical reader. The examples I have given
are not equally reprehensible; but the implication that their
authors 'move and live and have their being within the light', and
that there really is nothing to be said by way of qualification or
dissent, is their common denominator. The reader who snaps 'the
bond with the author' as radically as I have broken it here needs
to consider whether the detected common denominator implies
something more seriously wrong with our language today than the
widespread evidence of enlightenment. If there is no *debate*
between enlightened and conservative, perhaps responsibility for
the 'breakdown of communication' and the consequent debasement and stupefaction of the language lies with the conservative
as well? A friend has drawn the analogy of Northern Ireland –
the need to resist both the I.R.A. and the U.D.A., and the difficulty as well as the necessity of treading a *via media* shunned by
both sides. An article in *English in Education* for Autumn 1968
draws the battle-lines of entrenched attitudes from which the
Black Papers and *Education for Democracy* fought in the following
years: the subject is classroom English, but the attitudes are
representative of education generally.

Element	The Old	The New
Basis of Planning	Demands of the Subject	Pupils' Needs and Interests
Teaching Unit	The Class	Individual or Group
Teaching Staff	Isolated Teacher	Teaching Team
Books	Class Sets	Small Sets or Single Books
Other Materials	The Blackboard	Charts, Films, Tapes, Paints, etc.
Teaching Aids	Few	Broadcasts, Visits, Visitors
Drama	Set Plays	Improvisation
Literature	Isolated from Language	Part of a Theme or a Topic
Language	Written Exercises	Talking, Drama, Writing
Examinations	External	Incidental Internal Tests
Movement in Class	Little or None	Movement encouraged
Noise	'Stop Talking'	Useful Noise Encouraged
Other Subjects	Isolated	Subject Integration

(NORMAN THOMSON and DAVID BRAZIL, *Productivity in English Teaching*)

The authors confess that 'the "elements" have been arbitrarily chosen ... and the contrasts sharpened', but claim that 'two features [are] obvious, the ramifications of the old curriculum and ... the way in which, in a revolutionary situation, traditional loyalties become treason to the revolutionary cause and what was a virtue comes to be seen as a vice'. One may object that the sharpened contrasts are not so neutrally presented as the authors appear to believe, that the insistence on 'isolated' or the qualification of 'noise' by 'useful' implies a partisan attitude. But the point to stress is that the battle-lines do reveal the frozen imperturbability of conservative and enlightened alike: no debate, no exchange of insights, no modifications are possible; rigidity is God, even in its most 'incidental' and 'improvised' form.

That both sides are to blame for the fatuous simplifications of the sharpened contrasts does not mean, however, that there is any present purpose in apportioning the blame. An essay which offered to do so would quote extensively from the *Daily Telegraph* and the *Black Papers*, and enjoy a slaughterous field-day at the expense of such examples as this:

Britain has a great cultural tradition of intellectual achievement. Even in the post-war period, Britain has won more Nobel prizes for science and literature per head of population than any other major country. Britain has been enabled to do this partly because of her outstanding educational system which has been so efficiently geared to producing an intellectual élite. This is the system that progressives are now demolishing...

But the important thing, and the reason for my particular brief, is to attack the winning side – hence the bias of my doubts over the sharpened contrasts and the orientation of my guns in this essay.

By invoking a Laurentian text against the enlightened I can

hardly be said to be aligning myself with the conservatives. Tradition and continuity in *The Rainbow* are to be seen as delicately
shifting their ground, gathering their complex weight and significance, in response to changing landscapes and human purposes.
Lawrence knew that his book (dismissed by a 1970 conservative
in a reference to 'the [overwhelming] apocalyptic Laurentian
manner')[6] was an original development from previous novels. The
elements in his art that recall George Eliot (compare Tom and
the child Anna 'suppering-up' the beasts with Tom and Maggie
sharing plumcake in *The Mill on the Floss*) are less obvious than
those which suggest differences from her relatively stable world.
The achievement of the first rainbow, for instance, is not only an
achievement for Tom and Lydia and the child 'playing beneath
the arch': it is a point of growth, not a point to dwell on; the playing child introduces a fresh vision and further problems, not only
for herself but for her parents. Conservative hatred of Lawrence
('in the eyes of non-conforming critics and scholars a symbol of
defiance who must be accorded unmeasured praise')[6] is understandable: his relation to tradition is too radical to allow the reader
to rest on 'certain certainties'; there is no pre-lapsarian innocence.

Yet it is powerful enough, his relation to tradition, to offer even
less comfort to the enlightened – as the increasingly common and
confident 'placing' of him with Eliot, Leavis and Arnold perhaps
unwittingly illustrates. There is no *progress* in *The Rainbow*, only
change and the fresh challenges that change puts to people. The
meeting of the generations in the girl Ursula's visits to Lydia, her
grandmother, represents the strength of Lawrence's sense of continuity, the curious dependence of the young upon the past and
the modest gift of old to young. The account of Ursula in Brinsley
St School is one of the great post-Arnoldian scourges of the
Revised Code, or of elements in 'The Old' as charted above;
but Lawrence sets it in the third generation of the novel, where it
represents what the nation has sunk to as well as what needs to
be improved. And in the enlightenment that Ursula encounters
through the Benthamite Skrebensky we sense Lawrence's vital
questioning of 'the greatest good of the greatest number'.

Those summary notes are not offered as a critique of *The Rainbow*. To show the greatness of that novel, warts and all, is not a
task to be attempted in the present context. For *The Rainbow* is
not a tract against enlightenment – or an anti-conservative manifesto, or indeed any sort of discursive polemic. It is peculiarly
suited to my immediate purposes in that, as 'the highest form of

[6] See the article on Lawrence in the *Longman Companion to Twentieth
Century Literature*.

thought', it raises the notion of a *via media* to the level of 'the best that has been thought and said'. And by 'the best' is meant 'a religious depth of thought and feeling'.[7] *The Rainbow* could not have been written had the *Authorised Version* not been a living influence in Lawrence's upbringing;[8] the allusions, the imitations and the parodies both induce and are induced by the religious quality of the novel – no arid biblicism there. The command of a style at once traditional and, in its heterodox originality, experimental qualifies Lawrence to speak with special authority against enlightenment:

'Fool and knave, how dare you belittle us with the darkness?'

---

[7] 'In coming to terms with great literature we discover what at bottom we really believe. What for – what ultimately for? What do men live by? – The questions work and tell at what I can only call a religious depth of thought and feeling. Perhaps, with my eye on the adjective, I may just recall for you Tom Brangwen, in *The Rainbow*, sitting by the fold in lambing-time under the night sky: "He knew he did not belong to himself." ' (F. R. Leavis, *Nor Shall My Sword*.)

[8] See Ian Robinson, 'Religious English', *The Cambridge Quarterly*, Vol. 2, No. 4, now published in *The Survival of English*, Ian Robinson, Cambridge University Press 1973.

8 The Condition of Music

JOHN McCABE

Art, we are often told, must mirror the life surrounding it; it must be a reflection of the predominant mood of its time, an abstract expression of the prevailing attitudes and feelings, a response on the part of the creative artist to the problems and modes of his day. Thus, during the nineteenth century the rise of political nationalism was paralleled by the growth of the national movements in the arts; music, as usual, was generally slower than the other arts to reflect this aspect of the time, but as each nation began to discover a new political destiny for itself, so its musicians gave expression to this aspect of life in their own work. One thinks of the strong national element in the work of such composers as the Hungarian Erkel and Liszt (the latter a particularly proud and fervent musical nationalist), the Italian Verdi (the Hebrew Slaves' Chorus from whose *Nabucco* achieved a status akin to that of a national anthem), or the Bohemian Smetana. In Russia too the progress of a strong national-revolutionary feeling among the people was echoed by the composers; Glinka, whose powers as a composer await full appreciation, has justly been called the 'father of Russian music', evoking strongly national feelings in his music as early as the first half of the nineteenth century, long before the outbreak of the people's political and human struggles for their rights. Russia, indeed, provides us with one of the few examples of a composer anticipating political events, for in the operas and songs of Mussorgsky the composer gives the most profound musical expression to the desires of the ordinary man; his works tell of the feelings of the man in the street, often with the most harrowing and vivid evocation of misery, poverty, and oppression, and it adds significantly to our understanding of the basic causes of the Russian Revolution of 1917 and its abortive predecessor of 1905. It is rare that a composer is able in his music to give expression to a current of feeling with such force before it has burst out into public utterance; usually the composer has been inspired to demonstrate his concern with what is happening at the time (Beethoven's *Eroica* Symphony is a prime example) or what has happened at some earlier point in time. In later years we can see the rise to nationhood of the Hungarian people as a simultaneous event with the growth of intense nationalism evinced musically by the devoted attitude of Kodály and Bartók, both in their collecting of national folk-songs and in their integration, as a matter of policy, of aspects of their folk-music style into a classical manner of composition derived initially from Western European traditions; but, politically, Hungarian nationalism was a force that had been in overt existence for many, many years before these composers took their own part in the final struggles towards some kind of success for the nation.

If one suggests that the nineteenth-century emphasis politically was on the rise of nationalism, one can equally suggest that the dominating feature of the twentieth century has been the growth of internationalism, either in terms of a large bloc of nations under one didactic control (as in the Soviet bloc) or in terms of a group of nations allying themselves in some way to form a common entity with inter-dependent parts (such as the Common Market). This is perhaps not the place to discuss the pros and cons of these large masses, but it might be apposite here to suggest that by forming themselves into a large macro-nation, the separate parts of which have their own semi-independence, the various nations concerned in a venture of this kind stand to lose a high degree of their own intrinsic character (the affirmation of which was, to some extent, what nationalism was about), the loss being the greater the more one governing power is enabled to impose its rule over the constituent parts of the particular mass of nations (Czechoslovakia 1968 gives a sad illustration of this). One can see this working on a smaller scale with the increasing tendency in Britain to form larger civic units, in which one town swallows up a number of smaller areas round it under some generic title, sometimes with faintly comic results; there was, not so long ago, a plan to call the new, enlarged Greater Manchester area 'Selnec' (a typically bureaucratic invention doubtless occasioned by the need for computerized brevity and derived from the words South East Lancashire and North East Cheshire). This undignified name was, however, dropped, largely, one gathers, as a result of extensive protests from the inhabitants of the area, who objected not only to the clumsiness of the new name but also to the off-hand manner in which it was proposed to banish at one fell swoop centuries of tradition and local association with a single generalized name that had no associations whatsoever for the people living there but which was simply an official device totally unrelated to the needs and wishes of the people concerned with its results.

With the contemporary leaning towards internationalism and the denial of local traditions and associations, then, it is not surprising that this has been reflected as profoundly in the arts as the previous nationalism was. It is now the fashion to write music which does not betray in a single bar any sense of its nationality; it is regarded as praise when a distinguished foreign conductor can say, of a modern British work, 'this is the kind of music one can play anywhere in the world', meaning quite explicitly that because it doesn't sound British it will be acceptable anywhere. The corollary of this is that most British music, by sounding British, is unacceptable anywhere else, a view that unfortunately has been assisted both by the general neglect of our own music by our own musicians when they have performed abroad and by our extremely parochial attitudes to our own music; look at the length of time it has taken for the music of Elgar to achieve something of its true stature in this country at least, and even then this has been partly due to the efforts of foreign conductors (the recent advocacy of Solti and Barenboim being a fine example), bringing with it the cachet that outside recognition brings to those British musicians who are amazed that any British music could possibly be of interest to 'outsiders'. But the attitude still prevails in international circles that only British music which sounds as if it could have been written anywhere is acceptable outside these shores (and consequently within them as well). There is a lingua franca in music today that denies tradition and national feeling and regards any music which, however slightly, betrays its origins as being in some way irrelevant; this is especially true of British music, where as far as one can see foreign observers make every effort to see in it evidence of typical British conservatism, regardless of the actual facts of style. One thinks here, for example, of those German critics who have seen this in Elgar's *Enigma* Variations, regardless of the late works of Richard Strauss, written years after the Elgar and far more conservative but hailed in their country as masterpieces, presumably because they are by a German.

We live in an age of the stateless, it is true; this is one of our tragedies. But music is failing in its duty to humanity if it tries deliberately to echo this by producing works that are themselves stateless, for the tragedy of the displaced person is precisely the dichotomy between their homeland and their displacement from it. Music that totally ignores the existence of its own nationality, by a deliberate adoption of a faceless international language, cuts out this essential element and thus cannot be said to be a true reflection of the stateless peoples in the world. There have been many instances of composers spending large portions of their lives in foreign lands without losing one iota of their inherent racial consciousness; Stravinsky (whose *Threni*, a work utilizing the serial techniques developed outside his native Russia, remains one of the most Russian of all his works) and Martinu, for instance, or Bloch, whose intense Judaism is reflected in his music wherever it was written. It is this racial/national consciousness that forms an essential part of the music, and one that is absolutely necessary to the deepest fulfilment of the composer's identity. Without it, he is a stateless person without even the benefit of knowing from whence he springs.

Yet it is precisely this inherited life-line that many of today's leading figures are bent on denying themselves. I am not for a moment pleading for a return of the kind of minor local nationalism which the imitators of composers like Bartók and Vaughan Williams purveyed, validly enough in their own time and in their own place but lacking the larger vision to enable them to have a wider application. Nor am I suggesting that a *self-conscious* nationalism is the answer. But it is interesting to ponder the extent to which the use of folk-song reflects the composer's own nationality. It was suggested to me recently that Vaughan Williams would have written exactly the same music had he been French. This, surely, is nonsense. Any composer who writes a good deal of vocal music will inevitably be affected by the rhythms, stress, and aural character of his native language (Janáček is an obvious example of a composer deeply affected by this); the use of folk-song (for all the close relationships between different folk traditions, such as between Hungarian and English folk music, which accounts for a frequent, and initially surprising, kinship between the music of Vaughan Williams and Bartók) is further going to relate the music of the composer to his own country. But beyond this there are questions of tradition, national temperament, and so on, questions which have so many ramifications (political history, geographical position, meteorology, etc.) that it would be impossible to start discussing them here; these all affect the composer. To make a deliberate attempt to cut these out of one's music, to deny oneself any relationship with one's roots, is an act of artistic suicide. The pursuit of internationalism at all costs, revealed by the *avant-garde* with depressing persistence, is a tragic spectacle, for in attempting to make music which has no national associations the creators are denying themselves the connection that is likely to have most validity for their home audiences. It should not be thought that music which in feeling or style shows clearly its roots must necessarily be valid only for its country of origin, either; were this the case, Dvořák, Tchaikovsky, Debussy, and Sibelius would only be played in Czechoslovakia, Russia, France, and Finland. Yet they are composers whose music, though by no means self-consciously nationalistic in any stultified way, shows in every bar its cultural roots, its inherited character. We would be much the poorer without the diversity and richness of the repertoire, and without any attempt on our part to make the effort to come to terms with the characters of other countries through their music; the true internationalism, it seems to me, lies not in trying to create an international style which owes nothing to any particular cultural tradition (and therefore tends to exist in a self-imposed emotional vacuum), but rather in listening to, and trying to appreciate the peculiar qualities of, music from many different lands and thus coming to grips with different cultures, however much their music may owe in some details to that of other countries (as Tchaikovsky, that deeply and movingly Russian composer, owes to German music for instance). The inter-relationship of different cultures, the way in which one composer will succeed through the strength of his own roots in conveying a sense of his national consciousness while perhaps using techniques derived from another land, is one of the fascinating and rewarding aspects of music; to deny us this pleasure and enrichment of our lives is merely negative. I can only illustrate my meaning in an example of the failure to apply this kind of appreciation, by recalling a conversation I once had with a German composer who said that French music was all 'pretty pictures'; when I remonstrated with him and suggested that Debussy's *La Mer* was really a tight-knit symphony based on a motif of two notes, he side-stepped this by, as he seemed to think, clinching his argument with the remark that Debussy could not have written Beethoven's Fifth Symphony. This remark clearly showed his total failure to appreciate the special qualities of French music, by attempting to judge it solely in terms of the equally strong but quite different nature of German music; he too was denying himself the joys of discovering a fresh point of view and the rewards of trying to come to grips with a different culture on its own terms.

It is a curious dichotomy that in an age when revolution is all the rage, nationalism is frowned upon; after all, the two formerly went hand in hand. (I should stress here that by 'nationalism' I mean a sense of national identity and character, not the kind of perverted nationalism used as a device by the politicians and Hitlers of this world.) But there was bound to be a reaction against nationalism, and similarly I believe there will be a reaction against the current internationalism. In so far as the international lingua franca of music deliberately eschews an application to any sense of cultural identity, it reflects current political thinking; but just as the growth of large, increasingly faceless organizations (whether political, economic, bureaucratic, or whatever) has the effect of turning people away from its manifestations and making them resentful of the total lack of consideration shown for their comfort or convenience, so in music the growth of an impersonal style repels the listener who demands from music a genuine emotional force to which he can respond and with which he can identify, rather than merely a collection of sounds which, by deliberately avoiding those musical elements to which a listener can most easily connect, aims at a kind of de-personalized aural wallpapering. One can see the reaction to present political trends in such things as the manifestations of a desire of various groups for the world not to combine in larger and ever more unwieldy blocks but rather to split up into smaller units; the Welsh and Scottish Nationalists, for example, both require at least some degree of autonomy and self-determination to replace the present state of affairs in which their lives are very largely directed, often with disastrous results, from London and may soon be directed to some extent from the central offices of the Common Market, thus removing at least some of the decision-making even further away from the people whom it most concerns.

The over-centralization of life in Britain today, in all its many aspects, has resulted, in the musical world, in an extraordinary self-satisfaction on the part of the London musical coterie, whose attitude resembles nothing so much as that of the eighteenth-century Quality, who saw all that was worthwhile, significant, and 'amusing' as happening in London and all that was dull, boorish, and insignificant as happening elsewhere. If you talk at any length to most members of the London musical establishment, the word 'provincial' will undoubtedly make its appearance in the conversation before long, pronounced with an audible curl of the nostril. There was one occasion, a few years ago, when one of the editors of a musical magazine, on its being suggested that the publication should contain reports from the provinces on musical events there, said that 'nobody is interested in what happens outside London'. Were this merely an isolated instance of this type of snobbery, it would be unworthy of comment, but it typifies an all-too-prevalent metropolitan attitude. One is reminded, though, of Ambrose Bierce's definition of 'metropolis' as 'a stronghold of provincialism'. In this country, the metropolis being London, everything that is of any value or interest tends to be thought of as coming from that city, an attitude which is unrealistic and which engenders a remarkably pervasive and profound bitterness outside. There is no doubting London's importance in the sphere of international music-making; it is one of the main musical centres of the world, and this brings with it undeniable prestige and cultural strength, just as it enhances the international scene by providing it with a valuable, and viable, focus. The danger is that by achieving this position London is encouraged to think of itself as the only musical place in Britain, with possibly the occasional side-long glance at Manchester, Birmingham, or Glasgow. But just as we need the cultural force of an important musical centre of international attention such as London, we need equally a healthy provincial musical life, which in many ways we undoubtedly have, and to ignore this, or to imply that it is so markedly inferior to that of London as to be musically worthless, is to betray a smugness and lack of intelligence that derives from an excess of Bierce's metropolitan provincialism. For it has to be appreciated that, though certain features are common to both, provincial musical life is organized along very different lines and has a totally different purpose. It is far less socially orientated than that of the capital; it stems to a much greater extent from the musical needs of a particular area, and correspondingly to a much lesser extent from the demands of fashion, commercial necessity, or that aspect of a travelling musical circus going the international rounds which the London musical scene so often resembles.

It should not be thought that I am chastising London for its musical life; far from it. It is necessary and salutary for us, presents us with a great many events of major importance (which, of course, focus attention on this country and help us to maintain our position as one of the foremost musical nations), and for all its faults produces a lot of very fine music-making (as well as much that is uninspired and routine, though for very different reasons from those that cause the same faults in the provinces). By closing its ears to provincial music, and by failing to appreciate the very real difference in purpose that obtains outside London, the capital's musical establishment is in grave danger of cutting the provinces off from a relationship with the capital that could be enriching both ways. There is, too, a danger that, since London increasingly holds the purse strings, any provincial schemes which do not coincide with current metropolitan attitudes (which may hold good for the metropolis but may not do so anywhere else) may be denied the opportunity for existence, though it is fair to add that those in authority in this respect seem to be well aware of this pitfall; equally, one might in passing suggest that the existence of a set-up with such a built-in danger is in itself obnoxious, however well run it may be at the moment. We need a healthy and independent provincial musical life, and on the whole we have one, whatever the meaner spirits in the capital may say, but even so one can point to the difficulties of certain regional departments of the BBC, whose every decision has to be submitted to London for approval, as an illustration of the dangers of the over-centralization from which we suffer.

To some extent, it is true, there is some degree of autonomy, and it seems but seldom that the wilder manifestations of musical fashion retain sufficient strength over a period of time to spread from London to the provinces (with the exception possibly of the many University music departments), though here too a warning note must be struck, for it is increasingly evident that in London there is a tendency to want to foist on the provincial public concerts of modern music emanating from London organizations. This is done very much along the lines of educating the poor old provincial public, whose ignorance of the latest *avant-garde* creations is regarded as regrettable and reprehensible (to abet this, there has always been a provincial element anxious to ape metropolitan fashions). It is interesting to think that when a fashion spreads from the provinces to the capital, instead of the more usual procedure, it seems to take a much deeper stranglehold on metropolitan attitudes; the deep impression the Beatles made on pop music, the face (or rather the sound) of which they certainly changed, has gone much further and lasted much longer than any similar pop fashion going the other way, and similarly the advocacy of Mahler and Bruckner in the provinces (not least in Manchester under Barbirolli's direction) was possibly the major factor in the spread of these two composers' works into the capital and to the status of a veritable performing industry which they have now achieved. Only a few years ago, long after Mahler was accepted as quite normal fare in Manchester, a London music critic, Colin Mason, felt confident enough to assail an audience for nearly half a concert review for being so unintelligent as to sit through Mahler's Sixth Symphony; one doubts whether he would have been so forthright about it now.

But the extent to which fashion, in the long run, has much to do with public taste is doubtful. We are currently being told that Sibelius is really rather old hat, but performances of his symphonies not only continue but are quite definitely on the increase; and the records of *avant-garde* music, with a very few exceptions, sell quite execrably, and seldom last long in the catalogues. It does seem to be that the ebb and flow of fashion belongs largely to cliques

that regard themselves as privileged to know the secrets of life
(and which certainly behave as if they had a vast superiority over
us lesser mortals), affecting the ordinary concert-goer hardly at all;
there is, too, an awful air of condescension adopted to any music
which (of all unthinkable horrors) dares to become popular. There
is a tendency to pick on some young composer of talent and acclaim
him or her as the great hope of the future; but since he is constantly
developing his style, and thus tends to change more rapidly than
when set in his or her ways, this seldom lasts very long, certainly
not long enough for the composer's work to disseminate itself very
widely. The danger is that the pressures of instant success may be
such that the composer goes under, becomes self-conscious about
work and either attempts to repeat previous successes in order to
please the critics or deliberately tries to find some new gimmick
in order to maintain a pre-eminent position and keep their attention. This is a grave danger, and one very hard to resist in a world
in which attention is increasingly paid to the superficial spectacle,
cleverness, or flashiness of a work of art; it is more difficult for the
composer to develop naturally and unselfconsciously.

That even a composer of the highest gifts is not immune to this
danger is evident in the career of Ligeti. He captured attention
with some relatively early pieces in which his particular trademark
(his own individual application of a technique of slowly building
up clusters of notes, influenced by the stylistic innovations of
Penderecki), sprang to sudden world-wide fame as a result of the
use of several works in the film *2001*, and has fallen prey to
the serious pitfalls opened up in the international musical scene by
this success. Many of his works seem interchangeable, so similar
are they in technique and effect; each composer today is expected
to find his own gimmick and exploit it for all he is worth, and in
Ligeti's case it seems to have been damaging to his progress. This
is shown the more clearly because he has produced at least one
work which is among the masterpieces of twentieth-century music
and encourages one to believe that, if he could only break the
restricting bonds of a style into which he seems to have been forced
back in subsequent works, he could become one of the most significant composers of our time. Ligeti's masterpiece is his Second
String Quartet, a work that, while recognizably Ligetian in every
bar, derives its strength from a much wider set of stylistic resonances and bases than his other pieces known to me, and which
correspondingly has an immense range of feeling. It is a work in
which Ligeti integrates his own individual style with a development from this, and with resonances from the past; there are even
hints of the influence of Bartók, though Ligeti is far from a mere

imitator but a personality of great force in his own right. It is this ability to combine an unselfconscious acceptance of modern chamber music traditions with a development of his own style that is technically so encouraging about this profound work; but sadly the immense coverage his music received soon after the composition of this work, a coverage devoted largely to those works used in *2001* and thus most simply limited to the basic stylistic device of his music, seems to have forced him back on himself. The works subsequent to this success, such as the Chamber Concerto and *Ramifications*, echo the works previous to the Second Quartet; and even the orchestral work *Lontano* seems for the most part to be so like the earlier *Atmosphères* as to be virtually indistinguishable from it, despite a passing reference to Sibelius's Fourth Symphony that is doubtless unintentional! The result is that the Second Quartet shines out like a beacon in a landscape generally composed of fog; one can only hope that Ligeti will find his way out of the murk of a restrictive style and discover once again the ability to draw on the wider range of sources that makes the Quartet such a rich work.

But he is not the only currently fashionable figure to have fallen prey to the restrictions of a style which often seems to be geared exclusively to the promotion of a single compositional idea, for Penderecki too seems to have got becalmed in a welter of huge note-clusters, moving ever more slowly. Penderecki's rise to world-wide success derived largely from his string work *Threnody for the Victims of Hiroshima*, a prolonged scream of horror which initially seems technically very exciting in its application of a wide variety of what were then new techniques in writing for strings and also moving in its impassioned sense of outrage. It has given rise to an immense number of works devoted to themes of a similar nature (Penderecki himself calls his *Dies Irae* an Auschwitz Oratorio), the very frequency of whose appearance calls into question the motives behind the works; it has become not only respectable but highly desirable for a composer who wishes to be taken seriously as a committed artist, in an age when commitment (preferably political, I regret to say) is seen to be a mark of 'conscience', to write at least one major work expressing his horror at some manifestation of man's inhumanity to man. It has long been a claim of film-makers that by showing violence as it really is, or by showing the horrors of war, they are doing their bit in ridding the world of these evils, laudable aims in which they have signally failed. (Indeed, it has become something of a cliché to announce one's serious intent in such terms, though by now one is tempted to regard any such pronouncements with equal suspicion one gives to the familiar remark of rumour-bound actors and actresses, 'We're just good friends'.) The writer P. J. Kavanagh, interviewed in *The Guardian*, has discussed this type of instant conscience thus: 'I hate to see [the concentration camps] used to shock. When artists use the camps to say, "You slobs don't think about this sort of thing enough", that's incredibly crude and arrogant.' He could have added that it devalues the currency, demotes conscience to a kind of passport to respectability, and also makes it more difficult to descry genuine intent from merely band-wagon travelling; though when a genuine and personal vision of a man-made hell emerges, its power usually lifts it above its more cynical fellows (Picasso's *Guernica* and Sam Peckinpah's film *The Wild Bunch* spring to mind as works of this kind of exceptional power). Nobody can be immune to feelings of horror about many aspects of life today, or in the past; but to use this as an excuse for trying to lift oneself into artistic acceptance as a 'committed' creator is merely obscene. In Penderecki's case one cannot doubt the sincerity of his emotions; a first hearing of a work such as the Hiroshima piece can be a shattering experience. But it emanates, like so much 'advanced' music today, from very narrow stylistic premises, which, in the long run, work against the music's retaining its full force (not to mention the weakening of its ability to withstand the swing of the pendulum of fashion). One demands more from a piece of music than an emotional assault sustained at the same high pitch of shock throughout, for the listener soon begins to tire of a constant aural battery maintained at one level of intensity. One also demands some intellectual sense of control other than at the most primitive level, a sense of growth and of stylistic resonance. Penderecki's music, in his 'committed' works, shows a deeply-felt response to the human condition, but it is expressed in stylistic terms so narrow as to deny us any of the variety of means and techniques that would throw the emotional intensity into relief by giving us different facets of it. It emerges, simply, as a scream, devoid of the pity and gentleness that by their human contrast throw into sharp relief the inhumanity that is intended to be portrayed. One compares this to a work like Walton's *Belshazzar's Feast*, where the composer conjures up vividly the most harrowing sense of cruelty and barbaric power partly by means of the contrast with pity or rejoicing. The range of the Walton work, stylistically, is enormous, always controlled by the composer's own individual stamp throughout; the range of both intellectual and emotional qualities is equally vast. These are the elements one looks for in a major work of this kind, and they are the elements that have kept the work in the repertoire, because the audience is drawn into the music's all-too-human world.

The emotional and intellectual restriction of so much of Penderecki's music becomes more apparent when one hears the enormous choral works, the *St. Luke Passion* and *Utrenja*. There are moments, especially in the former, when a warm lyricism breaks out, and the Passion draws on quite a wide range of stylistic sources, including plainchant (the *Stabat Mater*, originally written separately and later integrated into the Passion, is a particularly successful piece on its own, not outlasting its welcome even after many hearings); the vocal and instrumental techniques are immensely resourceful and often exciting in themselves. Yet ultimately this is a disappointing work, one that does not wear well, and the reason for this is that despite the great stylistic range of the work, it depends ultimately for its effect of the familiar Penderecki clusters, moving with monolithic slowness. In the long run, after repeated hearings, the effect of this is deadening rather than moving; admittedly there is nothing more conducive to serious acceptance than an air of massive gravity, but it can work to the detriment of the music if overdone. *Utrenja* goes even further; the slowness and ponderousness of the music are quite staggering. Yet its effect is exactly the same as that of music in which there are far too many dramatic contrasts – it all comes out sounding like an endless aural sausage. The composer seems, like Ligeti in his most recent works, to have become the prisoner of his own stylistic discoveries, upon which he concentrates with all the avidity of a cat watching an ever-diminishing mousehole; yet both these composers have the ability to do so much more, if they could only break out of the confines they have set themselves, or perhaps rid themselves of the fear of losing their public persona by developing their styles. They are as genuinely musical as Lutoslawski, who has emphatically succeeded in pursuing his own path with an increasing depth of vision and without losing one iota of his following.

Part of the intended effect of music of such dense concentration on one type of sound must be to achieve a kind of ecstatic sense, in forcing the listener in upon himself – the exploration of the self. More 'advanced' composers have taken this a stage further. Stockhausen's *Stimmung* explores a chord of B flat for an hour or more, with six singers devoted to this musical navel-contemplation. The intention is to induce the listener, via the stages of interest and boredom, into a kind of cataleptic trance (though the third stage is often irritation rather than hypnotism). Stockhausen has described the work thus: 'Certainly STIMMUNG is meditative music. Time is suspended. One listens to the inner self of the sound, the inner self of the harmonic spectrum, the inner self of the vowel, THE INNER SELF. Subtlest fluctuations, scarcely a ripple, ALL THE

SENSES alert and calm. In the beauty of the sensual shines the beauty of the eternal.' One is irresistibly reminded of the similar pronouncements of an earlier composer preoccupied with ecstasy, Scriabin. Whereas Scriabin's grave deficiencies as a composer of large-scale works prevent his most 'ecstatic' pieces (the orchestral ones) from being other than a shameless mish-mash of romantic clichés surrounded by hot-house verbiage, however, Stockhausen has adopted far simpler musical styles in recent years, though he too is prone to Messianic public utterances. Witness a remark he made in an interview in *Rolling Stone*: 'One day, all of a sudden I became the way music is. I became a multiple being, a being which changes perspective, I became more flexible, I no longer have one standpoint. You cannot separate me from the music any longer, and you cannot separate the music from the listener any longer. And by that the music is influenced by the listener because he changes the music. What is music? I don't know.'

This is too simplistic by far; it says nothing new about the composer-listener relationship (it is, indeed, a collection of truisms), given with the air of uttering profound new discoveries. Stockhausen's band of followers will unhesitatingly view it as a statement of the utmost significance, in much the same way they accepted without question his almost cynically banal and simple-minded introductory talk before a London performance of *Mantra*. Yet Stockhausen is far from simple-minded. He has, however, found a way of tapping the current preoccupation with Self, the present-day liking for any language that disguises its innate poverty of thought with a frame of seemingly impressive verbiage, and the contemporary fad for self-deluding mock-philosophy (one regrets that a far more significant composer, and one who has already conjured up with infinitely more success a sense of ecstasy in his music, Tippett, seems currently in danger of falling into the same trap, as witness the over-elaborate and confusing notes he has written for his Third Symphony). All this can be seen quite clearly in some of Stockhausen's works in which no musical notes are written, but merely sets of instructions to the players to play anything they like (along the lines of tuning into the vibrations in the air, and so on). This, of course, is total abdication of the composer's responsibility, but Stockhausen would doubtless argue that by allowing the performers their freedom of expression he is composing music that has great spontaneity, that does not belong to him (in line with his views about the composer not being a separate being who controls others), that is entirely an expression of the self of the performers (thus offering us great revelations), and so on. But if you allow any number of performers complete freedom to play whatever they like, you merely loose anarchy on the world, without form, cohesive content, or a unanimous expression that will enable the listener the chance to grasp what is going on.

The result of this total abandonment of coherent thought in a pursuit of the dissolution of the self is an excess of triviality. One can only really become aware of one's self in a relationship with others, even if, like a hermit, one eventually has to come to terms with the self by removing from such a relationship, a decision which, though isolationist, is arrived at by a contemplation of others. It seems a purely selfish art that insists on making the listener concentrate entirely on himself, and furthermore it is one that pursues an inexorably ingrowing, incestuous circling motion of feeding on itself in ever-diminishing relevance to anything outside the self. Perhaps in this respect this kind of art does in a sad way reflect the society we live in, for do we not see every day some instance of a section of society pursuing a suicidal course of self-destruction with every apparent lack of concern for the long-term results of their actions? But can any art which relies so completely on a purely selfish ethos expect to have any real life force, any genuine appeal to listeners who want art to enrich life? Dr Johnson's words about writing ('The only end of writing is to enable the readers better to enjoy life, or better to endure it') spring to mind; music can hardly be said to be fulfilling this essential purpose if it merely drives the listeners in upon themselves in a spiralling introversion concerned solely with self-gratification. How much more rewarding it is to be swept by music in which the composer's aim has been, however much his emphasis may have been on self-expression, to 'communicate' (that dreadful but useful word) with other human beings in the curiously vague yet clear and direct way music has, to be taken out of oneself and into the vast human arena of feelings, to be moved by a sympathy that is unselfish! The absorption with the self that a composer like, say, Tchaikovsky demonstrates is one that has in it all the elements of humanity at large; as such it speaks in terms of human feelings which call forth a deep response from peoples all over the world; how different this is to Stockhausen's brand of pseudo-ecstatic self-gratification (not to say self-glorification). Stockhausen himself would claim to be writing music not for himself but for the whole world (my old school motto might well have been written just for him: 'Non nobis solum sed toti mundo nati'), but as Desmond Shawe-Taylor pointed out in a review of a Stockhausen concert, 'and yet in these insistent howls and squeaks an autocratic self seems also to be imposing itself, all too successfully, on the inmates of a concentration camp for masochists'.

The pity of it all is that, like Ligeti and Penderecki, Stockhausen has a genuinely musical mind, as occasional works throughout his career testify. He has been one of the very few composers to use electronic techniques and those of *musique concrète* so successfully as to produce pieces of real music, with coherent shape, sensuous sound, and a moving emotional feeling (in *Telemusik* and the earlier *Gesang der Jünglinge* respectively), perhaps because, unlike most electronic creators, he is capable of being a real composer; *Gruppen* is a virtuoso orchestral work of immense panache and excitement; and his *Klavierstücke* are a major contribution to twentieth-century piano literature. These works alone should keep Stockhausen's name in the forefront of contemporary composers. But alongside them we have so many recent pieces in which his apparent contempt for his audience, who will certainly swallow anything he cares to throw at them with hysterical avidity, has resulted in a rag-bag of non-ideas not even put together, let alone put together with any genuine creativity. It might be argued that, since I fail to appreciate his recent music, I am not therefore one of those listeners at whom he is directing his music, but in many cases my objection is not to his ideas but to the lack of real consistency in carrying them through. *Stimmung*, for example, is for me a failure not because I do not like or value the idea behind it, but because I do not think it is carried out with sufficient rigorousness; the serenity with which the single chord is explored at such great length is disturbed by the introduction of other elements (such as the pronunciation of what are described as 'Magic Names') which, though calculated to add to the metaphysical ramifications of the work and enhance its hypnotic other-worldliness, disrupt the rapt sense of contemplation much of the music achieves. In other words, Stockhausen's anxiety to give his music this aura of mystical revelation has become cluttered up with unnecessary details which obscure the very valid central point of the work.

But since *Stimmung* the details seems to have become the be-all and end-all of the whole thing, the central thought to have got lost altogether. Stockhausen, in fact, has become a total convert to the present cult of complete randomness, and like most converts is the most jealous purveyor of the doctrine. This return to primitivism, shown by the great emphasis now placed upon improvisation, is perhaps a reaction against the over-mechanical, 'progressive' civilization in which we live. This reaction shows itself in many ways – the extreme simplicity of some *avant-garde* music, in which one simple phrase will be repeated over and over again for an hour or so, is one instance. But improvisation is a more complex

matter. The current view has been well expressed by the composer
Barry Guy (in the 1971 Review of the Guildhall School of Music
and Drama): 'the radical rebirth of interest in group improvisation,
[is] surely a healthy sign. In saying this, we must bear in mind that
spontaneous improvisation on the part of the group is a natural
function of any "primitive" society and is an aspect that music of
"advanced" cultures has repressed or patronized at its peril.'
This is all very well, and contains a good deal of truth, but there
are certain dangers in adopting this approach without question.
In the first place, most 'primitive' musics have some kind of simple
rules, often enough derived from the melodic and harmonic limitations of the instruments used, so that even the freest improvisation
by a group will have a simple and easily appreciable sound; and
rhythmic structures, though often complex, have an infectious in-
telligibility. None of these things apply to the disorganized chaos of
the kind of fake primitivism of much modern collective improvisation (such as that in *avant-garde* jazz) produced by our contemporary neo-primitives; the sound is, simply, anarchic. And I doubt
whether the people of the baroque era, when improvisation within
a set context was normal procedure, regarded themselves as any less
'progressive' than we regard ourselves today; they did not find it
necessary to indulge in fantasies of primitivism to excuse their
musical techniques. The true nature of improvisation, it seems to
me, only emerges when it is combined with some restrictions,
whether derived from the nature of the instruments or from some
set of harmonic and melodic rules (whether strict or fairly free).
That it is possible to combine improvisation with fairly advanced
compositional techniques has been shown by many present-day
composers; Lutoslawski's *Livre pour orchestre* (possibly the finest
work he has yet written) is a masterly technical display of this,
allowing a high degree of controlled improvisation within a set
framework and producing a work that is both exciting and profoundly moving. Lutoslawski, like Ligeti in his Second Quartet,
shows an awareness and acceptance of his traditions, and an ability
to derive his strength from these, a strength which, coupled with
the profundity of his personal vision and his great resourcefulness
as a sonic inventor, produces a development of his own personal
style which does not involve a denial of his heritage but rather an
enrichment of it in his own terms. He has integrated new musical
developments with his own traditions and style; evolution rather
than revolution, in fact. However the past has often shown that
those who take one innovation of music to its limits, and explore
only that to the exclusion of all other elements, may be striking
pioneers, but the very narrowness of their vision works against any

wide application their music may strive for. It is not so many years
since total serialization was seen by its devotees as the only true path
for music to take. Now we can find Barry Guy saying, about European music, that 'Postwar developments were in the main devoted
to various ways of mathematically perpetuating the act of composition, after the *reductio ad absurdum* of the twelve-note row in the
shape of total serialization. In the last few years, we find by way of
contrast a far freer musical discourse and a healthy emphasis on
improvisation.' This again is perfectly true as far as it goes, but it
merely shows that the pendulum has swung from total rigour to
total freedom; neither can be satisfying in the long run, for neither
has that built-in balance between freedom and control that music
demands for its richness and expressive variety to come over. There
is, for the listener, no difference between the chaos produced by
mathematically permutated (and thus over-controlled) sound or
that produced by an anarchic (and thus under-controlled) babble.
The present pre-occupation with improvisation (an inevitable
reaction, perhaps, against the over-rigorous nature of total serialization) is possibly a further symptom of our concern with self-
expression in the peculiarly selfish manner which manifests itself
in every aspect of our lives, when even violence and militancy
are regarded as acceptable methods of stating one's case. And when
it comes to freedom for the performer, if he cares to take advantage
of it there is just as much freedom and spontaneity for the performer in a Haydn sonata or a Beethoven concerto as there is in a
performance with the Scratch Orchestra; every performance an
artist gives of a classical work is, or should be, a spontaneous one,
for all that the composer's instructions are fairly detailed. The very
conditions of concert-giving, where a pianist will be playing each
night on a different piano, for a different audience, in a different
hall, means that this element is built in; the joy is in realizing it in
a context that is otherwise set, in finding the equilibrium between
the restriction of the frame and the spontaneity of the moment.
This is a narrow application of the word 'spontaneity', but it is as
valid an interpretation of it as the opposite extreme in which one
is allowed complete freedom to play anything at all. Indeed, I am
not sure that complete freedom of performance, where the composer has totally abdicated his control, can possibly realize the true
value of improvisation as such; Charlie Parker's superbly improvised solos would not be nearly so affecting were there not a solid
basis underlying them to throw into sharp relief his magnificently
free-wheeling lines.

But the musical world is full of narrow little bands of people
all proclaiming theirs as the only right way; it has always been thus,

but today there are more departments of composition, all bent on pursuing their own compartmentalized purities. We see this in classical music, where there are so many different schools of thought, and in pop music, where pigeon-holing has reached quite ludicrous proportions. Pop music, indeed, is in a rather curious state, for it has become something of a pseudo-intellectual phenomenon, a state of affairs which might be said to have started with the Beatles. It will be remembered that they were at one time so respectable that a British classical music critic felt emboldened to suggest that they were the greatest song-writers since Schubert. Since then, pop music has become more and more accepted as worthy of intellectual consideration, and has responded by becoming more and more self-consciously serious. Words like 'profound', 'significant', 'the human condition' and so on appear with great frequency in the context of a music that is frequently infantile on both technical and imaginative levels. This is not to deny the best pop music its real qualities, its vitality, the occasional depth of feeling revealed in it; but we have reached a stage when, as Michael Smith in an article in *Melody Maker* put it, 'Every time some pop group oaf in a transport café delivers some asinine comment through a mouthful of egg and chips, there is a brilliant pop writer to pounce on the precious pearls and reproduce them as some apocalyptic truth which proves that pop music is the panacea for civil rights problems, Vietnam, economic squeezes, empty churches, drug addiction, incest, acne and piles.' How right he is! Pretentiousness is as much the order of the day in pop music as it is in concert music; fun seems to have gone out of the window (at a time when we desperately need some genuine music to take us out of ourselves). Doubtless, with the massive publicity machine ready to promote these notions, the pop fans genuinely think that by listening to this kind of self-consciously 'committed' pop music, they are appreciating the world's problems, but it often seems that the whole thing is an exercise in commercializing the problems for the benefit of those people in the business who stand to make the most money (not necessarily the artists themselves). There is an awful air of inevitability about so much of it; every few months some new pop star is found who is supposed really to know how to convey his 'commitment', but the singular thing is that so very few of them last very long. Perhaps this is because their music does not develop. The pop business, after all, is very largely devoted to the exploitation of hits, and the attempted repetition of them, a process that has its own built-in destructive properties. Musicians like the Beatles are able to last longer precisely because their music does develop over the years, and if the claims made for them seem excessive, one cannot doubt that much of their music was not only lively and inventive but also touching. But even towards the end they too fell prey to the simple-mindedness (neo-primitivism) that infects music in many directions; people who dislike pop music often refer to it as jungle music, a remark intended as an insult but which ought to appeal to the pop musicians, if they think about it. The attempt to go back to primeval bases ignores civilization as it has so far gone, and any music which does this can only be regarded, on the deepest level, as irrelevant, no matter how much it may give itself a veneer of contemporaneity. But, just as concert music is regarded as respectable if it concerns itself with political or human 'commitment', so pop music seems to think that, if it contains the words 'Vietnam' or 'Hitler', it must therefore be relevant to our times; we are back with the film-maker showing violence as it really is. Possibly all this is the reaction to the Victorian attitude that if you ignored something it would go away. Today we seem to think that if you shout about something it will go away. The facts do not bear either view out.

Nowhere is the cynical exploitation implied in so much pop music more evident than in so-called religious pop. The quasi-mystical self-delusion which infects so much music of all kinds shows itself clearly here. The churches seem increasingly inclined to use pop music in order to show themselves aware of current trends and the needs of young people; indeed, one would often think that the only people in the world are under the age of twenty. The results are often too embarrassing to bear; there is a serious dichotomy between the sensuous, essentially fleshy sound of pop music and the spiritual nature of the religious lyrics. Victorian hymnody may have been far more 'comfortable' and sanctimonious, but it was never as utterly divorced from any spirituality as this. Commercialization, whether it be of church music or any other, is one of the banes of our time; the *avant-garde* jet-set is just as blatantly mercenary in its own way. The irony of our present culture, in which pop music is regarded as being young people's ideal music (despite the evidence of great numbers going to classical concerts, buying classical records, and playing classical music), is that in the long run there is more money to be made out of classical music (though it takes much longer). Buy a record company executive a good lunch, and when he is sufficiently relaxed he will admit that the vast majority of pop records actually lose money; it is the rare million-sellers that pull it in.

The aspect of religious pop that disturbs me most is the depressing purpose that lies behind it, a debasement of the currency in order to appeal without effort to the lowest common denominator allied with a submission to the false image provided by the publicity machine. The lack of effort, the failure to apply oneself with real purpose to the task of listening to music, is fostered by the strange aura of inverted sanctity that surrounds the pop world, which is presented as something glamorous and exciting, though in actual fact it is no different for the people who make the music from the world of classical musicians; they stay at the same hotels when away from home, play in the same towns, and so on, the only real differences being the music itself and the audiences. The passive acceptance of the idea of glamour is perhaps a handy let-out from having to make an effort to think for oneself and make a choice based on personal response; it is too easy to accept the response that the machine says you should have. And today is the age of fun (though we take our fun with ever-increasing gravity), the pursuit of pleasure today for tomorrow we may die. This is a compensation for the boredom and sterility of life, perhaps. Dr Erich Fromm puts it thus: 'Two hundred years ago the same man would have said, "I have faith in myself." Today he says, "I have faith in the machine." ' The impersonal nature of the machine, of which man is part, reduces human beings to mere cyphers lacking their own identity, invaded constantly by a stream of events designed to relieve the resultant passivity, yet this very passivity enables man to receive these events without the bother of thinking about them. The exercise of filling up spare time has become the compensation for boredom, but the means for doing so are so diverse, and require so little effort, that it takes real trouble and application to sort out what one really wants to do to fill in the time. The more extreme manifestations of music, of whatever kind, often seem designed solely to catch the attention in a world where only the spectacular rouses man out of his lethargy; yet the effort of looking around and seeking something of real worth, something which will genuinely enrich one's experience and enable one the better to enjoy or endure life, is an exercise that is constantly made more and more difficult by the sheer pressure of the meretricious, the shoddy, and the showy. It is increasingly difficult, in an ever-diversifying world, to sort out the events from the non-events; and the events are not always those which shout their existence from the rooftops. The great tragedy of this is that life need not be so boring anyway; the effort of thinking for oneself, rather than passively accepting, questioning the values and trends that are paraded before one, gives infinitely greater variety and richness to life in general, and banishes a good deal of the sterility that can too easily be allowed to take control.

9 Pop Song, the Manipulated Ritual

CHARLES PARKER

Most of the time, you know, at work where the wireless is on nearly
all day, you sort of accept pop music. I mean you're not really given
anything else. But I like it.... I mean it's all put in such a way that,
you know, it's easy to listen to. I mean, it's just to capture the hearts
of young people I suppose; which it does, mostly.

16-YEAR-OLD SALFORD GIRL, *Vox Pop I*, June 1967

For twenty-four years, I worked as a documentary producer in the
BBC, and from around 1956 one of my main preoccupations was
to give expression, on radio, to the exhilarating rediscovery of
popular music which marked the trad jazz folk-song and skiffle
movements of that period. One of the results was Ewan McColl's
Radio Ballad series, which began with *The Ballad of John Axon*
in 1957/8 and finished with *Romeo and Juliet* in 1966.

These were musical documentaries rooted in the common speech
and in traditional song; they were as popular as limited exposure
on the then Home Service would allow, they were successful (*Singing the Fishing* won the Prix Italia documentary award in 1960)
and they were chopped by the BBC in 1964 (*Romeo and Juliet*
was an attempt by Schools Broadcasting to salvage something from
the pieces left over).

This same period saw the genesis and luxuriant growth of the
pop song industry, which I consider an aberrant and manipulated
expression of the same social realities which informed the Radio
Ballads, and this chapter is an attempt to demonstrate how and
why. I embark on it, not because I am an expert on the history of
pop song, which I am not, but because my experience in the field as
a documentary producer has forced me to confront the glaring
contradiction between the image of youth cultivated by pop, and
the actuality as expressed to me on a tape-recorder. It is out of
this contradiction that I write, and out of a growing suspicion

of the motives which led successive generations of programme planners in the BBC to discourage and ultimately destroy, not only the Radio Ballads, but subsequent attempts to explore the relationship between everyday speech and experience, and popular song.

In 1967, while I was still a BBC features producer, I tried to establish at least the beginning of a critical dialogue with the mass radio audience on the subject of pop song. The result was a series of eight half-hour programmes, compiled by Geoffrey Reeves and Stuart Hall, which we called *Vox Pop*. After a protracted struggle, we managed to get them broadcast – on Midland Home Service only, VHF only! They were dismissed by the then Controller of the Home Service, Gerrard Mansell, as unsuitable for the network, and of course they were not allowed anywhere *near* the real audience for which they were designed – the then Light Programme.

And yet these programmes were by no means negative or patronizingly superior in their attitude to pop; indeed as I now realize, our unforgivable sin so far as gaining BBC acceptability was concerned, was to have the gall to treat pop (or indeed any aspect of popular culture) seriously. Not that they were solemn either; they were in fact hilarious, as for instance when we discovered something like 150 songs listed in the catalogues under one and the same title – 'I Love You'; selecting from this spellbinding collection, we created a montage spanning the years from Al Jolson through Paul Anka and Peggy Lee to Cliff Richard and the Zombies ... with devastating effect! They were also analytical, confronting, for instance, the incontestable fact that Miss Sandie Shaw is an unright singer – if one assumes that her distinctive flair for singing consistently off pitch is deliberate....

> I think it's the visual thing that made Sandie Shaw, but obviously possibly the very flatness of her voice; I mean it has a sort of plaintiveness and wistfulness and is given very pretty songs....
>
> GEORGE MELLY, *Vox Pop 3*

But oh! the tussle we had with the legal department over this, so fearful was the BBC that such comment was actionable! And we ran into more trouble when we tried to quote the last 28 seconds from the Beatles' LP 'Sergeant Pepper's Lonely Hearts Club Band'. The track 'A Day in the Life' had been banned for broadcasting for its psychedelic/drug-phantasmagoria orchestration; yet still we found the accepted Beatles image was that of nice young men daring to walk on the grass, as compared with the Stones' and the Animals' more aggressive barbed-wire non-conformity; an image in no way borne out if the Animals and the Beatles are put in immediate juxtaposition when at their most phantasmagoric. Which meant quoting that 28 seconds. Which was denied us! Such stark critical exposure by context seemed to outrage the programme planners; almost as much as the outspokenness of some of the Contributors.

> I see pop music, and indeed pop art generally, as a defiant relinquishing of responsibility towards this society. The responsibility of thinking, the responsibility of being committed to any idea, to any point of view, to any course of action. And it's this negative attitude to society, to human thought, to historical processes, and all the rest of it, which it seems to me, permeates the whole of beat music, the whole of pop art.
>
> EWAN MACCOLL, *Vox Pop 2*

But outspokenness not, of course, from one standpoint only –

> There's a certain genuine freshness and vivacity in the Beatles which comes out in the nature of tunes in the first place; perhaps the fact that the tunes are of course quite intuitively modal or even pentatonic ... tunes which come more out of the way in which human beings in the state of relative nature instinctively sing.
>
> WILFRED MELLORS, *Vox Pop 3*

And not, of course, limited to the established critic, or the artist of an older generation –

> I think it's a bit maladjusted really to scream at a pop singer. I think it's sort of sex going the wrong way! I don't think it's right to have ideals in that sort of way, 'cos you don't know anything about a pop singer; you only know he can sing or he's good looking. Well isn't it better to have an ideal with a set of principles you'd like to follow? Say if you were a communist you'd want to follow Marx or Lenin, or if you were a Christian you'd follow Christ...
>
> I think it's mostly schoolgirls – girls from single-sex schools, mostly, who think boys are sort of off a different planet.
>
> 17-YEAR-OLD LONDON GIRL, *Vox Pop 1*

Statements like these, punctuated by extracts from the relevant discs, and set in a context of the origins, history, and development of pop song, made an informative, entertaining and stimulating series of programmes. The question is – *why* were they so frowned upon by a BBC establishment actually engaged in moving more and more overtly into the field of pop, under pressure from the pirate radio stations, and already laying the foundations of the pop-dominated Radio One and Two Channels? (To say nothing of Local Radio.) I was, of course, then still under the impression that the BBC was a Public Service Organization which was not dictated to by the market, but by its own tradition and developed sense of social responsibility! This question is, I believe, central to any examination of popular music, however cursory (and this paper cannot pretend to be more than an opening up of the subject). How is it, that pop song, the outstanding cultural phenomenon of the twentieth century, persuasive penetrator of Church and State; of Academic, Cultural and commercial Establishments, the dominant musical social environment of the 1960s, how is it that this phenomenon has on the whole been allowed to develop unchecked and unchallenged? Has it in fact been deliberately fostered and encouraged to the point where we can now expect State-organized pop concerts and University Chairs in Pop Song. Where are the critics and questioners of this process? My own experience would suggest that they have been deliberately ignored or suppressed, or identified exclusively with a Mrs Grundy school of anti-lifers wishing to re-establish puritanism! (in fact, of course, one is simply trying to re-assert the power of genuine and untrammelled popular creation). And the anti-critical attitude extends even to the sacred groves of Academe – even to that most sacrosanct intellectual shrine, the Third Programme, as it then was!

An earlier programme, *Instant Salvation*, which examined the meteoric rise of the fundamentalist preacher/hymnwriter team Moody and Sankey in the 1870s scandalized the then Controller of the Third Programme, P. H. Newby, who dubbed it 'tendentious', only broadcasting it because it was by then too late to withdraw it from the *Radio Times*, but rejecting out of hand a second programme 'Blessed Assurance' which brought the subject of 'sacred' song up to the era of pop.

> I just telephone upstairs when I'm troubled
> Never need to drop a nickel in at all,
> And the Boss is there a-waiting
> I'm not exaggerating!
> He's sitting waiting for my call – my call....
>   THE GOLDEN GATE QUARTET (Col. DC 636)

> The danger of individualistic evangelism is that it can very easily turn away the attention of people from the actual situation in which they are involved, the social evils of the world, the social conditions which have to be fought and dealt with and so on....
>   CANON DOUGLAS RHYMES, *Southwark Cathedral*

> Precious Lord take my hand
> Lead me on to understand
> I am tired, and weak, and alone

> Through the sun, through the night
> Lead me on to the light
> Take my hand, Precious Lord, Lead me on....
> ELVIS PRESLEY (RCA RCX101, EPA-4059)

Again the question is why? What is so scandalous about attempting
a serious critique of this fundamental aspect of pop song – its
manifest tie-up with religious exhortation and the possible dangers
and confusions this holds for both Church and Society? Again it
seems that any attempt to apply the sort of canons of criticism
long accepted in literature or fine art, is regarded as tendentious,
and is slung out! What is it that makes pop this sacred cow in
our society?

> Radio must adapt itself, not only to changes in other media, but
> to changes in society. I myself, like many in this hall, belong to a
> generation which was brought up on radio. To people of our age,
> radio was as important a formative influence as television is to our
> children, and as the Northcliffe revolution in newspapers was to our
> parents.
> IAN TRETHOWAN, *Radio in the Seventies*[1]

That the mass media exert a formative influence is indisputable.
That these media are in fact controlled by a power élite, with
money and position, is obvious – they are the people who own and
manage the major newspaper, film, television, recording companies
and so on. And for all its tradition of Public Service Broadcasting,
they are the people who control the BBC which, since the Television Act of 1954 has had to 'compete' in the market place of
cultural commodity, so that whatever may have been the reality
of its independence before, after 1954 the BBC has increasingly
conformed to the dictates of this same commercial class who control
the market.

> The immense demand for the popular music of the day was
> 'prompted by circumstances over which we have little or no control'.
> FRANK GILLARD (then Director of Sound Broadcasting, now
> consultant to EMI), *Guardian*, June 1964

Under the terms of its Charter the BBC did not *have* to enter
this market place; it did so because it believed that only in this
way could its credibility be maintained – could it continue to
command a mass audience. That this implied the drastic devaluation of that audience, hitherto accorded at least a measure of
critical respect, was ignored; but this volte-face, and its consequence, underlines what I believe to be the crucial factor in any

[1] BBC Lunch-time Lectures, Eighth Series-4. 5/3/70.

discussion of the media in general and pop song in particular. The drive towards bigger and bigger audiences is justified by the commercial companies as a drive to bigger profits; by the BBC as a self-evident public service good with no thought of commercial profit! But why this compulsion anyway to fill the waking hours of the entire population with entertainment? The BBC phenomenon, I believe, gives the game away, revealing that there is much more to the media than profitability – their real *raison d'être* is social control. And nowhere, I contend, is this more powerfully (and cynically) exercised than in the sanctioning and manipulating of pop song as it has been developed since the Rock'n Roll revolt of the mid fifties. Indeed pop is a master tool of social control by a ruling class precisely because it has its origins in the genuine protest song of Black America.

> Large segments of the general public and the music industry establishments looked upon the growing popularity of the rock and roll with uneasiness ... rock and roll songs had too much sexuality, the attitudes in them seemed to defy authority, and the singers either were Negroes or sounded like Negroes.
>
> CHARLIE GILLETT, *The Sound of the City*[2]

And even though such pop song is now the prime property of the music industry establishments, the illusion of rock-protest has been carefully sustained by a sort of shadow-boxing between the rulers and the ruled, authority and the young.

This, then, is my thesis, that pop is, in fact, now cherished by a ruling class as a peerless form of social control. And that consequently, any opening up of critical dialogue with or between those who are so controlled is inadmissible, since it will inevitably establish the sort of criteria and critical consciousness which works against such control, and towards the genuine ascendancy of the artist. And this, in our present social and cultural dispensation, is subversive, 'tendentious'.

> The department of the Environment could become a pop festival promoter, if proposals being considered by the Government advisory committee on such events, is accepted ... Committee members are also studying American urban programmes which present festivals in parks paid for by local taxation.
>
> MARTIN WALKER, *Guardian*, 7 October 1972

> The BBC set up Radio I in 1967 at the request of the Government of the day.
>
> DIRECTOR OF PROGRAMMES, Radio, *Anatomy of Pop*
> BBC Publications 1970, p. 97

[2] Sphere Books, 1971, p. 21.

But there is, of course, very little overt fostering of pop; there doesn't need to be! the social system within which such show-biz operates requires only that any operation be manifestly profitable; the real sanction is the gravy!

> EMI's shares are now 212p., sitting on a princely 33 times last year's earnings ... UK sales of records are expected to do well, helped by lower purchase-tax and the change-over to VAT next April. Profits could grow from £7,719,000 to £8,300,000 this year and £9,200,000 next.
>
> *Evening News*, 12 May 1972

> Decca shares rose 18½p. to 400½p. yesterday ... pre-tax profits for the six months ended September have more than doubled from £2,128,000 to £5,240,000 on sales of £47.2 millions.
>
> *Guardian*, 7 February 1973

Put but money in thy purse! In the past eighteen years we have seen the ethical standards of our society overturned; the humanist values involving respect for the individual and the cherishing of community relationships, and affections and loyalties, the unselfishness, the concern for others; the rich humour and laconic strength found in the working class, all the values which in the teeth of an acquisitive society, yet made social relationships meaningful for the mass of the people (and which Church and State at least paid lip service to), all have been attacked and discredited by the cynical 'I'm All Right Jack', anti-community attitudes of the world of pop. While the cash registers have rung up bigger and bigger profits; and socialite and intellectual have scrambled on the gravy train with never a care, and seemingly no concern any longer for the 'high culture' so expensively nourished in them, and so lightly discarded.

> This yellow slave
> Will knit and break religions; bless the accurst,
> Make the hoar leprosy adored; place thieves
> And give them title, knee, and approbation...
> *Timon of Athens*, iv I.

Anarchy moved in. For thirty years you couldn't possibly make it unless you were white, sleek, nicely-spoken and phoney to your toe-nails, suddenly now you could be black, purple, moronic, delinquent, diseased or almost anything on earth and you could still clean up. In a way, we were moving towards some kind of democracy... all you needed was dollar potential: earn, baby, earn.

NIK COHN, *A Wop Bop a Lop Bop*[3]

[3] Paladin 1972, p. 52.

One of the highlights of the BBC 50 exhibition in London, celebrating 50 years of Broadcasting, was a close-circuit television performance by Chuck Berry of 'Ding-a-ling', providing perhaps as good a demonstration as any of what this anarchic democracy has led to. His audience was not the Rock 'n Roll or Rhythm and Blues hardliners of his hey-day, but girls in their early teens. They looked like butterflies drowning in treacle, except that treacle is too wholesome an image for the salacious matrix in which these beautiful young people were being snared. It was like some latter day slavemarket – but with the ultimate hideous twist that the victims were conditioned to enslave themselves by some monstrous invertion of group therapy, which led them to publicly defile themselves and so be trapped and exposed on this altar of anarchic democracy, to go through the motions of exerting choice by buying the disc in such numbers as to send it to the top of the charts.

> Popular franchise in the hands of the masters of a great body of slaves were the worst instruments of tyranny which were ever yet forged for the oppression of mankind.
>
> JAMES STEPHEN C.1800

> I knew a very wise man, that believed that if a man were permitted to make all the ballads, he need not care who should make the laws of a Nation.
>
> ANDREW FLETCHER OF SALTOUN C.1690

Repressive tolerance is the phrase coined, I believe, by Marcuse to describe this self-enslavement, and although James Stephen was, on the face of it, standing against emancipation and humanity, his words carry a chilling ring of prophecy. For this, it seems to me, is the power so mercilessly deployed by 'democracy' in the developed West today, the power sanctioned by ballot box, gallup poll and audience rating and the top twenty. And it is so potent because it is rooted, at whatever remove, in something *real* in the people's response, which is then manipulated to become the very opposite of what the people intended, but in a way which is extremely difficult for them to perceive.

Thus, for instance, the social forces which powered the explosive emergence of pop song in the Rock 'n Roll bonanza of 1955, were essentially healthy! From the post war revival of Trad Jazz to the Skiffle movement of the fifties, the younger generation in Britain were vociferously rejecting the then popular song industry based on the Musical, and performers like Crosby and Sinatra, Vera Lynn and Gracie Fields; but once this was recognized, the musical moguls moved in, first on Trad Jazz, then on

Skiffle, which was successfully identified with Rock 'n Roll, despite the fact that this home-made string-bass and wash-board music had already rediscovered the indigenous folk music of the British Isles, and was rapidly shedding the American dust-bowl or Deep-South accents of the Woody Guthrie and Leadbelly songs where it began.

> Right from the very beginning the skiffle movement was split into two sections – one of which argued that this music could never really have total significance for English, Irish or Scots people because it was music in a foreign idiom – you had to adopt an American accent. And the people in the skiffle movement who were trying desperately to create a British popular music said that we must find a music, the idiom of which, the intonation of which was English, Irish or Scots. The others said we have all been exposed to some twenty or thirty years of television and so on, therefore it's unrealistic to expect us to abandon the effects of this – you know, what the anthropologists call 'acculturation'. We would finish up with a type of singing where everybody sounded alike, would use the same generalized American accent.
>
> EWAN MACCOLL, *Vox Pop* 2

The most cursory listening to Radio I today leaves you in no doubt as to which wing of the skiffle movement won out – so far as the mass audience is concerned – (and not only Radio I! as the 'generalized American accent' consumes more and more spoken word on every channel). And of course given the commercial interest, it was inevitable that the values of the market should prevail, and skiffle become identified with the new and profitable consumable pop.

> It's quite clear that around 1955/56 you have an absolute revolution. One immediate consequence was that it showed how much greater the potential market for pop music was to what had always been thought before, but as soon as a working-class oriented music appeared in the middle fifties, the market widened and really multiplied.
>
> ERIC HOBSBAWN, *Vox Pop* 2

> I remember coming out of the Elephant and Castle, the big theatre on the corner – Trocadero – and it was after seeing the Bill Haley film *Rock Around the Clock* – and we all went down the Old Kent Road; and at the end of the Old Kent Road all the fire engines were there and they all got their hoses all ready and it was a big thing, this was, terribly big thing. The world belonged to us and it didn't belong to the conspirators in Denmark Street. The world belonged to us.
>
> RAY GOSLING, *Vox Pop* 2

It is the commercial exploitation of genuine aspirations and attitudes which have developed the enormous market for pop – although of course a hard core of artists and audience stuck to their social and aesthetic guns, to carry through the second trad jazz revival in the late fifties and the movement comparably committed to the blues in the early sixties, but these in turn were all but absorbed into the mainstream of pop, and in particular nurtured groups like the Rolling Stones. By the end of the decade, the Blues survived only as one attenuated element, rock culture. The other great stand against tin pan alley was the British Folk Revival, which withstood the blandishments of the commercial operators to greater effect and to which I shall return later. But it is interesting that the common assessment of skiffle by the present generation of pop song apologists is that it came *after Rock Around the Clock* in 1954-55, by which they mean that the commercial success of skiffle came with Lonnie Donegan and 'Rock Island Line' in 1956; as an 'underground' music it had, as Ewan MacColl says, existed for many years before this (the Crane River Jazz Band included a skiffle group in 1949 and Ken Colyer's Jazzmen in 1952) but skiffle had been ignored by the media and the manipulators, despite its spread like wildfire through Britain in defiance of the established (and middle class) popular music of the day. But once it dawned on the industry that a hundred thousand guitars a year were being sold (and in the early fifties the guitar was still a rather exotic instrument in Britain) then the skiffle competitions burgeoned in every cinema and holiday camp and the bland identification of skiffle with rock and roll took its toll; and the new big business revolt of youth found its million dollar archetype!

> If one had wanted to create a pop-cultural demi-God, then one would have created Elvis Presley and set him down in Memphis, Tennessee in 1955. The timing was everything. For the first time the Western World was healthy enough to support an economy aimed at affluent teenage. With no external threats to promote boys into men or girls into widows, before their time, adolescence was able to develop a culture of its own.
>
> RAY CONNOLLY, *Anatomy of Pop*, p. 71

Mr Connolly is a journalist, who dealt with 'Personality in Pop' for the BBC I series *Anatomy of Pop* in 1971; and it's statements such as his, riddled as they are with internal contradictions, and disposing the sort of trendy cool which in fact is cynical cold-bloodedness, that are typical of the way in which pop has been dealt with by the media analysts and reviewers and columnists.

The affluence of the fifties did indeed enable the young to develop something of a distinctive life style, but it was their own (in the sense that skiffle was their own) only while the economy was *not* 'aimed at affluent teenage'. And the fact that, as Charlie Gillett points out, the big record companies were slow in readjusting their sights does not mean that the independent companies who were first on target were any more committed to the needs and aspirations of youth; their committal was to youth as a wide-open market, and the life-style they engendered was designed for commodity consumption – which is not at all the same thing as culture!

> It's some bloke in Paris running around in a dirty big Rolls or Mercedes says 'I think next week we'll have 'em up an extra inch.' You see? You haven't got any option. Why have you got to have them up an extra inch? Because everybody else has got them up an extra inch, that's why.
>   17-YEAR-OLD LONDON BOY, Radio Ballad *On the Edge*[4]

Such an assessment of this life-style as fundamentally one of exploitation, is of course challenged by the apologists of pop.

> Audiences and creators can determine the content of a popular art communicated through the mass media. The businessmen who mediate between the audience and the creator can be forced by either to accept a new style. The rise of rock and roll is proof.
>   *The Sound of the City* (Introduction p. 1)

Charlie Gillett calls this his most important assumption, and I agree with him. The role of the businessman is crucial – but I believe decisive! And it is naïve of Mr Gillett to assume otherwise. And that he himself is uneasy, or at least confused, is evident in his unwitting exposure of a contradiction which, it seems to me, cannot but be fatal to any serious analysis – that of confusing 'content' with 'style', a confusion further compounded when he goes on to discuss function.

> For many people in this age group, popular music provides a sense of change, as records and styles replace each other in the instant history of the hit parades. At any time in this history, each listener has a few records that enrich his feelings, extend his sense of love or despair, and feed his fantasies or fire some real relationship. He switches on the radio and waits for this music, or buys the records and plans his own programme of moods.
>   (op. cit. p. vi)

[4] Argo Records, DA 136.

Surely this spells out the essentially synthetic nature of the pop experience? Phrases like 'a sense of change', 'instant history', 'program of moods', reveal a preoccupation with form at the expense of substance, style and not content, sensation not experience, which is precisely the object of cultural exploitation, whether for money or power, or both. The businessman does not mediate, he castrates. (The subsequent fall of rock and roll is proof!) Now if this were merely the exploitation of certain wholesome but marginal qualities and responses in the young, say the appetite for ice-cream, or pop (in the old sense of mineral water) we could perhaps accept it as we have perforce to accept so much else in our consumer society. But to exploit the condition of adolescence is to interfere with the whole structure of society at its most delicate and vital; for whether we call it Confirmation or Initiation or just Growing-up, the safe and confident passage from the lost innocence of childhood through this distressful ugly-duckling stage to conscious adulthood is vital both for the individual and for the community. Yet for the businessman it now seems merely to present him with a golden opportunity of precisely assessing the marketable areas of vulnerability in that most vulnerable of potential consumers, the uninformed adolescent. Could there be a more inhuman manifestation of what Marx calls the 'icy waters of egotistical calculation' in which the bourgeoisie have drowned religion and chivalrous enthusiasm ...

> When you sell a kid on a product, if he can't get it, he will throw himself on the floor, stamp his feet and cry. You can't get a reaction like that out of an adult.
>
> ADVERTISING MANAGER for Oscar Mayer

> Well it's one for the money, two for the show
> Three get ready now go, cat, go! but don't you
> Step on my Blue Suede Shoes.
> Well you can do anything but step on my Blue Suede Shoes...
>
> ELVIS PRESLEY (RCA RD 27120)

> 'Blue Suede Shoes' was important – the idea that Clothes could dominate your life ... it was the first hint of an obsession with objects that was going to become central.
>
> NIK COHN, *A Wop Bop a Lop Bop*, p. 26

> Sun recording studio, Memphis, said 'If only we could find a white man who had the Negro sound and the Negro feel, we could make a billion dollars.' And in walked Elvis ... All Elvis did was translate

pentecostal hellfire and damnation into 'Good Rocking Tonight' ...
but he paid his taxes. Elvis was the regular guy....

RAY GOSLING, *The Times*, 10 July 1972[5]

Elvis. The golden boy in the golden suit and golden slippers with
the solid gold Cadillac. Latest on the gravy train of Sun Kings
who have held mankind to ransom since Acamapichtli the Aztec
and beyond.

> In 1969 I visited Las Vegas to see Presley's stage comeback ... 'Elvis,
> you still the best' the men were whooping, and the women were still
> the same too, clutching their thighs and loins in excitement, trying
> to pull him off stage down among them ... the man who brought
> back their adolescence and forgotten fantasies. And still he's playing
> the young boy, overcome at the effect he's creating, embarrassed but
> flattered by his simple sexuality.
>
> RAY CONNOLLY, op. cit. p. 71

Overcome, as they say, all the way to the bank; a multi-million-
dollar industry, incubated in that 'simple sexuality' so blatantly
deployed to simultaneously assault those vulnerable in pocket and
crotch, whether regressed middle-aged women such as now swoon
over Tom Jones in a frenzy of fake pubescence, or the genuinely
aroused teenager.

Adolescence is the period of sexual as well as economic imma-
turity and vulnerability; it is, or should be, the period of initiation
into adulthood, and from man's earliest days the ceremonies and
implications and deep poetic meanings attached to initiation have
been central to human society; and to manipulate initiation is
to *savage* society at its cultural and psychological roots. This is
the dangerous game that the hustlers of pop song are playing, and
it's a diabolically clever one worthy of its origins in historic cultural perversion. Because the erotic response aroused in the adolescent is a real one, and in giving himself to this response the
adolescent is only too justified in so rejecting the bankruptcy of
the received culture as it is presented to him and which seems to
be his only alternative. The perversion lies in the use of primitive,
atavistic, orgiastic stimuli, not in order to initiate the subject
into adult society, but to hold him down mercilessly in the sensations aroused by those stimuli as ends in themselves. So that
instead of the controlled progression from ignorance to understanding, childhood to adulthood, economic liability to economic
asset, virginity to fruitfulness, using the classic concept of the death
of the old being – the child, in the rebirth of the new – the man

[5] From a review of *Elvis* by Terry Hopkins, Macmillan.

or woman; instead of this vital social function, the activity is made functionless and celebrated for itself alone. The engine fires but the vehicle's on the chocks; the engine screams, the wheels race – but there's no road and no destination.

This essentially orgiastic basis of pop song, as it has developed from rock 'n roll, provides its apologists with their weapon against any would-be critics – they simply assert that because of this, pop by-passes all established canons of criticism, literary or musical or ethical, since the response is one of sensual spontaneity and the intellect is not involved (and this even though paradoxically 'Rock' today can mean music with a distinct intellectual content – but for a progressive minority; the music of the mass audience remains the essentially mindless pop).

> ... the (largely white) pop explosion that occurred in the wake of the Second World War is a rediscovery of music as orgiastic magic, now relevant, in its caprine potency, not merely to a Black minority, but to the young at large .... In the Rock and Roll explosion which initiated the new pop after the Second World War the word, with intellectually communicable meaning, is almost, totally insignificant.
>
> WILFRED MELLORS, *Times Literary Supplement,*
> 19 November 1971

Later on in this brilliantly argued – and I contend ultimately irresponsible-article which he entitles 'Pop as Ritual in Modern Culture', Professor Mellors asks us to remember that 'pop is ritual in an emergent stage'. I must quote him in full, because it is a crucial point.

> It is easy to say – and it is true – that there is a fundamental difference between ritual that supports inherited beliefs, and a ritual that seeks to destroy or obtain fulfillment only in regression and dream. We must remember, however, that pop is *ritual in an emergent stage*, and that its ambiguity, given its association with youth, may be its strength.
>
> WILFRED MELLORS, op. cit. (my italics)

But what, one must ask, is this pop ritual emerging from, and whither is it directed? And how does this statement relate to the actual process whereby any comparable ritual has emerged in the past? Certainly its association with youth can mean only one thing – Initiation. I must therefore spend a little time on the history of Initiation, since it is the relationship of pop to the psychological needs and drives of the adolescent, which, I believe, explains the hold it has on the teenager.

Early man, confronting a material environment for which he was not physically equipped and which he was only beginning to understand and control, yet survived and developed by first creating, in imagination, an environment which he could control. This illusory technique of magic effectively, at this stage of man's emergence, supplemented his deficiencies of actual technique, and was a total collective possession and experience of the group or tribe, for only together was survival possible. It involved the most consummate mastery of mimesis, and combined poetry, music, and dance in meaningful and utterly functional ritual. To catch the animal on which the group subsisted, it was first necessary to enact the hunt, after which group confidence was such that the success of the actual hunt became inevitable.

> Thus poetry, combined with dance, ritual, and music, became the great switchboard of the instinctive energy of the tribe, directing it into trains of collective action.
>
> CHRISTOPHER CAUDWELL, *Illusion and Reality*[6]

> The common speech of these savages is rhythmical, melodic, fantastic to a degree which we associate only with poetry. And if their common speech is poetical, their poetry is magical. The only poetry they know is song, and their singing is nearly always accompanied by some bodily action.
>
> GEORGE THOMSON, *Marxism and Poetry*[7]

> On no occasion in the life of primitive people could dance be dispensed with. Birth, circumcision, and the consecration of maidens, marriage and death, planting and harvest, the celebration of Chieftains, hunting, war, and feasts, the changes of the moon and sickness – for all of these the dance is needed.
>
> CURT SACHS, *World History of the Dance*[8]

It would seem, therefore, that a condition inconceivable to primitive man is isolation and loneliness – the condition endemic in the adolescent.

> Loneliness. If you're lonely and you won't tell no-one what you really want. If you're lonely, people sort of think you've got a disease, you're unwanted. Loneliness ... loneliness is an awful thing.
>
> SALFORD 15-YEAR OLD, *On the Edge*

> You just sit on the edge all the time, nobody wants you to come in and sit round the fire in the middle.
>
> GLASGOW 17-YEAR-OLD, *On the Edge*

So that one immense attraction for the young, of anything which smacks of such primitive ritual, is its fundamentally collective

[6] Lawrence and Wishart, 1958, p. 27.
[7] People's Publishing House Ltd, New Delhi 1954, p. 8.
[8] W. W. Norton, New York 1963, p. 4.

nature, putting to flight loneliness and the fears of loneliness.
There is of course a large area of pop which exploits that other
refuge of the lonely, the private world of the daydream, but this
is really a throw-back to what Stuart Hall in *Vox Pop 3* calls
'the self-regarding enclosed world of the Crooners.... Bing Crosby
or Vera Lynn waiting in the wings!' Pop song proper is rooted
in the shared ritual. Then again such ritual is essentially egalitarian, meshing in with the revolt against adult authority, necessary if the adolescent is to achieve independent adulthood; and in
the ailing, hypocritical, corrupt society which seems to be the
adolescents' inheritance, the personal revolt is understandably
allied to the social revolt and provides a further pull towards
primitive ritual.

> The group is the only authority that has real existence ... for the
> authority of a chief is largely if not wholly symbolical, a convenient
> fiction.
>
> PAUL RADIN, *The World of Primitive Man*, p. 226[9]

And, perhaps most potent for all of us, but especially for the
adolescent, there is, in the developed forms of primitive magic,
a frank and unforced celebration of human sexuality.

> For few other facts in life is it possible to show so direct a relation-
> ship between man and his animal forbears as for those of the sex
> cycle. It is not strange then, that the sex cycle should have been the
> first to become socially crystallized, reorganized, and reinterpreted.
> Nor is it strange ... that this never attempted to disguise the bio-
> logical facts and acts involved.... Not only was there a polarization
> of nature into male and female – the male sky and the female earth,
> the male sun and the female moon – but sex (was) brought into
> immediate and fundamental connexion with the whole life of the
> group, particularly with regard to the assurance and the perpetuation
> of the food supply.
>   There was, however, another side to this socialization which has
> had a direct bearing on the history of civilization. One of its con-
> stituent elements, puberty, became not simply the recognition that
> an individual had reached the age of sexual maturity; it became
> dramatized as the period of transition par excellence; the passage of
> an individual from the position of being an economic liability to
> that of an economic social asset ... The simplest tribes, the food
> gatherers and fishing-hunting peoples, have already developed
> intricate and complex initiation rites around it. These puberty
> rites are the fundamental and basic rites of mankind.
>
> PAUL RADIN, op. cit., p. 152

[9] Abelard-Schuman, N.Y. 1953.

In Neolithic Art, when hunting or food-gathering man becomes a crop-raising or cattle-raising tribe, the object is not merely sought by society, but changed by it. The dance becomes the formal hieratic movement of chorus and incipient Tragedy ... It emphasizes the magical and world-governing power of the gesture. The circling sun obeys the circling dancer; the crop lifts with the leaping of 'young men', life quickens with the dizzy motion.

CHRISTOPHER CAUDWELL, op. cit., p. 256

Our own May Day memories are survivals of this great tradition of the fertility rite (surely misconstrued by Frazer as originally a human sacrifice – a construction which goes utterly against the grain of primitive art as rooted in mimesis). On May Day the young boys and girls go in procession to the woods and meadows while the community mourns their 'death' as children. They return as men and women, carrying with them the sprigs of May as symbols of the procreative power reviving in the earth, and burgeoning in themselves since in the course of the night they perform for the first time the act of sexual union.

> Unite and unite; and let us all unite
> For Summer is a-comin today
> And whither we are going
> We all may unite
> In the merry morning of May....

As the Padstow May song so recognizably celebrates this ancient ritual. So that the instinctive response of the mid-twentieth-century adolescent to the ritual sexuality and orgiastic form of Rock and Roll, to Elvis the Pelvis, Little Richard, Chuck Berry and the rest, is understandable, commendable and altogether in a tradition which, whether or not it's openly acknowledged, his parents share.

So what has gone wrong? Why is it that the pop scene seems always to manifest not the creative, zesty and healthful qualities of man and nature but the negative, obsessive side, the ugly qualities, the reverse side of the coin? I contend that it is because, once such a popular form is manipulated in the interests of a minority group, and for their profit, there inevitably ensues a process whereby its original function is transformed into its opposite; hence the life-asserting fertility rites, in the hands of an emerging priest-king class of property-owners living off the labour of the masses of the people, becomes the death-asserting fearful rites of ritual sacrifice so honoured by Sir James Frazer in his *Golden Bough*. And this exploitation of popular ritual has all too long a history too, for it dates from the emergence, with the achievements of domesticated animals and agriculture, of the possibility of property! As man gained command over his natural environment, he lost it over his social environment; the united tribal society becomes divided against itself; man, alienated from society, and ultimately from himself, steps on to the stage, held in the grip of an authority in which he has no effective say.

> Fear, let it be remembered, is no instinct, man was not born with it. Fear does not create anything. It is self-created within man through ... economic and environmental insecurity. But economic insecurity has the mental correlate.... A marked subjectivism. Subjectivism, in its turn brings about the dominance of magic, of coercive rites, and emphasizes the strictly coercive aspects of religion.
>
> In all aboriginal societies, attempts are continually being made by the medicine men and the priests, to free themselves from the drudgery of securing food and to concentrate in their hands whatever wealth they can, in order to exact privileges and obtain this power over others.
>
> PAUL RADIN, op. cit., p. 138

> The convulsive dance is a characteristic of shaman cultures. It makes its appearance where priestly dignity and magic powers are in the hands of the witch doctor or the medicine man, where as a result of a peculiar racial tendency or a cultural influence, religious experience and its cult formation rest solely on the rule of hypnosis.
>
> CURT SACHS, *World History of the Dance*, p. 20

> Initiation ceremonies retain their democratic and tribal aspects only in societies which have not emerged from that primitive stage in which all social control is in the hands of the tribal elders.... with developing political centralization such functions tend to become obsolete.
>
> HUTTON WEBSTER, *Primitive Secret Societies*[10]

> When that system begins to disintegrate, initiation loses its tribal character ... the rites become perfunctory ... or else form the basis of the magical sodality or secret society.... The privileges exercised by the initiated have lost their economic foundation and are exercised more or less consciously for the purpose of social exploitation. In Mexico and Peru, the most advanced areas of primitive America, this hypertrophy of magic ... reduced the people to a state of absolute subjection to a bloodthirsty theocracy, whose progressive refinement of human sacrifice was only terminated by the extinction of their culture in the even greater horror of the Spanish conquest.
>
> GEORGE THOMSON, *Aeschylus and Athens*, pp. 100-102[11]

[10] New York 1932, p. 75.
[11] Lawrence and Wishart, 1941.

I have spent so long seeking to establish the history of cultural manipulation and its consequences in ancient society, because it seems to me central to a real understanding of the contradictions which bedevil the pop scene. Only this sort of historical perspective can make sense of the grotesque nonsense perpetrated in the name of pop song and a permissive society. The fact that a ruling class has, on the face of it, sanctioned overt erotic licence in flat rejection of all its precedent shibboleths is only the further twist in the control mechanism techniques; for the permissive society is *not* a liberated society, but one ruthlessly controlled in the interests of hedonistic consumer capitalism, and to understand the nature of this control, and thus be able to combat it, it is necessary to understand its history, and see through the successive disguises in which authority cloaks its real nature, from priest-king to the latest incarnation as pander-superstar. And always the smoke screen of official outrage at excesses officially if discreetly engendered, so that in the consequent confusion and cultural anarchy the debauching of the people is made to seem their own fault while a ruling class clean up on proceeds – and no matter if all that was once held sacred is thrown to the dogs in the process!

'The spectre of mankind without memory', raised by the German philosopher Adorno, is fleshed in the instant and only sensation of discotheque and DJ show; history, folk lore, ancient loyalties are rejected as irrelevant, and youth is alienated from age, dismissively identified with archaic concepts like Commonwealth and Patriotism – or Cornish pasties and Yorkshire pudding. Which is all very convenient at a time when a British Government is so feverishly dismantling traditional British society in the name of monopoly capital, multi-national corporations, the European Common Market, and Hamburgers and Coca-Cola. A cosmopolitan facelessness, as drained of identity as the new British Rail uniforms, is being stamped onto a people whose rich vernacular identity is seen as a threat, and is therefore identified for the young (and with just enough truth to carry weight) with an outmoded, censorious and duped adult world.

And the teenager, in throwing out the devil of a restrictive official morality identified with everything the adult world stands for, is like the man in the New Testament who, having got shot of one devil, took in seven far worse devils, 'and the last state of that man is worse than the first'.

A selection for the rock vocabulary might proceed as follows: incongruous, trivial, mediocre, banal, insipid, maudlin, abominable, trite, redundant, repulsive, ugly, innocuous, crass, incoherent, vulgar, tasteless, sour, boring.

RICHARD MELTZER, *The Aesthetics of Rock*[12]

As I read that passage, Meltzer is making two points. First, don't try to assimilate rock by applying the hooray words used for conventional forms of art – mellifluous, eternal, new, etc. Secondly the words he quotes are not empty. A description of the Stones, for example, should allow for the fact that they mean to be ugly, and are good at being ugly, and why is it that wrong? since the world isn't all a garden.

GEOFFREY CANNON, *Guardian*, 20 November 1971

The monstrosities do appear to satisfy, by their very disorganisation and violence, the private urge to express, and personally to get hold of, the trigger-end – instead of having always to face the muzzle-end – of the same disorganisation and violence of the world in which the listeners-to, and buyers-of these 'arts' find themselves entrapped. What thus appears to be the fondling and possessing of something that is palpably (to those who hate it) ugly and disorganised and impossible to love, is therefore in a deeper sense the arming of oneself with precisely the weapon with which one is attacked: noise when one is attacked by noise, ugliness when one is attacked by ugliness, machines when one is attacked by the machine. That this is practically a form of suicide – and the cure almost worse than the disease – is irrelevant.

GERSHON LEGMAN, *The Horn Book*[13]

And surely the most cursory glance at the world of pop song reveals the betrayal of the real aspirations of the adolescent, who asks for bread and is given a stone. The hunger for acceptance into society, for participation in the collective experience, for participation in the deep poetry and root rhythms of primitive ritual, for the routing of the fears of loneliness and rejection – how is this hunger assuaged?

Blues singers tended to be concerned with experience or relationships between people. The abstract nature of the relationship in gospel songs between the singer and God was rare in the blues, but it was close to the unreal ideal conception of love which adolescents often have. Between 1948 and 1952 the potential connection between the emotions of gospel singing and the expectations of adolescent listeners ... occurred to various singers, record company executives, and composers. Indirectly and directly, gospel styles and conventions were introduced into rhythm and blues – and constituted the first significant trend away from the blues as such in black popular music.

CHARLIE GILLETT, *The Sound of the City*, p. 178

[12] Something Else Press, New York.
[13] New York 1964, p. 334.

The compulsiveness of rock critically changed the emphasis of attention in pop dancing! jivers were dancing *to*, not with (each other). A few years later the Twist reduced contact even further. Since then ... totally solitary dancing is becoming increasingly common, from the snaky convulsions seen at open-air festivals to the bland clockwork of the Go-Go dancers.

> RICHARD MABEY, *Anatomy of Pop*, p. 83

Across the past decade, soul has become progressively stylized, formal even, and now tends to be as ritualized as some religious festival ... Groups and soloists alike indulge in standardized bouts of dialogue with their audience (Is everybody all right? 'Yeah.' 'Let me hear you say Yeah.' *'Yeah'* 'No let me hear you say Yeah louder "YEAH" ') What makes all this such a bringdown is the total lack of any real involvement. Most soul singers don't act like people and they don't treat their audience like people either.

> NIK COHN, op. cit., p. 115

And Nik Cohn compounds his own critique of this audience betrayal, by going on to dismiss his *own* criticism!

I'm being too prissy: pop is a business first and last. It has always been full of fake messiahs and bring down is an essential part of the game. (p. 117)

It's this sort of trendy cynicism, trying to have it both ways, which I believe is the ultimate betrayal of the young by those who could and should be continually appraising the scene and exposing its aberrations and hypocrisies (which go far to outstrip those the teenager in revolt is against!) As witness, for instance Peter Hall's critique of *Jesus Christ Superstar* in the *Observer*, 14 May 1972.

Jesus Christ Superstar is already a classic of the seventies – an event which will describe our decade to the future.

The odd thing is that the authors have taken over one of the world's most dramatic stories and turned it into something passive and undramatic ... This Christ has no point of view, political, social, or human to communicate. He expresses a generalised love....

The record (it began life as an LP) was very dramatic. It was alive (*sic*) with howling guitars and the infinite variety of the Moog Synthesiser.

The live performance had to reproduce the record meticulously, and yet bigger, louder, and better. The musicians are sealed off in the pit as if it were a recording studio. The sound comes from a vast array of loud-speakers ... The effect is startling. I did not hear one word from start to finish.

And so on; but set in a full page spread with touching 8×6 picture captioned 'Broadway's Jesus (Jeff Fernolt) comforted by Mary Magdalene (Yvonne Elliman)'; and for all Peter Hall's scathing words about the manner of the production, the matter goes all but unremarked – 'It's not blasphemous, but it sounds as if it is going to be.' The whole effect is to excite interest in the show while seeming to damn it. Above all at no point does Peter Hall question the validity of the rock idiom, which he casually extolls as a 'lingua franca for the world' ... In the beginning was the Word, and the Word was with the Moog Synthesiser ...

> You'd have managed better if you'd had it planned.
> Why did you choose such a backward time and such a strange land?
> If you'd come today you'd have reached a whole nation
> Israel in 4 BC had no mass communication.
>
> *Jesus Christ Superstar*[14]

> Riding high on the success of the *Jesus Christ Superstar* production, which contributed 29 per cent to earnings, Stigwood produced its best pretax profit of £1,250,000 for the year to the end of September. This represents a 133 per cent improvement on the previous year.
>
> *Guardian*, 28 February 1973

> Gerry Marsden, the pop star, is to lead a one-day pop festival 'Godbeat' in Chester Cathedral. It will be part of the all-church 'Call to the North' campaign during Holy Week. The Archdeacon of Chester said ... 'We are not going to preach at people though, just express Christian love and concern.'
>
> *The Times*, 24 January 1973

Such clerical eagerness to embrace pop song is surely a betrayal of all that the Church stands for, but all of a piece, perhaps, with the relegation of the King James Bible to the waste bin and the bowdlerizing of the *Book of Common Prayer*, and I suppose that *Hymns Ancient and Modern* makes such an uncritical acceptance of the trite but trendy inevitable. But the betrayal is at a level deeper than the aesthetic; it involves basic doctrine. For take that crucial Christian concept, the family, 'Honour thy father and thy mother' is surely an inescapable injunction for the Christian. How then, in the name of some lip togetherness, can the Church so adulate a pop song manifestly rooted in the precise opposite?

> As manager, what Oldham did was to take everything implicit in the Stones and blow it up one hundred times ... he turned them into everything that parents would most hate, be most frightened by. All the time he goaded them to be wilder, nastier, fouler in every way

[14] EM MFP 5280, Leeds Music Ltd.

than they were – they swore, sneered, snarled and, deliberately, they came on cretinous.

It was good basic psychology: kids might see them the first time and be not so sure about them, but then they'd hear their parents whining about those animals, those filthy long-haired morons, and suddenly they'd be converted, they'd identify like mad.

This, of course, is bedrock pop formula: find yourself something that truly makes adults squirm and, straightaway, you have a guaranteed smash on your hands, Johnny Ray, Elvis, P. J. Proby, Jimi Hendrix – it never fails.

NIK COHN, op. cit., p. 153

A culture that tries to be exclusively adolescent can ultimately justify itself only at the expense of adulthood, which means, inexorably, the dishonouring of the parents. So the generation gap is ruthlessly widened and deepened and its bridges blown, and the surrogate mummies and daddies get to work milking the micro boppers. And if this is good commercial psychology, how much more is it good political psychology of the grand old divide-and-rule school! For what can more effectively destroy the disturbing relevance of the past, and defuse the explosive potential of the present, than this fanning into flame of the tensions between father and son, mother and daughter ...

My father has got one word that fits every teenager he can see who wears a long jacket or a tight skirt. That's *Tripe*; pop music, that's *Tripe*; anything to do with teenagers, that's *Tripe*!

NOTTINGHAM 17-YEAR-OLD GIRL, *On the Edge*

They got to realize that what we want out of life is not what they think we should have. It's what we *want*! And you don't seem to be able to pass that over in any form, to the adult world.

LIVERPOOL 16-YEAR-OLD BOY, *On the Edge*

But if you break away, you're regarded as something strange, like a beatnik or something like that!

RUTHERGLEN 14-YEAR-OLD BOY, *On the Edge*

There can be no doubt that we are confronting a mounting crisis in social and personal relationship. The skids seem increasingly to be under the traditional concept of the family (as another of our *On the Edge* teenage speakers said – 'It's out of Enid Blyton, isn't it?') but there can be no resolution on the basis of mounting hatred and alienation; and this is what pop song surely engenders, battening parasitically upon the breakdown of the old cultural patterns and substituting the spurious community of shared sensation.

The breakdown of aboriginal cultures brings to the fore the intermittently religious individuals ... being fundamentally unanchored; they became more easily terrified and psychically disorganised. It is to these factors that we must ascribe the role played by collective hysteria in all the new religions that spring up on such occasions.

PAUL RADIN, op. cit., p. 96

... the incremental repetition of brief, non-developing phrases, with or without intelligible words, generates and at the same time is generated by an unremittent beat. The continuity of the beat destroys the sense of temporal progression, so that one lives once more in mythological, rather than in chronological time. The trance the music induces may be enhanced by narcotics: as was certainly the case in primitive music rituals.

WILFRED MELLORS, op. cit.

It is no new thing to engender collective hysteria as a lucrative – and spurious – social therapy for a disrupted community; what is new is the monstrous scale given by twentieth-century electronics to what are still, in essence, age-old manipulative techniques. I recently had occasion to demonstrate this in a sound sequence. It began with Tom Jones singing 'Delilah', and at a high point in his atavistic vocal, I made a direct segue to a Yaruro Indian Shaman from Venezuela, and thence a further segue to Otis Reading singing 'Sweet Lorene'. The family likeness was startling! And on the orchestration/Moog Synthesiser/electronic manipulation level, for a radio documentary on Transcendental Meditation called *Peace of Mind*, a similar cross from Tibetan Ritual Music to 'World in a Jug' by the Canned Heat made an equally devastating aural point. There is, indeed, nothing new under the sun, as anyone listening to an extraordinary programme some years ago by A. L. Lloyd, *The Voice of the Gods*, can bear witness; it was like listening to stone-age Rolling Stones! The social objectives of these Shaman and medicine men, priests and monks and religious howlers, in developing their outlandish and perverted vocal techniques, was to engender fear in their audience by emulating the voice of God – an abstraction whose modern counterpart is surely the brilliant but dangerously potent electronic sounds of electric guitar and recording studio. These can have a psychological effect as devastating, and indeed as terror-inducing, as the Voice of the Gods – but amplified to overwhelming proportions, and capable of inducing hysteria on a mass scale. The film *Gimme Shelter*, on the Rolling Stones tour of the United States in 1969, reveals the dilemma of a pop group facing such hysteria and having to resort to manipulative shamanist techniques to control the audience. This is the death of community, and at Altamont it was the death of four people when the

Stones really came up against it and a crowd of 300,000 got out of control. For this total aural possession is, I believe, the more or less desperate attempt to conceal and compensate for the absence of the true community of shared experience; sheer electrical energy is no substitute for passion.

> The Negroid voice, simulated by White men, substituted aggression for nervosity ... Percussion was more violent ... both because it was metrically cruder and because in amplification it was so loud. Similarly, whereas the Negro's guitar was often savage but sometimes, like his voice, intimately expressive, and whereas the White man's country guitar or banjo was cheery if insensitive, pop's vastly amplified electric guitars and organs became a plangent resonance that engulfs consciousness ... In primitive music, demonic possession devils 'personal' expression; in modern Rock the immense sea of sound has a comparable effect on a vaster scale, and loudness becomes paradoxically more silent than silence, since one is no longer aware of gradation.
>
> WILFRED MELLORS, op. cit.

Paradoxically indeed: since we are now told that the sound level mandatory in some discotheques can transcend the threshold of pain for the normal eardrum, and medical opinion has it that the 'loudness more silent than silence' may well result in the absolute silence of deafness. This manic assault upon the aural sensibility makes nonsense of any identification of this activity with 'art' in any meaningful sense of the word. The attempt is to achieve actual physical feel (with echoes of Huxley's 'feelies' and Lewis Mumford's 'Megatechnic Primitivism'). The physical pulsing of the loudspeaker and of the surrounding air-space must be perceived for anything to happen.

> When I was listening to pop records professionally, I found one very good way was to put your hand on the loud speaker and get the vibrations from it ... You enjoy it more that way.
>
> ADRIAN MITCHELL, *Vox Pop 6*

> Spector ... knew more about the actual mechanics of recording than any other producer before or since ... So what he did, simply, was to assemble all of the noise in the world and then ride it.
>
> His most persistent image of himself was paranoid-creative Phil Spector hemmed in by cigar-chewing fatties, beautiful Phil among the uglies ... His records were his best revenge.
>
> So when you bought Phil Spector records, you were buying huge frantic outpourings of spite and paranoia, rage and frustration and visional apocalypse. And if you were teenage, you probably felt exactly the same way and you loved it. That's how Spector came to make two million clear at the age of twenty-two.
>
> NIK COHN, op. cit., p. 96

Even making allowances for Mr Cohn's exotic style of writing, this is an analysis which conforms to the evidence of the ear; and yet a serious musicologist can confront this manic eclecticism, as taken up and extended by the Beatles (Phil Spector, incidentally, now produces for Apple) and after expanding on the poetry of *Sergeant Pepper's Lonely Hearts Club Band* which, though remarkable, is fortunately 'at a poetic level beyond intellectual formulation', can go on to say this:

> Yet if 'Sergeant Pepper' is, in this relatively traditional sense, art, it is also a ritual involving the young – through its electronic extension of musical sounds into the environment of the external world – in a ritual togetherness, without the prop of Church or State.
>
> WILFRED MELLORS, op. cit.

As a documentary radio producer it was my business professionally to explore the aural 'environment of the external world'; I found that the sounds and rhythms and tonalities, expressive of the actual human communities in which people work, struggle, and live together, bear no relation to those of 'Sergeant Pepper'. The way, for instance, girls in *On the Edge* actually talk about leaving home makes nonsense of the lyrics and lachrymose banalities of 'She's Leaving Home'. Yet this song has been hailed for its concrete content and specific reference – exposed by such a comparison as generalized and spurious – but by this very token, of course, immaculately geared to the multi-national pop market. This, it seems to me, is the real meaning of 'ritual togetherness' – the false community of the cosmopolitan teen-scene where the identity is submerged in a common, conditioned response of the viscera. Professor Mellors, who should surely know better, is taking at its smirking multi-million-dollar face value the utterly synthetic and deliberately abstract environment which the whole pop song industry and its pop-art ancillaries have built up as the 'external world' in complete rejection of the *real* external world in which men and women have to make a living and confront the harsh facts of life. The Beatles syndrome is the most masterly confidence trick ever perpetrated on a self-captivating audience, who really believed they sang with Liverpool accents and confronted reality!

> All the lonely people, where do they all come from?
> All the lonely people, where do they all belong?
>
> Eleanor Rigby

If you didn't have an idol, I suppose it's because you didn't like them, and you didn't like anybody ... of the pop stars. You'd probably wouldn't like very many people at school they wouldn't

like you. If they'd ... huh! *they're* not very up-to-date, you know?
That ... that would make you feel lonely.
                    15-YEAR-OLD GIRL in *This Week*, television documentary
                                   on David Cassidy, 22 March 1973

So much, then, for the way in which pop, in seeming to combat
loneliness and the loss of community, in fact intensifies their effects.
And similarly with the other two aspects of primitive ritual which
I mentioned – its essentially democratic, egalitarian quality when
not exploited by shaman or priest, and its frank sexuality. In pop
ritual these too become their opposite.

> He had become, in fact, a godhead – unseen, unreachable, more
> than human. The demon lover had been turned into a father, an
> all-powerful force that could rule his fans' lives without actually
> being there. His distance was a positive advantage, his artistic mis-
> takes irrelevant, and there seemed no reason why anything should
> ever change. Worship, after all, is a habit that's hard to break.
>   NIK COHN, *A Wop Bop a Lop Bop*, p. 29

Elvis 'where pop begins and ends', the regular guy, ex US Army
Specialist Fourth Class, as described during his nine-year seclusion
in the sixties:

> Elvis lives, honoured by the State of Tennessee and in Mississippi –
> which made September 26th Elvis Presley Day.
>   RAY GOSLING, *Guardian*, 10 July 1972

> You have to be a real square not to love the nutty, noisy, happy,
> handsome Beatles. If they don't sweep your blues away – brother
> you're a lost cause. If they don't put a beat in your feet – sister
> you're not living.
>   Editorial in the *Daily Mirror*, November 1963

And does democracy survive the dogs and the wire and Securicor
guards of the Pop Festivals? Or the bombardment of admass
promotions?

> They're the mummies and daddies! They're the things that are
> really telling you what to do, although you don't really know
> it.
>   HACKNEY 16-YEAR-OLD, *On the Edge*

Or just consider one other implication of the electronic stranglehold. Skiffle was poor man's music, washboards and string basses,
music that could be made by everyone – which is one reason why
it caught on so fast in Britain. But you try to start a pop group
now! To acquire the bare minimum of electrical and electronic
equipment you need to mortgage yourself as if you were buying
a fair-sized house – at least before Mr Hyams and Co. decided that

the prices of property needed hiking to more realistic levels if Centre Point was to pay off a million per cent! And as with democracy, so with genuine sexuality.

> Presley's breakthrough was that he was the first male white singer to propose that fucking was a desirable activity in itself and that, given sufficient sex appeal, it was possible for a man to lay girls without any of the traditional gestures or promises.
>
> GEORGE MELLY, *Revolt into Style*[15]

Now the trouble with this is that without the 'traditional gestures' the activity is reduced to the most mechanistic rutting – which by and large seems to be the ultimate effect (Curt Sachs points out in his analysis of dance that the creative development of erotic dance is precisely in the area of 'traditional gestures'). But what is more is that even the rutting is not real. Elvis was carefully presented as not in fact laying the chicks, and when the Teds did the roof fell in. In this crucial aspect of the activity, the utter perversion of function is perhaps most damaging.

> Though the sex act is, to be sure, never really completed on the dance place, the various phases of the act are depicted here and there very fantastically. It would be difficult to imagine the motions of onanism and cohabitation, the suggestion of enormous sexual organs, and the exposure of their own, the frenzied shrieking of obscene words and the chants of unprintable verse which the dancers of both sexes alone or in couples bring to their dances ... White men have often become excited over the 'shamelessness' of such dances. But ... for the primitives it is not a matter of sensation and pleasure, *but of life and unity with nature.*
>
> CURT SACHS, op. cit., p. 93

These primitive dancers and musicians are indeed shameless, for no shame can attach to an activity on which the very survival of the group depends. But wantonly to exploit these same areas of erotic fantasy for utterly subjective and self-indulgent ends is damnable, dangerous and degenerate. Consider Nik Cohn's description of the aftermath of a performance by the Rolling Stones in the Odeon, Liverpool, 1965.

> After the show, I hung around in the dressing room. The Stones were being ritually vicious to everyone ... and I got bored. So I went down into the auditorium and it was empty, quite deserted, but there was this weird smell. Piss: the small girls had screamed too hard and wet themselves. Not just one or two of them but many, so that the floor was sodden and the stench overwhelming ... the empty cinema (chocolate boxes, cigarette packs, ice-lolly sticks) and this

[15] Penguin, 1972, p. 36.

sad sour smell. I've kept on saying how great the Stones were but all I've shown is evil and the question finally needs to be asked: what's so good about bad?

NIK COHN, op. cit., p. 155

There can be no question that the eighteen years since 'Rock Around the Clock' have seen a remarkable change in our society so far as the external trappings of permissiveness go; although it cannot be sufficiently stressed that this has not meant real sexual liberation as between fulfilled and adult human beings, in the full meaning of the word adult, but the sexual licence of the pop festivals or the suburban wife-swapping key parties as between pitiful human ciphers, trapped in the over-heated unreality of an unresolved adolescence. The sanction now given to four-letter words and full frontals and the rest may also have allowed the open publication of Burns's *Merry Muses of Caledonia* and Gershon Legman's *Rationale of the Dirty Joke* in paperback, but the extent to which any such positive aspects of this change are due to pop is questionable. What is unquestionable is the disastrous contradictions and perversions which we now fear.

It is this prurient permissiveness (now slithering into pornography) which makes it so difficult for anyone to take a stand against the abomination of the media, without seeming to espouse the Festival of Light and Lord Longford *et al*. And it is precisely the hideous legacy of sexual censorship which the pop song panders exploit so viciously.

> The evil residue of censorship is exactly this: that the new and partial literary freedom has immediately been seized upon and accepted strictly as the freedom to print and gloat over the most nauseating details of the sadistic and other sex-linked abnormalities.
>
> *The Horn Book*, p. 306

and whilst Legman, writing in the early 1960s, asserts that in no sense has a comparable freedom been allowed the mass media, a proposition not so self-evident today! he yet goes on:

> the same substitution of an allowed sadism for a prohibited sexuality in the folk literature and electrically promulgated 'entertainment arts' of mass circulation can only result in the most dangerous and most sinister abnormalization of the whole psychic structure of future generations.
>
> op. cit., p. 306

The Family is the most horrific book yet written on the death of rock idealism on the seamier side of California – not just because it details the life of would-be rock star turned murderer and fanatic, Charles

Manson, but because it puts his killings into a gruesome perspective ... Manson is seen as a product of this environment.
That is what is most frightening of all.

ROBIN DENSELOW, *Guardian*, 18 May 1972[16]

Gershon Legman is a learned and controversial American scholar who has specialized in erotic folklore. His book is a passionate assertion of the genuinely erotic as central to human survival, but he is also concerned to explain the desperate aberrations of a society, alienated from itself, trampling on what it holds most sacred. And sacred not in the theological or liturgical sense, although at root the genuine religious experience partakes of the same essence, but a humanist sense of the sacred; of the qualities of human love and fellowship and creativity, and the organic relationship between these qualities and the material world in which we live. The sacrosanct quality of the truly erotic, the truly lyrical, the truly epic is man, and in the tradition of struggle and sacrifice and achievement and refinement of perception which is man's history (as opposed to the monstrous perversion of all this, officially presented as History). This is what we can find in folklore, in the articulated experience of working people today, in the concentration of children at play, in the beauty of adolescents themselves even as they are drawn to the pop song panders who would sap their beauty and debauch their vigour, pressing into their hands the tools of self-destruction. Gershon Legman again, at the end of his chapter on Bawdy Song:

> In the days when priests ordained ritual public coitus at dawn, at the winter solstice, under the mistletoe-laden boughs of sacred trees, to bring back the dying sun from fearfully remembered glacial night; in those days there was no need of bawdy song, yet that was perhaps its heyday. The remnant that we have of it is strange and misshapen, more often monstrous and repellent – as the world it mirrors becomes monstrous and repellent – than simple and unashamed as it once was, in the days of the Song of Songs. Even so, there is more honesty and nobility – and immeasurably more life – in even the worst bawdy songs than in the ephemeral slubberdegullion of so-called popular songs. That the sexual impulse is, and involves, a sacrament as profound as that of any religious formula, is hardly to be sensed in the tepid love-droolings and paeans to frustration of modern popular song; yet it remains, immanent and unmistakeable, in the power and surge of bawdy songs in all languages, for all its uncouth humour and savage trappings. It is of that power, and not of that uncouthness, that people, are afraid.

The Horn Book, p. 426

It may seem a bit of a contradiction that I should go to an expert

[16] On *The Family* by Ed Sanders, Hart-Davis.

in erotic folklore for a statement about what is sacred, but within this seeming contradiction is the essence of our critical dilemma. The frank sexuality of folk-song, as recorded at its source – the field singer – is utterly devoid of the prurient suggestiveness which makes the 'permissive' pop song so offensive.

> More than once, on being told an indelicate song, I had great difficulty in persuading the rustic informant that I could not show the piece, and therefore should not write it. 'But why not?' I have been asked 'there was nothing wrong with that ...' Neither was there, really... the unsophisticated villagers feel hurt at the decision and often discover considerable embarrassment.
>
>   ALFRED WILLIAMS, *Folk Songs of the Upper Thames*

> An old man came a-courting me, hey ding dooram down
> An old man came a-courting me, hey dooram down
> An old man came a-courting me
> Fain would he marry me
> Maids when you're young never wed an old man
> For he's got no falooral faliddle-i-ooral
> He's got no falooral faliddle-i-day,
> He's got no faloorum, he's lost his ding doorum
> So maids when you're young never wed an old man.
>
>   SAM LARNER, 1959, of Winterton, Norfolk

> My ding-a-ling, my ding-a-ling
> I want you to play with my ding-a-ling....
> This little song it ain't so bad
> The cutest little song you've ever had
> Those of you who will not sing
> You must be playing with your own ding-a-ling.
>
>   CHUCK BERRY, 1972

Now why should I find a rich and genuine hilarity in a folk club singing the chorus of the first song, and a sick and tawdry degeneracy in teenage fans singing the chorus of the second (as was shown every hour on the hour on the TV monitors at the 'BBC 50' exhibition in London)? The answer, I submit, is because in the one, my response to the erotic implications is directed to a manifest social purpose – confrontation with the social injustice of wealthy old men marrying nubile young girls, and imaginative release in the subsequent ridiculing of the impotent husband. In the second, my response is essentially narcissistic, masturbatory almost in the physical satisfaction of erotic caress, by another or by my own hand, being suggestively induced – and I am being titillated so that Mr Chuck Berry can get another number in the Top Twenty. And the almost derisory manner of the delivery of the song is the final insult to my manhood or womanhood, this mocking manipulation of youthful sexuality, so adroitly done that the young people are themselves made the agent of their own emotional debauching, is the ultimate damnation of such pop. And it has been present since the days of Juke Box Jury, and before. I can remember seeing a Lonnie Donegan Road Show at the Birmingham Hippodrome in which the resident comedian's stock-in-trade was precisely this manipulation of an audience to self abuse. As for instance one 'joke' as I remember, was of a group of teenagers witnessed after a showing of *Rock Around the Clock*, having a ball around the lamp-post outside the cinema; the pay-off line being that they were paraplegics.

Now it is conceivable that I am misreading the signals of 'Ding-a-ling', and taking insufficient notice of the traditional American black's 'black' humour at his own expense, the derisive sexual flyting which is a feature of black society bitterly resenting its own deprivations. Maybe – but deliberately used *outside* such a society, and in a commercial, exploitative, mass media context which makes a mockery of those deprivations, it still becomes an abomination I believe (and in any case, compare this Chuck Berry with the 'blue' blues and he falls flat on his face). But then the whole of the pop-song industry is based on the exploitation of folk-lore, of grass roots musical and poetic forms, and in the process of that exploitation, destroying their original social function and draining them of any meaning other than the induced self-gratification of an audience (and money pouring into the till!). This is why I get so angry with Professor Mellor's white-washing of this sepulchre with his talk of emerging ritual and the identification of 'Hair' with Dionysiac initiation. Because while such apologists hold the field, the way back becomes that much more difficult for us to find.

But there *is* a way back, an alternative to this Witches Sabbath of meaningless orgiastic utterance, as deliberately sanctioned and utilized by the power élite to safeguard their position, diverting and controlling popular modes and aspirations which would other-wise pose a threat to them; devices which, as I have tried to show, can be traced back to primitive society and the emergence of shaman cults and the like, and which I believe can only be under-stood in an anthropological context. This is our predicament. But the alternative was always actually present in pop itself from the days of skiffle onwards, the continual re-assertion in the very heart of corruption, of the astonishingly tough quality of the human spirit. For it is only the genuine energy of youth which powers the tin pan alley perversions, and as the tide of events forces a more and more direct confrontation with reality, the unreality of pop will, I believe, stand mercilessly exposed – like the pathetic attempt by a Bogside Rock group to confront the social agony of the Derry Catholic community in a Rock number 'Bloody Sunday'. The instincts and concern of that group are so true, their commercially corrupted form of manifestation so grotesquely inadequate – and utterly, *utterly* unrelated.

But as I said earlier, the folk revival withstood and, praise be, in essence still withstands, the blandishments of commercialism. In A. L. Lloyd and Ewan McColl it had two scholar/artists who had laid the foundations of the revival aided by the arrival in Britain of Alan Lomax, well before the skiffle movement took off. Above all it had the Public House as the immediately available venue, which led to the emergence of the Folk Club, able to exist independently and free from commercial necessity. This gave the British revival a local small-scale coherence which its American precursor had never had (there the emphasis had been on Carnegie Hall concerts and University campuses, and the overblown Folk Festivals on the Newport Model). In the Folk Club it was possible for revival singers to explore the folk tradition for an increasingly aware and critical audience. And while this was a minority, it was still a sizeable one, because it is an extraordinary fact that today, when the folk revival has been penetrated by pop and there is great confusion reigning, still in every town and city – and in many villages – folk clubs proliferate, plenty of whom still stand out against tin pan alley. But there was another aspect of the British folk revival which made it a tough nut to crack.

> The most striking thing about the whole British scene, and one which filled this singer with envy, was the large numbers of really first class songs being made up – which seemed to grow so naturally out of their older traditions.
>
> PETE SEEGER, 1959

Any assertion of the contemporary relevance of traditional song to repertoire, singing style, and instrumentation, constitutes a threat to commercial popular music. Even more does it pose a challenge to the whole apparatus of ad-mass culture, if within the traditional folk forms can be found modes of creation immediately relevant to the mass media needs of today. It was this which Ewan MacColl's Radio Ballads began to demonstrate; from *The Ballad of John Axon* in 1958, to *Romeo and Juliet* in 1966, he showed how documentary radio and folk music have a consonance which is immediately recognizable.

SINGER/STUDIO: Through the months and through the years
While you're bringin' up the bairns
You man's awa' tae here and there
Following the shoals o' herring.

And when he'd back there's nets to mend
You've mebbe got a score or twa,
And when they're done, he'll rise and say,
'Wife it's time I was awa'....'

FISHERMAN'S WIFE, Its been a wor' life, mending nets. A' wor'life;
CAIRNBULG: gutting herring and mending nets.

FISHERMAN'S WIFE, If I was to live my life again, I would never marry
PETERHEAD: a fisherman. I would not. It's a good job ye dinna
ken what's in front of you!

FISHERMAN'S WIFE, We used to sing a song –
CAIRNBULG: Fa would be a fisherman's wife,
To gang to the creel, the scrubber and the knife,
A foul fireside and a raivelled bed,
And awa' tae the mussels in the mornin'.

SINGER/STUDIO: Work and wait and dree your weird,
Pin your faith in herrin' sales,
And oftimes lie awake at nicht
In fear and dread o' winter gales.
Singing the Fishing[17]

For the greatest – and most hopeful – contradiction in the whole confused state of popular culture 1973, is, I believe, that the very electronic tools which made possible the perversion which is pop, can also make possible the creation of works springing from the people at their still vigorous linguistic and ethnic roots and superbly fitted to meet the challenge of the times. Trad Jazz, Skiffle, the Folk Revival, the Radio Ballads, even elements in progressive pop, all point this way. But for their emergence, there has to be a major change of heart in the authorities who control the mass media. How to bring this about is, of course, the real 64 thousand dollar question....

[17] Argo LP DA 142.

10 Roads, Office Blocks, and the New Misery

FRED INGLIS

I

I went, recently, to a public inquiry about a proposed piece of what, in the nauseatingly vacant language we have all learned to speak in public, was called a striking modern development. The occasion was all you might have expected; it filled you with a sense of dull, beaten fury. If it was, for the people on the right side of things, to all appearances a victory, that was only because, like the plague, the enemy had retired in order to reappear elsewhere.

The proposal was to build a large extension onto the rather sprawling and debauched elegance of an early nineteenth-century spa hotel set on the rim of the gorge at Clifton, Bristol, high above the river Avon. Above the hotel, the ground rises gently to Brunel's amazing suspension bridge; fronting it is the extraordinarily lengthy eighteenth-century terrace, Caledonia Place, with its massive, solid pediments and lintels, and broad carriageway in front. It was widely believed in the area that the proposed extensions were for new hotel rooms. But this was to underestimate the developers. In the first place, the hotel owners had decided to build a discotheque on the end of the building. When they submitted plans for the extension, they agreed that the changes were likely to mean a drastic increase in the number of cars using a narrow, steep road, itself serving the hotel as well as the terrace houses which wind up and down and along the densely built-up escarpment. In these circumstances, the only place to build any accommodation for cars was upwards, and plans were accordingly submitted to the local planners for a multi-storey car park high on the edge of Clifton gorge, lining the route of one of the most stylishly vertiginous Georgian terrace developments in the country.

The plans went through on condition that recognition was made of the area's official zoning, which was residential. This was not difficult; simply a matter of replacing the last of the car-park storeys with a series of bijou penthouse flats, leased by the hotel and giving onto a sensational view of the gorge, the Bristol water-front and the Mendips in the distance. And at this stage, the adaptation was discovered to be wholly appropriate, since the Government was offering £1,000 subsidies for every new hotel room built in an effort to liquefy the congealing flow of capital investment in building developments. The only difficulty was that to qualify for this generous subsidy to the most expensive rentals and the most exclusive flats in Bristol, the plans and submissions all had to be in before the end of 1971. It was by this stage late summer. It was also at this stage that local conservation groups began to press much harder for attention to what was going on.

This isn't the place to report in detail the intrigues and the trivial evasions practised both by officials and councillors in an effort to forestall this pressure. Enough that a public inquiry was forced. At the inquiry the resisters' barrister was able richly to display both technical address and a stylish, stylized forensic mode of interrogation which left the developers reeling.

In the most silky and insinuating tone, then: 'Let us suppose that we are watching a modern primary school project, Mr Dunnett, and the teacher, considering the environment as many good teachers now do, asks her class of bright, quick ten-year-olds, "Children, where do you think is the *most unlikely* place to build a multi-storey car park? Which would be the really *silliest* place to put a building full of cars? Silly because it blocks up the road, spoils the view and so on?" And then in the back row, Mr Dunnett, little Hymie puts up a hand and says, "Next to the Royal Spa, Miss."'

Prolonged laughter in the big court room. Well, the pleasure to be taken from the laughter is real and satisfying; the occasion is a public drama, right enough, and the villains have been jeered at. But it is not enough to tell the developers that a ten-year-old would see and judge for what it is the insensitive irrelevance of such an idea. The developers are not children, they want the subsidy and the rents, and they want them badly. They have been granted detailed planning permission by the council, and now these absurd groups of people, worried about the completely minor defacing of the local architecture, have forced them to justify their plans in public according to standards they do not recognize. Who wouldn't be angry and frustrated in their shoes? There is a lot of money to make if they move fast enough.

'Now, sir, you are the chief architect of these plans, are you not?'

'I am.'

'You know, of course, the bye-law pertaining to the diameters of the turning circle for cars both inside and outside a multi-storey car park, I'm sure; but on the plans I have before me your provision is nothing like these?'

'Well, I...'

'And you know, further, that the road camber is exceptionally steep at this point. What sort of access gradient have you designed? I cannot find any measurement on your plans.'

'No, well, I'm afraid we haven't yet gone into that sort of detail.'

'But these are supposed to be final plans, Sir; do you know how steeply the existing cars would have to climb in order to see whether anything was coming?'

Pause.

'You *have* seen the site, haven't you, Sir?'

More laughter. Embarrassment. Apparently the architect has *not* seen the site....

And so on. The barrister, in a slightly shaming but deservedly triumphant way, cuts his enemies to pieces. Behind the exchange, the story went, lay months of scandalous horse-trading between factions swapping development favours paid for by political support in drawing up the battle-lines of local parties in new local government areas. The speculators found that in return for planning permission, those of their number who were councillors prominent in the very popular effort to keep their areas out of the new county borough of Avon would be expected to reduce those efforts in the interests of consolidating the strength of their party *within* the new county. Tit for tat. In this case, the government inspector rejected the plans and the developers promptly sued for compensation of the cost of plant already hired, after permission was first given. This compensation is far too large for the authority to pay; a compromise solution now in the air is that the development will be resubmitted with a new hotel slightly lower down the gorge.

II

Who would be surprised at this long, messy, occasionally evil-smelling history? Isn't this simply the greed and rapaciousness of many men? To be surprised is to declare oneself an innocent. But to say this is to make certain assumptions not, as in the premisses of classical liberalism, about individual morality, but about the morality which is presently made possible by the dominant institutions of society.

The two most powerful institutions of our present culture are the institutions of production and capital. They are of course strongly and inextricably linked and bonded. And it is a typifying feature of institutions that one lives within them as part of the framework of one's life. To collide with an institution, to step outside its premisses, is to declare oneself in part an exile or an outlaw. Hence it is the case for most people that they take for granted the unspeakable power of capital; they see it as having the greater right over natural beauty and certainly as representing in itself those rights of property which override other and reasonable considerations of freedom, or even of convenience. Thus, in the case of the Bristol hotel, many people ignored the petitions and the hearings because 'it was none of their business'. If a hotel was built on the gorge, too bad. The executive was elsewhere.

Now clearly not everyone felt like this about the hotel, otherwise the bulldozers would have rolled in by now. And this fact is one minor signal among many, I think, that evidence a collision between major institutions of the culture. The combined forces of production and capital are clashing, intermittently and quietly, with those of a more loose-limbed network of symbols and institutions: the family, for one; certain key individual liberties (of home, of movement); some educationally traditional ideas about townscape and its scale, about 'man-sized' areas of living; a longer-lived tradition of resistance to the onslaught of industrialism. The conflict between the vast, supple, and destructive power of capital and its mild-mannered antagonist, the suburban garden, is still a small one. It is far too optimistic to see it as part of the unmistakably more historic and global struggle of exploited peoples the world over to throw off that same power. Nonetheless, certain surprisingly uniform groups of people in this country are coinciding in their resistance to capital when it threatens central values. They have gone beyond the misery of vague uneasiness which characterizes men who sense that they are threatened, but cannot identify their enemy. These groups have begun to identify their issue. To that extent, they have become exiles in their own culture. What, in their perception of things, is the nature of the enemy and his warfare?

Once, the enemy of the Englishmen conscious of this issue was the speculative builder and his ribbon development. In that pioneering pamphlet of his, *England and the Octopus*, the visionary architect Clough Williams-Ellis diagnosed the threat to the landscape as the long uniform lines of gabled, owner-occupied semi-detacheds curling out from the big industrial cities. In an unforgettable bestiary *From Pillar to Post*, he was joined by Osbert Lancaster, and then by John Betjeman, Thomas Sharp, and others. But the tastelessness they so sharply indemnified was in fact much more than a matter of visual barbarism – serious enough in itself, but not lethal; it was the headlong destructiveness of concrete social processes. Their environmental and aesthetic argument critically lacked any grip on society. Even as recently as 1965, Lionel Brett, ex-president of the RIBA, maps out in a wonderfully witty and pointed manner in his *Landscape in Distress* the depredations of bungaloid growth, the choice examples of bye-law philistinism and builders' allsorts, without seeing that the ruin of Oxfordshire is not due to these local buccaneers, so much as it is and will increasingly be due to the massive momentum of a whole social mechanism. This mechanism is the structure of capital and production, the impetus of which in its hunger for returns on investment is the dominant force behind the destructiveness of the Western industrial nations over the whole world.

But to attribute the evils of a blitzed and poisoned landscape to the accumulation of capital is simply to redescribe the problem. It gives us slightly more purchase on the ideas, but not much in the way of diagnosis. Capital and production are not surrogates for the march of History or the will of God; they become apparent in the thoughts and actions of men; they are features of consciousness in those who need power; they fix the contours of consciousness. If a man wishes to understand their operation in the present context, then he can only do so by attending time and again to the particular examples and seeing whether the pattern they yield to his analysis can be generalized. What, then, are the manifold relations between capital and the landscape?

Put the question in a more everyday fashion. More bluntly. What do you most notice these days about the English landscape as you travel it?

The road-builders. Wherever you go by road or train you pass the great scars smashed for miles across the land: the huge piles of ripped out trees and hedges, thick with loam and dust, mysteriously charring, sometimes blazing up in big flames, for days; the colossal yellow bulldozers with a wheelspan big as two men; and then the roads themselves, smooth and polished, sliding away into the blue distance, bewitchingly empty, with perhaps a knot of three or four men in hard yellow helmets squatting at the bare verge and opening their bottles of sweet, cold tea. As the roads are, under construction, I like them; nothing specially horrible, a certain magnificence sometimes in the long curve of the six empty lanes; something both amazing and touching about their solitude, the sense one has that those three or four men built the whole road on their own, or sat about watching the thing unroll of itself. None of the awe and magnificence of Dickens's railway trampling across Stagg's Gardens:

> The first shock of a great earthquake had, just at that period, rent the whole neighbourhood to its centre. Traces of its course were visible on every side. Houses were knocked down; streets broken through and stopped; deep pits and trenches dug in the ground; enormous heaps of earth and clay thrown up; buildings that were undermined and shaking, propped by great beams of wood. Here, a chaos of carts, overthrown and jumbled together, lay topsy-turvy at the bottom of a steep unnatural hill; there, confused treasures of iron soaked and rusted in something that had accidentally become a pond. Everywhere were bridges that led nowhere; thoroughfares that were wholly impassable; Babel towers of chimneys, wanting half their height; temporary wooden houses and enclosures, in the most unlikely situations; carcases of ragged tenements, and fragments of unfinished walls and arches, and piles of scaffolding, and wilderness of bricks, and giant forms of cranes, and tripods straddling above nothing. There were a hundred thousand shapes and substances of incompleteness, wildly mingled out of their places, upside down, burrowing in the earth, aspiring in the air, mouldering in the water, and unintelligible as any dream. Hot springs and fiery eruptions, the usual attendants upon earthquakes, lent their contributions of confusion to the scene. Boiling water hissed and heaved within dilapidated walls; whence, also, the glare and roar of flames came issuing forth; and mounds of ashes blocked up rights of way, and wholly changed the law and custom of the neighbourhood.
>
> In short, the yet unfinished and unopened Railroad was in progress; and, from the very core of all this dire disorder, trailed smoothly away, upon its mighty course of civilisation and improvement.

The motorway builders aren't any the worse for not being like this. The only time their scenery takes on anything of this furious busyness is when the road begins to butt on its blunt, stubby stilts into the hearts of big cities. The dense thicket of struts and scaffolding below the platforms of the road is alive with the bright hats of the men; there are the tall rigs which hold in the pile-driver, the dull, slamming weight which shakes the pavements below the road every few seconds; there is a little village of shanties, caravans and hutments, with bits of washing hanging over the craters and duckboards and deep mud ruts of the site, where the nomadic army of roadbuilders has made itself a spontaneous new community.

Well, there too – the bystander says – is the march of progress incarnate. It's got to come, there's no stopping it, you must have progress. And so forth. But walk a little further along the perimeter of the construction site, and the costs of progress begin to look more sombre. There are the half-wrecked houses, the blind windows and nailed-up doors, the heaps of old mattresses, gas cookers, crumpled prams and fridges, and the vacant lots, the waste land behind the dull façades. A little further on, and the houses stand which were left as the dozers and the wreckers' ball-and-chain swept their long swathe through the district. No shops open, though. If you look harder, no doctor's surgery, no dentist, no police station. Nowhere for children to play except across the fascinating, dangerous rubbish of the demolition site, and along the road stodged with the unmoving cars, the giant sneezing lorries whose massive immobility has insisted on the necessity for the motorway. And if you pick your way across the bombed-out ruins to the dark, close streets beyond, you find all the symptoms of the dismal contagion which spreads out from any such upheaval. For it is a truth universally acknowledged that an urban motorway in possession of a good fortune must be in want of a site on which one finds the highest correlation between suitable geological conditions and unskilled working-class residential areas. The blight stains whole communities for life. It is not only a matter of waiting months and years in the twilight to be rehoused; it is for many people in the muddy zone between the road and freedom from the road, a sentence to a twilit life for life.

Walk back along the demolition site to the stretch of road which is in use. A tremendous ramp propped on its blunt curves above the roofs of the dull little run of ribbon development, inclines gradually downwards and enters a low culvert at the foot of a long sequence of seventeen-storey point blocks. At this point, a six-lane motorway in full play unrolls a thick carpet of noise and lead-poisonous fumes well beyond the point blocks whose vision of city life is now the roofs of the traffic thirty-five yards across the dreary brize-block patios which serve their hundreds of council tenants for playground and garden. If you walk across from the ground-floor flats to see the traffic, the road-planners' rationalization and flow-chart efficiencies are visible for what they are: a brutal and irrational effort to solve a trivial difficulty by destroying everything in the way. There was never a more telling occasion to accuse men of intellectual tunnel vision; the urban motorway is the symbol of their condition. It is as if, like American policy in Vietnam, you annihilate all natural and human life in an area, strip the trees and drive out the homesteaders in order to call the country pacified. It is of the same order of insanity as to tear out all the bluebells and primroses in a wood so as not to tread on them. Motorways transform time into a narcotic.

I am describing a large portion of townscape in Bristol, a couple of miles from where I am writing. Consider the many places where the same wintry report could be presented.

London, where the proposed motorway box linking the four major motorways is already partly built. The miles of elevated carriageway on the west-bound M4 exit, the bitter resistance from the Notting Hill Community association make clear the developing nature of the struggle in the capital, and the weaponry and warfare of the two sides.

York, where a proposed circuit road costing £10 million, dilating to eight lanes in two major architectural approaches to the city (Bootham Bar, Bishopthorpe Road) destroys 340[1] houses of (strictly) priceless and irreplaceable significance in the first two phases of the plan alone. The major report commissioned by the Labour Government in 1965, published in 1970[2], recommended that, as well as discouraging rather than encouraging drastic increases in traffic quantities, a simple and cheap reversal of the depopulation of the city be attempted. The study sets out how some of the close, intimate streets of the medieval city centre could be closed to traffic and returned to the use of pedestrians; it goes on to suggest how the centre of a city, which after 6 p.m. is silent and abandoned, could be recaptured for city living by the cheap reconversion of the derelict offices and packed, brown storerooms which stand above the elegantly renovated trinket and antique shops, the surviving greengrocers, the chainstore butchers, chemists, and sweetshops. The scheme represented a courageous effort to recreate, to plan *and* cost a living city. It was an effort to return normal domestic living to the rich, commercial texture of the city centre in which it began. York is an unusually suitable place to attempt such an experiment: it is close-knit and strikingly beautiful; it is obviously insane to permit traffic to go where it goes at the moment; there is an itinerant population of students which needs the sort of housing which could have been easily provided, housing which itself is built in materials and styles both beautiful and fashionable. All these reasonable considerations were ignored by

[1] All details from *York 2000*, a series of broadsheets published from 142 Micklegate, York.
[2] As *York: A study in Conservation*, Viscount Esher, HMSO.

the dominant preoccupation of planners and councillors with the making of roads. And the consequence is a brutal throughway which would destroy the very possibility of walking round the medieval walls and shake hundreds of inner-city (largely poor and elderly) homesteaders out of their beds as the juggernauts grind past.

Newcastle upon Tyne, where the city fathers have disembowelled one of the finest Victorian centres[3] in England and where the fabulous devastation caused by putting the A1 on stilts through the poor areas of Gateshead and downtown Newcastle has, as in Bristol, London, York, Southampton, Leeds, Derby, Leicester, Birmingham (a choice early example), Northampton, and uncountable other examples, shattered whole neighbourhoods and left their remnants living in solitary confinement. Without shops, schools, protection, or the commonplaces of social care. Without a society. The classical terms – expropriation and alienation – are there to read in the ruin, in the quite conscious wretchedness of the faces of local people. They are condemned to an intolerable unhappiness by the decision of men they do not know and who do not want to understand what is happening.

And so on. Through *Bedford* where, the immigrant neighbourhoods south of the river having been sacked, the proposal now is to run the usual four-to-six-lane motorway along the pleasant strip of parkland which lines the Ouse and its towpath; through *Glasgow*, where the road is intended to run across the roof of the Court House, through Glasgow Green, making J. J. Burnet's Barony Church[4] unusable and demolishing the remaining sections of Monreith Row[4] and Adelphi Street (working-class houses now, of course); through *Warwick*, where *their* proposals tear out the St Nicholas and Priory Parks, the main public open spaces of the town, split the town in half along its most distinguished historical axis (Guy St and Cherry St) and demolish a hundred minor city buildings; *Worcester*'s centre is already destroyed, worse than *Newcastle*'s; so are *Preston*'s, *Chester*'s, and *Bradford*'s. On and on; an endless, identical roll call.

III

Very well then, whose interests *are* being served by these mammoth schemes? Production and capital. But what does it mean to say that? In the case of the rate of roadbuilding it means the irresis-

[3] See particularly the demolition of the masterly Eldon Square.
[4] See A. H. Gomme, *The Architecture of Glasgow*, Lund Humphries 1968.

tible combination of the car industry, the heavy transport lobby, the heavy engineering and construction industries, all backed up and linked across that wide front by enormous government support, institutional and economic. The government in this case sees much of its plans as tied to this complex of industries for the maintenance of economic growth and stability. The car industry is one of the main regulators of the exceedingly delicate and uncontrollable balance of the economy.

This frame of mind in governments is the best kind of help the vampires of the development trade could ask for. And it is a particular frame of mind which is the real subject of this essay. For it is consciousness which creates and recreates culture, and the manifold lineaments of consciousness are not to be accounted for in any simple description either of the systems of production (the Left) nor the free-ish play of the modern mixed economy (the Right). Least of all will these simplified terms do to explain the astonishing variety of culture which takes its form in great cities.

Nonetheless, governments in the West can be identified as preoccupied by short-term ends. They are increasingly aware that their alleged control of long-term social reconstruction is a fraud; all they can do, in a series of drunken lurches, is hold a reeling, pitching sort of balance between short-term expansion and short-term recession. Between boom and slump. Between stop and go. And then as the thing pitches unsteadily along, there is the giant effort to pull its bows around as against a colossal weight of water and to set a new course.

The nautical metaphors are irresistible. In the circumstances, no government risks its neck far enough ahead so as to change this plunging movement into something utterly different. It counts on the profits seeing it through, on their providing enough wealth for the government to drain away a sufficient quantity in social benefits and wages. It then creates for itself a frame of mind in which this programme comes to seem the only realistic one, and people speaking of different plans can be dismissed as impractical and unrealistic. It isn't hard to see how this picture of things perpetuates itself. Transport, steel, and heavy construction compose a structure which admits a crude but manipulable system of control. A government can to a very marked degree adjust consumer spending by changing purchase or value-added taxes; its desperate release of pressure on sterling by devaluation (in 1967 and 1972) pays off immediately in car sales and therefore in export figures. At the same time, by authorizing national road-building, they can aim for a measure of long-term stability, and encourage the movement of capital and investment into regions abandoned by the decisions of private or multinational enterprise. In these circumstances they are hardly likely to be sympathetic to claims made that car manufacture should be drastically curtailed and the road-building programme halted. For the circumstances are not only as I have described them – that construction, steel, transport are key industries – they are figures in a frame of governmental mind which works to conserve the existing economic order and to suppress not only radical alternatives, but also the criticisms of the existing order which subvert or challenge its apparent rationality. Thus we find a situation in which ignorance is systematized and the conclusive demonstration of appalling waste and profligacy can be disregarded. The point is easily made if one looks at the development of the heavy lorry industry. There is no doubt that the sensational increase both in the size of individual lorries and in the number of the lorries themselves[5] has caused severe social damage. A main response to this has been to build bigger roads, both in an effort to reduce the damage and to increase the efficiency of the lorries themselves. But this measure has been met by the production of bigger lorries (in 1972, 32 ton axle weight) and the proposal of even bigger ones ($41\frac{1}{2}$ ton, if we agree to EEC conditions). Going along as these increases have done with the quite fabulous increase in car ownership, the next response on the part of local and national government has been to keep the dominant industries where they are, and to build more roads for the traffic to occupy. This practice is then justified both by economic and practical arguments. It is held that traffic jams waste money; that road-building helps make money (increases liquidity, investment, regional development etc); that in any case traffic must be kept moving and people must get to their destinations. But these beliefs are held and these arguments offered in such a way as to make refutation almost impossible. We have a situation in which the fanatics of profitability and their helots fight to conserve a set of arrangements which can be shown convincingly to be squandering huge sums of money. And when their spokesmen are challenged not in the name of decency and social justice, but in the name of their own totems, cost effectiveness and profit, to do their sums better, they react not by rational argument but, in the classic modalities of the bureaucracy, by threats, black magic, and by suppression. Max Weber diagnosed the nature of the bureaucracy first and best, much more pointedly than Kafka:

Wherever increasing stress is placed upon 'official secrecy', we take

[5] See *Heavy Lorries*, Civic Trust Report, October 1970.

it as a symptom of either an intention of the rulers to tighten the reins of their rule or of a feeling on their part that their rule is being threatened.

Consider the lorries again. Their opponents argue that trains could take much more heavy freight; the transport lobby says the trains are losing money. Yet road construction and maintenance exceeds income from vehicle duties by £400 million.[6] The costs of environmental damage and congestion are put at £2 million *per day* (i.e. £700,000,000 per year),[7] but the transport lobby makes busy play with the alleged cheapness of its dreadful mastodons, hammering along roads subsidized by public money at the rate of £7.90 for every 50 pence of private money.[8] Time and again spokesmen for human reason and decency show that the official practice is lunatic and unprofitable; time and again their arguments are dropped into the bucket. The insolence, casualness, neglect, and overbearing loutishness on the part of local and national government officials is now a byword; it serves to confirm that already powerful mythology of impotence and apathy which invades every corner of English public life. The universality of pattern in the reaction of the bureaucracies to outside challengers makes it clear that no banal explanations about 'the sort of people who become officials'[9] will do. The pattern is attributable to the structure; and all horror stories can only take on their significance if we understand them as the product of the whole structure, and of the way in which an inhuman structure makes impossible to its natives the natural feelings of gentleness and affection which they would be well able to show as members of the other institutions which shape their life and its meanings. Our public bureaucracies are by custom and legislation impotent. First, as a matter of the intellectual histories inherited from poor laws and Victorian charity systems; second as a consequence of their legislated responsibilities, the written definitions of their callousness and careless nonchalance; third and finally, in the nature of their systems, their ignorance and incoherence, their distance from local life, their essential pointlessness. All these qualities, inherent in the structures of public administration, make it impossible for the vast planning institutions to express the tenderness, intelligence, resilience and dauntlessness the absence of which makes public life so waste and windswept, and leaves it vacant for the occupation of the hordes of the Philistines and the Armies of the Night. The

[6] *Heavy Lorries*, supplementary circular, Civic Trust, 10 October 1972.
[7] *Railway Review*, NUR, 29 September 1972.
[8] *Trade and Industry*, 25 August 1972.
[9] See John Gower Davies' valuable study *The Evangelistic Bureaucrat*, Tavistock 1972.

desperadoes and tricksters express in *their* structures of intent only too well the greed, rapacity, and slaughterous indifference to human life which remain the distinctive marks of untrammelled capitalism, ever since they were first named for what they are by Marx, Dickens, Bakunin, Dostoievsky, Conrad and Rosa Luxembourg.

These deadly and momentous qualities are far harder to fight than the undoubted philistinism so wittily inventoried by the pamphlets from Clough Williams-Ellis on.[10] The deep blankness which is the real thing strange about our bureaucracies gives the pirates all the rope they need. The highly protected market of property development and speculation is the perfect expression of 'mixed economy' capitalism. The dreadful office-blocks are the complement of the packed and hurtling motorways which twist about their giant plinths and their dead rectangles of dirty ornamental water which serve to fill up the spaces between the traffic.

In either case, the officials – planners and administrators alike – can be counted on to perpetuate the official consciousness.

I recently telephoned the chief planning officer of Bristol corporation to make inquiries about the negotiations between the department of the environment and the authority. Angry beyond discrimination at the challenges made to his work by local resistance groups, he shouted more or less hysterically that 'bungling amateurs' had no business interfering with 'years of work by experts', and had in any case no right of access to 'private, I say *private* discussions' – discussions which decided the fate of several thousand people and their houses. In another encounter, a resistance group on Teesside so raised the temperature of what are laughingly called 'participation meetings' that the vice-chairman of planning encouraged the process of democratic participation by telling one of their more fluent committee members to 'sit down and shut up', and explained in an agony of neurotic self-defensiveness to the single applicant for an improvement grant that he couldn't have his money in case they knocked his house down, but that

> this information is based upon the present policy of the Council. It is given on the distinct understanding that the Council does not warrant the accuracy of any of the replies and on the basis that

[10] See, nonetheless his classics, *England and the Octopus, Britain and the Beast*, Denys Thompson's trail-blazing school pamphlet, *Your England* (Chatto 1952); Ian Nairn's brilliant special issues of the *Architectural Review, Outrage* (1955) and *Counter-Attack* (1962), *Landscape in Distress*, already cited, and Fred and Enid Inglis' *Blotscape* (Chatto 1967). Last and best in the line is Nan Fairbrother's *New Lives, New Landscapes*, Architectural Press 1970, Penguin 1972.

neither the Council nor any officer, servant or agent of the Council is legally responsible, either in contract or in tort, for any inaccuracies errors or omissions herein contained whether arising from inadvertance or negligence or from any other cause whatever.[11]

Time and again the pattern of individual atrocity stories recur: the distance between the dense texture of local life and the drawing board; the brutal insistence of city bosses on the absoluteness of their power;[12] the bullying resentment of planners when challenged by the community; the deliberate mystification, the silence, the evasiveness; perhaps worst of all, this remote exercise of repressive powers takes to itself an aesthetic rhetoric, a mingling of the higher technicality and the fulsomely progressive. Here is Julian Amery, until December 1972 Minister for housing and construction:

> The Government is determined to control inflation and create conditions in which business can operate and invest with confidence. And we have already introduced measures which should be helpful to the construction industry.
>
> The re-casting of investment incentives, the increased rate of building grants in Development Areas, and wider use of powers to make grants towards the cost of providing basic infrastructure services and clearing derelict land should all be useful.
>
> These, and our cuts in company taxation, should give new vigour to the industry. I will continue to seek for further ways of stimulating demand....
>
> There is also the grave question of urban renewal. For some parts of our inner urban areas the only answer is clearance and rebuilding.
>
> Urban renewal is a huge subject which has received far too little attention until now. It bristles with difficult problems of finance, planning and engineering and social balance and a great deal of work needs to be done before a coherent approach can be evolved. There are no short cuts here but the work is rewarding and worthwhile.[13]

Well, you can't be too hard on him; he has his mythologies to believe in. But what would it be like to hear a Minister who spoke precisely of human need and meaning in such a way as to break with the liturgical incantation of the false gods, 'inflation' 'demand' 'clearance' 'investment'. There is plenty of social wealth; it is

---

[11] Quoted from original: Teesside Dept of Planning Letter, ref. B6 9927/71 dated 22 May 1972.

[12] When 'final decisions' on the Bristol road were leaked to the local press, Labour leader and planning chairman Mr W. Jenkins swore that the informants would be sacked and made his group's vote on the scheme a leadership issue – 'vote against it, and I resign'. The vote was for, 51-17.

[13] *Municipal Review* 42, 496, April 1971, p. 116.

poured out as social benefits into the purses of the brigands.

Thus and thus do the bland lead the bland. In a special research programme, financed by Washington D.C. Bureau of Public Roads, a group of planner-sociologist mandarins intend that their study 'will reduce the number and intensity of costly and divisive highway controversies, will provide more attractive (*sic*) roads, will improve the urban environment and will help insure the continuance of the highway construction program'.[14]

After such victories, who needs defeat? The point being there as always to ensure compliance in a ruinously destructive enterprise in which the only clear profits go to a handful of people. It will not do to say that these wasteful and colossal constructions keep men employed: the whole impulse of the giant corporations so usefully exemplified by the construction industry has been to intensify subordination by reducing employment hugely. In the twelve months up to January 1972 the heavy engineering construction, concrete and heavy steel rolling industries sacked 5 per cent of their labour force.[15] The focus of, in the grisly euphemism, development, is the greater profit, and with the roads, the other grotesque forms of this are the office and shopping blocks which litter the gaunt and rainswept runways designated as precincts in every recently smashed-up town centre.

IV

These blocks are less hateful in their social effects than the roads, but even more horrible to look at. In a mad effort to catch the *Zeitgeist* and clasp it to him, the architectural critic Reyner Banham spoke of London's skyline 'as looking at last like a twentieth-century city'[16] and praised the freeways and the sheer size of Los Angeles as the true manifestation of the automobilized city.[17]

There you have it. Style for style's sake: the *Zeit* for sore eyes. The praise we were supposed to learn for modern architecture back in the fifties – for its 'elegance'[18] (Mies van der Rohe), its 'uncompromising clarity'[18] (Phillip Johnson), the 'ultimate'[18] in 'organic grandeur' (Frank Lloyd Wright), in 'splendour of concep-

[14] Quoted by Robert Goodman in *After the Planners*, British edition, Penguin 1972, p. 123.

[15] *Dept of Employment Gazette*, April 1972. See also A. Glyn and B. Sutcliffe, *British Capitalism, Workers and the Profits Squeeze*, Penguin 1972, p. 133ff.

[16] Reyner Banham, *The New Brutalism, Ethic or Aesthetic?* Architectural Press 1966.

[17] *Los Angeles, the Four Ecologies*, Allen Lane 1971.

tion'[18] (Le Corbusier) – this terminology has gone sour on us. Whatever the great achievements of these men, the lessons of the prairies and the plains around Chandigargh, of Manhattan and the Mediterranean, look dead and dreary when they are rinsed down to the office blocks and flats of contemporary England. Admiration for *shape* was always such an external business; it was so easy to be cheated by a little bronze cladding (the Seagram building, and hundreds afterwards) or the bogus imitations of *La Ville Radieuse* as at Roehampton, and all the lethal council block estates which followed Leslie Martin's broken-backed LCC experiment. Nothing was asked of human use and scale, and any tuppence-ha'penny architect could get by with talk of 'cellular construction' in his offices, and '*pilotis*' to dignify his ground-floor car-ports.

Anybody can document these generalizations from the first office blocks to hand. What they all so richly exemplify is the power of new technology to change a culture. Here we have the systems which produce concrete slabbing, girder grids capable of distributing a megatonnage stress unthinkable before 1960, and curtain facing for a fifty-storey façade. These systems make possible the overbearing dreariness of such monsters of the times as Stock Exchange House[19] in Edinburgh, Birmingham's Sparbrook Ringway, Bristol's city centre, the Wulfrun Centre, Wolverhampton, the Cambridge Lion Yard Scheme, Brighton Marina, the University of Aston, Manchester Piccadilly, the town centre, Plymouth, the C & A corner in Exeter, and the utter nullity, the oppressive vacancy of dozens and dozens of such schemes in small tidy towns like Stockton-on-Tees, Cockermouth, Godalming, Barnstaple, St Albans, St Neots, and stations north, south, east, and west. The philistinism and butchery of design in each place is complete. I shall take examples from London simply because it is on the whole an easy place to visit, and the evils are larger, and therefore more visible.

Centre Point at the crossing of Tottenham Court road and Oxford St is the most notorious of the buildings which provide London's so-much-to-be-welcomed brutalist skyline. The vulgar exterior is not to my point; vulgarity may be a virtue.[20] What is inhuman about the design is what everyone sees as such: the

[18] The casebook of these clichés is Peter Blake's *The Master Builders*, Gollancz 1960.
[19] Finished in 1967 by Kelly and Surman; now cracked and dangerous. See *Private Eye* 283, p. 6.
[20] Cf. the end of Margaret Drabble's new novel, *The Needle's Eye*, and its description of the Alexandra Palace.

simple boringness of the thing to look at and to work in; its overbearing size; all combined with the fact that you can't get into it,
can't walk round below it, and that you dislike its mucky little
pools of ornamental water.

Richard Seifert and Partners are probably the architects responsible for the most of the really nasty new buildings in London.[21]
Their projected Victoria Street block, which copies Mies van der
Rohe in its bronze-and-granite cladding and its high-toned colour-
supplementary polished bronze columns at its base, embodies most
of the vices I have named: pride, envy, hatred, avarice, gluttony...
It is the mausoleum of consumer fashions projected on a giant
scale: the over-expensive finish, the utter disdain of its predecessor
(Pilkington's Windsor House) and of the people round about and
inside it, the competitive, lumpy harlotry of the external detailing,
the brassy swank.

It would be impossible to chronicle the office blocks of Britain.
A brief report on the *cause infâme* of Piccadilly Circus will have
to serve as a close to this review and to complete a sketch of an
explanatory theory to account for the scale of the present exploitation. In the latest scheme for the Circus, 60 per cent of the new
floor-space goes to offices and hotels, and 3 per cent of the floor-space
to entertainment. The City of Westminster planning authorities,
like all the glad band of its peers over the country, proposes a happy
epic of destructiveness – including for example the flourishing,
profitable, and handsome Criterion Theatre in order, naturally, to
put a doubtless organically related office block there instead.
Small, 'man-sized' fragments of London's once living townscape
like Rupert Street and Denman Street are to be either flattened or
humiliated by the big bullies around them. Faced by the consequent certainty of more traffic, the authority plans simply to lift
pedestrians to a top deck at roof level where the delights of a day in
the Big City will be limited to imitating the boulevardier on a rainswept platform about as architecturally interesting as the flight
deck of an aircraft carrier. And below, threading its way through
the steeplechase of island, signs, crossings, lights and lanes, around
and about will go the dodgem route.

Of course it is a mad scheme; these decisions are the decisions of
an insane bureaucracy. But a utilitarian rationality is only too
clear in the actions of the developers who benefit from these
schemes. The suspicion is then inevitable that the mad schemes

[21] E.g. Grays Inn Road, High Holborn, Bishopsgate, Wandsworth, Knights-
bridge, Cromwell Road. See *Architectural Review*, August 1971, January
1972. *Private Eye* 280, *Sunday Times*, 27 July 1972, BBC Radio 4 *This
Island Now*, Nicholas Taylor prod. 1972 *passim*.

which serve the developers' cheque books so well may serve other pockets too. The only theory which is adequate to these conditions is a conspiracy theory: public planning in Britain smells very strongly of mass corruption. The old saw about the inherent waste-fulness and irrationality of capitalism is nonetheless true for being truistic. The 'free play' of restricted money-market forces has dis-covered the base anomaly that empty office blocks are more profi-table than any other land speculation in the world. The loans to be floated on the possession of such assets when they stand on the most expensive land in the richest city of Europe make for specu-lative gains which rise spectacularly faster than either the rents the buildings would yield, or the rates and taxes they absorb. They represent the safest gambling chips imaginable; short of a global slump, their investment returns cannot fall below the rate of profit in the manufacturing sectors, and because of present rates of inflation and heavy stock appreciation (to say nothing of develop-ment incentives) are likely to remain consistently above that rate, in spite of (some say,[22] *because* of) the present crisis in the world struggle for markets.

Whatever the complications of replacing empty office blocks with habitable houses for the homeless, restoring nice houses, build-ing beautiful schools, and however it may be true that you can't put the capital, the production and the labour down to build in Norwich if it wants to demolish in Reigate, it can only be revolting to contemplate a society in which the present devastation is wrought to provide profit for a few manipulators and to vindicate the encephalitic rigidity of local government bureaucracies.[23]

In the end, it is a question of manipulation, and of the relations of power to the meanings of a culture. In the Skeffington report,[24] there were the most minor suggestions made about 'participation'; they amounted to little more than telling people what had been decided. Nothing about letting people decide for themselves. I have no intention at this point in the argument of making sentimental claims for populism. The social roots of hateful beliefs and insensi-tivity towards alien and organic forms of life are too deep for that. Left to themselves, most people would probably vote for more roads ('but not just *there*') and another airport ('but not over *my* patch'). Yet the most deadly enemy of the times remains that combination of planner-bureaucracies and the drive for profits which seems at the moment licensed to destroy the world before the turn of the century.

[22] See Glyn and Sutcliffe, op. cit., p. 7off.
[23] For a choice case-study or two, see *Community Action*, 1- , issues from April-May 1972, 9 Pattison Road, London NW2.
[24] *Planning and People*, HMSO 1969.

I cannot sketch out much of its advances over the past quarter century. Roads and point block development will have to serve here as examples of what I mean. It would be valuable to go on to consider the irruptions of the transnational corporations in new forms such as the exploratory drilling of Rio Tinto Zinc in the Hermon valley near Dolgellau.[25] The Anglo-Welsh brigadier who owns the 10,000 acres has given RTZ lucrative permission to spend the £500,000 on exploration when no one knew much about it, least of all the Merioneth authority (though they did their best when they found out). RTZ has started work in the Lake District, in the Derbyshire Peak, in the Cleveland Hills. The promises of jobs for these thinly populated areas veer by anything up to 300 per cent (300 and 1,500 have been suggested for the Dollgellau area); there is no guarantee of a time-span. RTZ is, after all, in it for money. This colonialism accelerates daily. The attempted 'reconciliation' of economic growth and the environment by the Zuckerman report[26] turned out to be the patched-up, put-up devotional manual it was always certain to be.

But for this chapter the roads-and-point-blocks developments will do. There people can meet in most visible conflict the forces which are likely to destroy them. Sitting in the motor car, they can go by the daily 100,000 to the New Forest, by the daily 9,000 to the small corner of Borrowdale in the lakes, by the 4,000,000 pic-nickers per summer to the Peak District. The motorways make available to any car owner in England at least one national park within a maximum of $2\frac{1}{2}$ hours drive.[27] Sitting in a motor car, therefore, the people are sitting on the breaking point between the ethics of productivity and those of a free society.

A few people who live beside, on, and underneath the motorways are beginning to realize this. They have been preceded by those people – a rapidly growing number – who have seen that the present rate of invasion by hungry generations into the open countryside (as opposed to the millions of private square miles) will soon tread it down into beaten, sterile earth. They have been joined by groups of all kinds who dislike the disjuncture between homelessness and the empty precincts of shops and offices. The common element in these criticisms is the unrepentent if sporadic belief of men and women that they can run their own lives. To be

[25] See, for the story, Richard West, *River of Tears*, Earth Island 1972. Also Merryn Jones, 'Dilemma in Dolgellau', *New Statesman*, 7 April 1972.

[26] Zuckerman Commission on Mining and the Environment. See the review by Jon Tinker, 'A mouse that didn't roar', *New Scientist*, 21 September 1972.

[27] All figures collected from local authority reports and amenity groups by D. Rubinstein and C. Speakman in *Leisure, Transport and the Country-side*, Fabian research series 277, May 1969.

invited to participate is not enough, a grace note of the planners.

> *Je participe*
> *tu participes*
> *il participe*
> *nous participons*
> *vous participez*
> *ILS PROFITENT*[28]

Heigho.

It would be empty to close the argument with a description of what townscape a living culture would create for itself. My point is this. That it will be impossible to think out social and moral criteria adequate to the creation of a common culture, the most powerful and manifold expression of which would be the city,[29] the town, the landscape, and the house, until we insist on managing our lives for ourselves. The necessary condition for a common culture is free men and women in the streets. How this may be achieved is another matter; the struggle to make democratic and expressive forms adequate to the technology, the physics, and the chemistry in which we live must and will be experimental and aggressive for a long time yet. But it is not difficult to catch and identify those moments in the life of the land and its townscapes which embody that self-controlled dignity – the phrase tells in more than one sense – which if not a primary virtue, is a condition for virtue. You find such moments in the good primary school we have all grown used to. The neat, inoffensive lines of glass and stained pine or white slatting which punctuates doors and windows; the flat roofs, the trim, low rectangular shape; the single-storey cluster in which it is hard to pick out a front door where there is so much glass for the world outside to flow through; all the busy life inside given such ready access to the warm grass, the little flowering trees, the rosebushes, the hard, ungiving playground.

Or turn a corner down a courtyard still free to pedestrians in a big city. There are, as a matter of quite conscious planning, fewer and fewer such corners left. In a living townscape this corner will mix offices, shops, pubs, maybe stalls and barrows, maybe manufacturing workshops or small factories. In the unselfconscious way such successes of townscape have, the busy life of the place combines, mingles and separates again the multiple roles of city life. The corner allows for us to be customer, client, pedestrian, sight-seer, huckster, all in a matter of seconds. As Alison and Peter Smithson put it,

---

[28] *Atelier Populair* (ex-école des Beaux Arts) poster, May 1968
[29] The greatest argument for this belief is Lewis Mumford's classic *The Culture of Cities.*

.... it is the idea of street, not the reality of street, that is important – the creation of effective group spaces fulfilling the vital function
of identification and enclosure, making the socially vital life of the
streets possible.... Architects make a flat surface of everything
so that no microbes could survive the civic vacuum cleaner. To
think that architects are given to talking devotedly about space
while they are actually emasculating it with a void.[30]

They go on,

Somewhere there must be a place which not only allows for the
contact of mind with mind, but also symbolizes it. This can only
happen at the 'centre' (there can be only one place where the
experience of the community reaches its maximum: if there were
two there would be two communities). It is quite clear that in an
ideal city at the present time, the communication net should serve
(and indicate) places-to-stop-and-do-things in.

The consequence of most modern planning is that the contact
of mind with mind is chloroformed or forestalled. We have a
frame of mind, a state of consciousness which has learned its
procedure from the assembly line and flow chart. In the city, as
in the factory, operational management has destroyed the multi-
foliate play of social life in an irrational effort to rationalize action
in terms of single ends. In a brilliant paper which I first heard
given to the Town Planning Institute annual conference in 1968,
Christopher Alexander[31] translates this argument into a modern
mathematical set theory in which the 'semi-lattice' describes multiple overlapping sets, and the 'tree', sequences of separate dependent sets. In 'trees', work areas and dormitory are separate; in 'semi-
lattices', creative overlap is possible. A new town (e.g. Milton
Keynes) is a tree; an old one (Tewkesbury, Aberdeen) is a semi-
lattice. Alexander provides a marvellously lucid and usable model
for a regenerate planner's intelligence. But the first victories are
not conceptual, at least not the concepts of the drawing board.
They are political. For such a system of overlapping identities to
achieve its own social and architectural symbolism, men and
women would need to see that the many divisions of labour were
defined by a common social factor; that this factor was composed
of the rich and diverse meanings and productions of their lives;
that this was their social wealth.

They would then have to lay claim to their own.

[30] *Team Ten Primer*, A. and P. Smithson (eds.), Architectural Press n.d.
[31] A first version of which appeared in *Design* 206, February 1966.
Reprinted in Bell and Tyrwhitt, cited.

11 What's the Good?

F. R. LEA

He who ignores philosophy is condemned to repeat it.

SANTAYANA

The powers over nature which science has invested in man are already so vast that, abused much longer, they are certain to result in his extinction. Equally vast is the power over human nature which, thanks to biochemistry and genetics, will soon be at the disposal of rulers, elected and unelected. This power will be used. That we ourselves, if we chance to survive the twentieth century, will be changed as perdurably as we have changed our environment, admits of no doubt. The only question is whether the change is to be for good or for evil. It is up to us to decide – and decide quickly...

How often, over the last fifty years, we have been treated to such admonitions as this! And still they fall on deaf ears. We attend to the prophets for a moment; we admit that the danger is quite as great, the choice quite as urgent, as they say – and then go on as before. Small wonder they begin to lose heart, cry, 'what's the good?' and lapse into bitter silence. I would do the same myself, if only the decision they called for were one we could actually take.

But this it is not. We could no more respond to their summons than we could obey the injunction, 'Fly to another planet', unless we happened to know which planet to fly to. We cannot take the very first steps – cannot even discuss the first steps – towards changing anything for the good, until we have answered the question, 'What *is* the good?' And this, the old question of moral philosophy, is seldom so much as raised.

Traditionally, moral philosophy is said to be concerned with 'the Good'. I do not care for the expression. 'The Good' has a way of suggesting some mysterious entity, remote, immaculate and probably spherical. Nor is 'the Good Life' or 'the Good Society'

much improvement, since, as Hegel used to insist, there is no such
thing as 'life' apart from living beings, or 'society' apart from ourselves. I would sooner speak of 'the good man', if only because we
all have a more or less clear idea of him – clear enough, at least, to
doubt whether he is to be found in the mirror; and if we could
give sound reasons for upholding one such idea rather than others,
the main problem of moral philosophy would be solved. Knowing
who the good man was, we would know what we meant by a good
constitution, education or art: it would be the kind that produced
him. In the absence of any such moral criterion, we do not even
know what an evil kind is.

There have been periods in history – the longest – when this
problem was presumed to have been solved. To know what type
of man was 'good', what type he himself should aim at being and
seeing, the Confucian, Mohammedan or Christian had only to
contemplate the Founder of his Faith or consult His accredited
spokesmen. In Europe and America as recently as a century ago
most fundamental disputes could still be settled with the words,
'Christ said ...' or 'Christ showed ...' Widely as opinions might
differ as to what Christ did say or show, or what He actually meant
by it, few doubted that man's ultimate aim was to be 'more Christ-
like'. Even atheists, in their anxiety to rebut the charges of
immorality brought against them, vied with their Christian critics
in philanthropy, chastity and most of the other traditional virtues.
In those days, it still made sense to speak of using human powers
for the good.

Today it makes little or none. We ourselves live in one of those
periods – the shortest – when no such consensus prevails; when not
merely the traditional ideologies have gone by the board, but
along with them the traditional ideals; when, accordingly, words
like 'good' and 'evil', 'right' and 'wrong', have lost all point of
reference. Although we continue to use them, we have no clear
idea what they mean, let alone whether they mean the same things
to others as ourselves. Even when we talk of a 'good' constitution,
education or art, we are like travellers discussing the way to Cambridge, where some are thinking of Cambridge Cambs., others of
Cambridge Mass. – or rather, we are like tourists discussing the
way to Oxbridge.

Would a good education make a man healthy or wealthy, a good
art make him happy or wise? Or are the four terms interchangeable? Is the Healthy Man the same as the Wealthy, the Happy Man
the same as the Wise? If so, in what esoteric sense? It would take
a Wise Man to say. It would take *the* Wise Man, in fact, 'wisdom'
being once defined as 'the knowledge of that wherein man's highest

good is to be placed', and a 'philosopher' as one who aspires to such knowledge.

The object of moral philosophy is to propose a rational definition of 'the good', 'the good life' or 'the good man' – that is to say,
to adduce convincing reasons for bestowing the epithet 'good' on
one type of man rather than another. This, at all events, was the
object of moral philosophers in the past – and not only of those,
like Aristotle or Spinoza, who are commonly classed as such. There
was scarcely a major philosopher from Socrates to Nietzsche who
did not have this for his object. Kant himself, though treated
primarily as an epistemologist, saw the *Critique of Pure Reason*
as simply 'preparing the ground' for that ethical enquiry 'which is
in reality the peculiar duty and dignity of philosophy'. Whether
their point of departure was political, aesthetic or religious, most
philosophers wanted to know what was 'good'. It was because they
wanted so passionately to know that they pursued their enquiries
so dispassionately: they could no more afford to trip up than
engineers, surgeons or generals. The notion of the philosopher as
cool or uncommitted could only have occurred to a very ignorant
or academic mind.

But is the object attainable, or was their enterprise foredoomed
to futility? Can convincing reasons ever be adduced? There is
no lack of voices denying that they can – and I do not mean just
those voices which have been asserting off and on for the last two
millennia, always in the same tone of defiant originality, that ethical
judgements are 'merely subjective' or 'purely relative' to this, that
or the other. This assertion, since it throws no light on the question, 'To *what* shall we make them relative?' or '*Which* subject
shall we treat as authoritative?' may be ignored. The voices I mean
are those of philosophers themselves, and 'moral philosophers' at
that, not asserting, but arguing, that a rational definition of 'the
good' is chimerical. According to Professor B. Medlin,[1] these actually constitute the majority today. 'It is now pretty generally
accepted by professional philosophers', he writes, 'that ultimate
ethical principles must be arbitrary' – and if we are to understand
by 'professional philosophers' English-speaking lecturers in philosophy, his statement is almost certainly correct.

These philosophers are not unaware of their predecessors' efforts
to arrive at a rational definition. Such efforts, they will readily
admit, served as valuable a purpose as the search for the elixir of
life or perpetual motion: had they never been undertaken, we

[1] B. Medlin, *Australasian Journal of Philosophy*, Vol. XXV (August 1959).

might never have known that the object was a will o' the wisp. Even so, they argue, now that we do know, it would be a sheer waste of time to continue – and the philosopher's time is precious. For the old enquiry, accordingly, they have substituted a new one – namely, as to whether the proposition, '*x* is good' is equivalent to '*x* hurrah!' or 'I approve of *x*, do so too' or 'my approving of *x*, yes; your approving of *x* also, please'. Industriously prosecuted for the last forty years, though still unconcluded, this enquiry is said by its practioners to constitute a 'revolution in ethical theory'.[2]

Time is certainly precious. If the old enquiry is foredoomed to futility, we can as little afford to resume it as we can to indulge in the new one, profitable as this might be, were the value of *x* to be determined. If the value of *x* is truly indeterminable, the sooner we take our arbitrary decisions the better, and, since they cannot be defended by reason, propagate them by example or blows. Before resorting to either, however, it would be as well to examine the argument which leads to so paradoxical a conclusion.

It is ably summarized by Professor Medlin himself:

> One cannot derive conclusions about what should be merely from accounts of what is the case; one cannot deduce how people ought to behave merely from one's knowledge of how they do behave. To arrive at a conclusion in ethics one must have at least one ethical premiss. This premiss, if it be in turn a conclusion, must be the conclusion of an argument containing at least one ethical premiss. And so we can go back, indefinitely but not for ever. Sooner or later, we must come to at least one ethical premiss which is not deduced but baldly asserted. Here we must be a-rational; neither rational nor irrational, for here there is no room for reason to go wrong.[1]

Hence the need for an 'arbitrary' decision.

Professor Medlin, be it noted, is not suggesting that '*x* is good' is equivalent to 'I like *x*', or '*y* is right' to '*y* appeals to me personally'. He is not reviving the so-called 'emotive theory' of ethics – a theory that would hardly have attracted serious attention even in Cambridge, but for Moore's attempt to present a don's emotions as intuitions of 'non-natural qualities'. He sees as clearly as any classical philosopher that the terms 'right' and 'good' imply some

---

[2] Cf. G. C. Kerner, *The Revolution in Ethical Theory* (Oxford, 1966). 'Ethical theory' is here defined on the second page as 'the logical analysis of ordinary moral language – in other words, an investigation into the nature of the terms and modes of reasoning which are actually employed in discussing and settling moral issues in practice'. One should remember that 'actually employed', in this enquiry, always means 'in England just now'.

standard independent of personal predilections, and that the standard is normally that of the society we happen to belong to – the society whose norms, no doubt, are stamped on our super-egos.

When, for example, I ask myself whether or not I ought to behead a slave whose disobedience was occasioned, to my knowledge, by sudden loss of memory, I am not asking whether or not I feel like beheading him. My feelings have nothing to with the matter. What I am asking is whether the general precept, 'it is right to behead disobedient slaves' applies in this particular case. And the same would hold true were the precept itself to be challenged. However strongly I might feel that it was a good one, my feeling would be no answer to the man who told me it was bad. In order to discuss its goodness or badness, we would have to agree on some further premiss – the desirability, perhaps, of upholding the existing aristocracy. Extreme severity towards slaves, he might argue then, was more likely to endanger this end than secure it.

But what if he should go on to deny that the power of the aristocracy itself was pre-eminently desirable? What if, like a medieval Christian, he should affirm that it was desirable only insofar as it helped the Church to re-cast mankind in the image of Christ? As Professor Medlin says, we can go back indefinitely, but not for ever. Sooner or later, if our discussion is to continue, we must come to at least one ethical premiss upon which rational disagreement is impossible: and what sort of premiss would that be?

Prior to the fifth century BC it seems to have been generally accepted that 'the will of the gods' constituted such an ultimate premiss. What Zeus or Jehovah or Moloch had declared to be right *was* right. It took the Greek Sophists to ask what ground there was for presuming the gods to be good, even supposing they existed. It was by driving home this question, indeed, that they precipitated the first short period of general ethical confusion – and we have only to attend present-day discussions in advanced, 'sophisticated' circles to be carried straight back to the fifth century. There we shall hear Prodicus discounting the gods as personifications of natural forces, Critias inferring that wily rulers invented them to keep the people in order, Antiphon exposing the folly of compliance with any code or convention one could violate with impunity...

Yet, though intelligence was called for in those days to advance such antinomian views, and courage, even in a country without a powerful priesthood, to challenge such cherished convictions as the birthright superiority of master to slave, man to woman, Greek to Barbarian, those Sophists, we can see now, were in no better case than their opponents. They were no more rational, at any rate, since, when it came to justifying their own approbations, they could only appeal to Nature as traditionalists appealed to the gods: and what ground was there for presuming Nature to be good – even supposing a rebellious nature less conditioned by tabus than a conforming?

The rebel who pronounces the promptings of Nature right is in one boat with the priest who proclaims the will of Zeus. Neither really does more than dignify a particular predilection or prejudice – and to dignify is not to justify. To justify it, he would have to invoke some higher authority still. To prove that the Natural Man or the Godly was veritably good, he would have to carry his case to a court whose verdict was impossible to contest, if only because it left 'no room for reason to go wrong'. And such a verdict as this, quite clearly, could not be 'deduced': it could only be 'baldly asserted'.

So far, Professor Medlin's conclusions rest on firm ground – ground trodden firm by the classical philosophers who made it their jumping-off point. The question we have to ask, therefore, is whether they did well to jump off, or whether, as he would have us believe, they would have done better to leave off; whether moral philosophy must end where they thought it began; whether, in short, because an ultimate ethical principle has to be baldly asserted, it has to be 'arbitrary' too.

Let us assume for a moment that it has. Let us imagine that, thanks to our readiness to grant due weight to any argument, no matter how much it may offend our predilections, we have been won over to his point of view. We are agreed that 'most professional philosophers' are right. We are faced, accordingly, with the arbitrary choice of that principle which, since our enquiry was by no means academic, is to be the premiss of all our future judgements and actions. How shall we set about making it? How ensure that the decision is genuinely arbitrary, 'neither rational nor irrational'?

There is not much risk of its being rational. Granted that no sound reason can be given for any such principle, there is no risk whatever. All the ideals of the past and present being on a par, we shall not be behaving *less* rationally if we opt for Hitler's rather than Hume's, say, or Mani's rather than Mao's. But what of the irrational? How are we to make equally sure of not giving way to that?

There is still so much prejudice in the air; we are still so apt to be swayed by ancient convictions, modern conventions, or their emotional heritage – convictions harking back to times when some reasons did seem stronger than others, conventions deriving from metaphysics itself – from the belief, for instance, that the evidence for and against an after-life was germane to the issue. It would never do to relinquish our own judgement only to yield to our ancestors'; much less to let passion decide, ambition, conformity or revolt. We shall have to take every precaution, if there is to be no room for reason to go wrong; have to be vigilant indeed, if we are to be genuinely a-rational. What steps shall we take?

Rather surprisingly, in view of all that hangs on the question, our philosophers do not tell us. Having pronounced an arbitrary decision necessary, they leave the matter at that. To go further and divulge the appropriate procedure, they must feel, would be tantamount to renouncing their views on the point at which philosophy ends. Yet the procedure is not self-evident. It is not so to the ordinary man, at any rate, unused as he is to taking even minor decisions without any reasons whatever. How *does* one do it?

The feat would be less problematic were the alternatives only two. There is a well-established procedure for securing arbitrary decisions in cases of this sort. If the choice were between Zeus and Nature alone, we could simply toss up – 'heads' for the Natural Man, 'tails' for the Godly. But this will scarcely serve our turn today, faced as we are with a plethora of possible principles, a positive *embarras de richesse* of 'good men'. Some subtler method is called for. Would it, perhaps, be enough to draw up a list of all these, blindfold ourselves, turn round thrice and stick a pin in the paper? Is this how our philosophers themselves decide on their ethical principles?

I find it hard to believe. It would be impossible, if they did, for quite so many to end up pin-pointing John Stuart Mill. A few at least would be found committed to ideals less consonant with university status. Notwithstanding their silence on the question, the evidence is strong that they cheat – that they do allow rationality to intrude at some stage or other, and only take scrupulous care not to examine the reasons too closely.

However, as the Professor says, 'one cannot deduce how people ought to behave merely from one's knowledge of how they do behave'. It is no objection to any theory that its professors do not take it very seriously; and if I myself object to this one, it is less because of its psychological absurdity than because of its logical redundancy. They, after all, would no more be able to canvass than I to confute it – let alone charge them with 'cheating' – had we not already subscribed to an ethical first principle which, though neither rational nor irrational, is anything but arbitrary.

If the reader is in any doubt about this, let him inspect the two following propositions: (a) at least one ethical premiss must be arbitrary; (b) at least one ethical premiss need not be arbitrary. How will you decide which of these is true – by tossing up, or by using your reason? If you decide to use your reason, you need do no more: you have already given your assent to (b). Not only have you pronounced the value judgement, 'truth is better than un-truth', but you have subscribed to what Russell once called 'the most imperative of moral precepts' – to follow reason wherever it leads. So have I, and so (I fancy) has Professor Medlin. Had I not subscribed to it, nothing I write would be worth a politician's promise, and were I unaware of the fact, you should write me off as an ignoramus.

This ethical principle cannot, indeed, be deduced: it is neither rational nor irrational. It cannot be defended without being pre-sumed, or contested without being conceded. I can only 'baldly assert' it – can only announce to the world at large, 'my approving of honest reasoning, yes; your approving of honest reasoning also, please', R.S.V.P. Yet it is anything but trivial. If you cannot accept my invitation, it is all over between us – our enquiry ends here; whereas, if you can, it would be plainly absurd to go looking for any other principle, blindfold or open-eyed, before exhausting the implications of this one. And the implications are far-reaching. It was for this that Socrates stood, and by standing for this alone that he effected the first, and so far the only, revolution in ethical theory.

The obligation to follow reason wherever it leads I shall call 'the rationalist imperative', and one who professes it a 'rationalist'. In these pages the term 'rationalist', therefore, will signify a man who relies on reason, not indeed to find the true answer to a question ('the truth', for short), but to demonstrate that it *is* the true one, and who proportions his belief to the strength of the argument. The term will not be reserved, as it was in the seven-teenth century, for men who argue that there is a God, nor, as it was in the nineteenth, for men who argue that there is none. Still less will it be applied, as it is in the twentieth, to men who merely assert that there is none. The man who merely asserts such a thing I call an 'irrationalist'.

An irrationalist can only assert, or else keep quiet. He may assert things we have reason to think true, but we shall not call them true on the strength of his assertions. He may assert that his beliefs are derived from a higher source than reason, but we shall not call it higher unless we have reason to believe them; nor, though we may revere him as a poet or mystic, shall we call him a philosopher, since philosophy proceeds by argument. An 'irrationalist philosophy' is a contradiction in terms. Within philosophy, the important distinction is not between rationalist and irrationalist, but between the rationalist who remembers the rationalist imperative and the one who forgets it.

If you try to picture a man completely convinced that it is right to follow reason wherever it leads, and convinced of nothing else; who, accordingly, treats as evil whatever so-called goods interfere with the pursuit, and accepts whatever so-called evils it may entail, such as poverty, insecurity or death, you will picture Socrates. He is the embodiment – one might say, incarnation – of that imperative which is the presupposition of philosophy, moral or natural. In this lies his symbolic importance.

Needless to say, the importance of Socrates was not purely symbolic. He professed to be seeking 'wisdom', which is knowledge of the good; and, in addition to posing most of the questions his successors would answer, he suggested most of their lines of approach. Yet he committed himself to none of their deductions – nor did he need to, being wholly committed to their premiss. Had he claimed to be in possession of wisdom, he could not have persisted in his search; had he renounced the search, he could never have established, as he did, that to follow reason wherever it leads is itself the beginning of wisdom.

'The fear of the Lord is the beginning of wisdom', Solomon said, and the votaries of Zeus were of the same mind. Not that they objected to reason: they were quite prepared to argue their point. But if their arguments were refuted, they fell back on others, and if these were refuted, on force. It was for 'denying the gods' that Socrates was condemned. No rationalist can maintain that he was rightly condemned without contradicting his premiss; no philosopher who remembers the premiss can pronounce the Godly Man better than Socrates.

An irrationalist may perfectly well do so. Rejecting the arbitrament of reason, he is beyond or beneath refutation. But an irrationalist philosopher is a solecism. Take Jean-Paul Sartre, for instance, who is often dubbed one. He is certainly nothing of the kind. His philosophy, he tells us, is simply 'an attempt to draw the full logical consequences from a consistently atheist position',[3] and to an irrationalist it would matter not a whit whether his deductions were logical or not, consistent or inconsistent. If Sartre ends by pronouncing any one 'commitment' as good as another, including commitment to a cause that would silence such enquiries as his

[3] J.-P. Sartre, *Existentialism and Humanism* (London, 1948), p. 56.

own, that only proves him a rationalist *manqué*, who has forgotten his premiss. And the same holds true of the advocates of ostensibly arbitrary, actually conventional decisions. You cannot, in one and the same breath, exalt the Socratic Man and the Holy (or unholy) Idiot. The rationalist imperative imposes a limiting condition upon possible ideals.

'Man is the measure of all things', said Protagoras. But *which* man – the Natural? The Sophists, too, were mostly rationalists *manqués*, since they followed reason only so far as to impugn such ideals and institutions as they chanced to dislike; and if they disliked racialism or slavery, for example, it was not because it ran counter to reason, but merely because it offended some 'very strong feeling' or 'deep instinctive sense' that this, that or the other was right. Hence their discomfiture at the hands of a thinker who, far from employing reason, was her employee; for whom reason was a sovereign, not a servant, and a sovereign to be obeyed whatever her behests.

The rationalist imperative does more than impose a limiting condition upon possible ideals and ethical codes. It imposes a minimum code of its own. For, if it is right to follow reason, it is right to cultivate whatever propensities the pursuit may demand, and to curb whatever impairs them – not least those very strong feelings that prompt very weak rationalizations or that deep instinctive will to live which bids fly the hemlock. After Socrates no philosopher was thought worthy of the name who did not observe at least this minimum code. His death being of a piece with his life, and Plato's artistry of a piece with his insight, the *Phaedo* exerted the same spell over earlier antiquity as the Crucifixion did over later.

In the *Apology*, Socrates likens himself to a soldier obliged to die at his post. He is charged with a 'mission', which no power on earth will induce him to betray: 'while I have life and strength, I shall never cease from the practice and teaching of philosophy'. He is only saying the same thing more quietly when, in the *Crito*, he describes himself as 'one of those natures which must be guided by reason, whatever the reason may be which upon reflection appears to be the best'. But it is in the *Phaedo* that Plato reveals most surely and subtly what that 'philosophy' was that exacted so rigorous a discipline.

Is it Socrates's mission here to demonstrate the truth of preexistence, of 'recollection', or of survival after death? Assuredly not, though he is accredited with all three theories. He has scarcely begun to muster the evidence before he is adjuring his friends to challenge a demonstration which, in the circumstances, is only too likely to be biased: 'I would ask you to be thinking of the truth and not of Socrates: agree with me, if I seem to you to be speaking the truth; or, if not, withstand me might and main, that I may not deceive you as well as myself in my enthusiasm, and like the bee, leave my sting in you before I die.' He is not there for affirming, nor to affirm, the truth of any particular theory, no matter how convincing or consoling.

But neither is he there to instil a radical scepticism regarding all such theories. Far from it! 'No worse thing can happen to a man,' he goes on, than to let suspicion of rationalization harden into distrust of rationality. There have been only too many 'great disputants' who, finding first one argument and then another false, 'come to think at last that they have grown to be the wisest of mankind, since they alone perceive the utter unsoundness and instability of all arguments'. Let the thinker, rather, having scrutinized his first principles as closely as he can, proceed 'with a sort of hesitating confidence in human reason' towards 'the best and most irrefragable of human theories, and let this be the raft upon which he sails through life.'[4]

This was what the great classical philosophers did. They scrutinized the principle that Socrates stood for, saw that it afforded firm ground, and took off from that. Nor is there any reason why we, with their help, should do otherwise. Nobody has yet given us the least cause to believe their quest foredoomed to futility, or the history of western philosophy a tale told by an idiot – let alone to believe idiocy a necessity or make a virtue out of that. Everything goes to show, on the contrary, that the worst errors in ethics have arisen, not from setting over much store by Socrates's premiss, but from forgetting that it ever existed. That is why I have given it a name – *ne taceretur.*

Socrates has never been safe. The rationalist imperative has always been threatened, and not merely by the masses, whose reason is a tool of their sectional interests, but by philosophers themselves. Plato's own confidence in his particular, dialectical reasoning was so far from hesitant that he ended by claiming final truth for his conclusions and banishing Socrates in their name. Nowhere does he show himself further ahead of his time than in his anticipation, by close on a millennium, of the Holy Inquisition. It was not until Calvinists took to testing their deductions against 'stubborn, irreducible facts' that his procedure was seriously challenged, not until they transferred their exact observations from the Book to 'the

---

[4] My quotations are from Jowett's translation of *The Dialogues of Plato* (Oxford, 1871).

Book of Nature' that empirical science came into its own.

Had Plato or the Schoolmen prevailed, there would have been no science as we know it, dependent as this is on the decision, not only to reason, but to listen to reason. For that matter, there would have been none if Calvin had prevailed, his confidence in his conclusions being quite as unhesitating as theirs. He, too, would have subscribed to Lenin's maxim, 'first convince and then coerce'. It was only because his method resulted in so many contradictory conclusions that no single practitioner could impose his own on the rest that the competition of theories came to be seen as the condition of their mutual correction. It took Milton and Locke to envisage the 'search after truth', no longer as the peculiar vocation of this individual or that, but as a collective endeavour, prolonged from generation to generation and expanding to embrace all who, renouncing the claim to finality, adopted the one ethical principle indispensable to its pursuit – 'mutual forbearance'.[5]

I believe that the establishment of this principle, which, like the rationalist imperative, can be contested only where it is conceded, was the greatest contribution of the English to moral philosophy. Certainly its concession alone made possible the rise of a 'scientific community'. It may well have been their greatest contribution to political philosophy too, since there sprang directly from this the idea of the 'rational society' as itself a scientific community, ascertaining, through discussion and concerted experiment, the further conditions of 'forbearance'. In Locke, Godwin, Rousseau and Kant, one can follow the emergence of a new, intellectually unassailable ideal. Their 'good man', whatever else he may stand for, stands for toleration; their political and educational theories take shape accordingly. It is just because they value toleration, not as an end in itself, but for the sake of truth, that they are equally hostile to the indifference that comes of not knowing what is good and the permissiveness that goes with not caring.

It is strange that scientists should so often forget this ethical principle, the presupposition of all their activity; that even they should still be heard chanting after Hartung, 'Any set of customs or institutions, or way of life, is as valid as any other'; 'I could just as logically [sic] adopt the conventions of any other culture I chanced to learn about ...'[6] Not that these choristers are as

---

[5] Locke, like Milton, couples 'mutual forbearance' with 'charity', but gives no reason for thinking the latter indispensable.

[6] Quoted by C. Kluckhohn, *Culture and Behaviour* (Glencoe, 1955). 'Ethical Relativity: *sic et non*'.

numerous as they were forty years ago. Though it may have taken the light of burning books to open their eyes, many would now endorse Kluckhohn's opinion, that 'emotionally and practically this extreme position is hardly tolerable – even for scholars – in the contemporary world'. But – why in the *contemporary* world? Why *even* for scholars? Why, above all, *emotionally*, not *intellectually*? They have only to preach what they practise to spare themselves all those forlorn appeals to 'certain universal human norms', which, even if they really were either certain or universal, would impose no ethical obligation – since, as our philosophers are so fond of insisting, 'one cannot derive conclusions about what should be merely from accounts of what is the case'.

If it is strange that scientists should be so forgetful, however, what is one to think of philosophers who, having intoned their response, imagine nothing further required of them – and this at a time when Socrates is threatened as never before? For, while the Marxists may be alone (at the moment) in claiming final truth for their ethical criterion, not only is that criterion itself of English origin, but it has been propagated so much more effectively in England and America than in Russia or China that if nobody tries to enforce it here, it is mainly because nobody needs to. Here what was once the reasoned conclusion of a handful of philosophical radicals has long since acquired the status of an unquestionable axiom: namely, that 'The Good = Happiness' – not the Happiness Hereafter which Locke upheld as the reward for truthfulness here, but Happiness Here, 'The Greatest Happiness of the Greatest Number'.

The success of an ideology – *alias* a moral and political philosophy – bears no proportion to its soundness. The more inconsistent a philosopher is, the more prejudices can be rationalized in his name and the wider will be his influence. It is not hard to understand why Bentham's definition of 'the good' should have supplanted Locke's, least of all when the condition of its fulfilment were laid down as Equality, Security, Subsistence and Abundance. The wonder is, not that bourgeois and proletarian in turn should have devoted their lives so devoutly to fulfilling these conditions, but only that the ideologies themselves neglected to set the example – that they, on the contrary, when taxed with courting insecurity, deprivation and destitution, would unblushingly affirm that the happiest man of all was a man of sorrows and acquainted with grief. But even this stood in their favour. Once the Nonconformist Conscience had been so affected that Christians, too, would come to talk as though a papal edict – on abortion, say, or contraception – was sufficiently refuted by the unhappiness it occasioned, there was nothing to stop Happiness Here from becoming the accepted ethical criterion of all who profess ethical neutrality, from the sociologist who presumes the Happy Man wealthy to the psychiatrist who presumes the Healthy Man happy.

Yet the Principle of Utility did not supplant Locke's entirely without protest. Even after the Utilitarians, by a master-stroke of propaganda, had appropriated the title of 'rationalist', there were still some philosophers to insist that the goal of philosophy is truth, that truth makes nobody happy except the man who happens to desire it, that it makes most men so acutely miserable or indignant that they would happily requite it with hemlock, and that to exhort them to pursue their happiness is to exhort them to do just that. Nor were these philosophers content to protest. Genuine rationalists themselves, they took up the task of determining a viable ideal – an ideal on which men might agree, not because it chimed with their predilections nor because it was the will of a god (History, for instance, or Progress), but because the same reason prescribed it that challenged both.

Now that their forebodings have been so amply fulfilled, therefore, that half the world denies them a hearing, might we not have expected the other to take them all the more seriously? Might we not have expected their ideas to command some attention at least – to be expounded, explained and, if not adopted, replaced?

Elsewhere[7] I have tried to follow that quest for a viable ideal, as it was taken up amateurishly by the British Romantics, professionally by their German coevals, Kant and his successors. But why was it left to an amateur to follow? Why do 'most professional philosophers' ignore it? The answer usually given is that those nineteenth-century thinkers were 'metaphysicians', and metaphysics is now a lost cause. The answer would be more convincing if either we or they knew what 'metaphysics' denoted.

Originally the name was bestowed by Aristotle's editors on that 'first philosophy' which, as the coping-stone of his classification, stands 'over and above physics'. 'Physics' being his word for the natural sciences, psychology and sociology included, what stands over and above is the study, first of those principles (like 'the law of contradiction') which govern research in them all, and secondly of those which govern all their objects of research. The special sciences investigate special kinds of object. Physics (in its modern sense) deals with what is material – the inanimate being; biology

---

[7] My book, *The Ethics of Reason*, has been refused publication, but may be privately issued.

with what is living – the animate being; psychology with what is mental – the human being. Metaphysics deals with what *is* – Being.

'The science of Being' it used to be called, and as Aristotle conceives and conducts it, it appears to be a 'second-order' science. The specialists having determined the common denominators of this, that and the other kind of being, the metaphysician is there to determine their highest common denominators. His aim might be simply stated, therefore, as the unification of the sciences.

Such a unification has always been the scientist's dream. As Kant pointed out (in the now most important and neglected part of the first Critique), science is founded on the faith that nature will invariably lend itself to classification or explanation in terms of such common denominators as 'species' and 'laws' – that it will invariably conform, in other words, to those three sovereign principles of reason, *Variety*, *Affinity* and *Unity*; and consequently that, by subsuming species under genera, particular laws under general, it is approximating ever more closely to that 'systematic unity of cognitions' which would account for the phenomenal world as a whole. The word 'species' itself, transferred from logic to the animal kingdom, commemorates Aristotle's faith that the laws of thought were laws of nature: and if he had done no more for all three kingdoms than he did for the one, his metaphysics might have been just as fruitful for science – as fruitful, perhaps, as Democritus's.

Unfortunately, he did do more. For all his antipathy to the Platonic Forms, he lived too near Olympus to be proof against the typical Greek temptation to hypostatize – or, if they were really important, personify – common denominators. When it came to Being itself, even he succumbed. Before he knew what he was about, he had endowed it with independent – though necessarily indemonstrable – existence. Being had become a Divine Being, 'over and above' the natural sciences in an altogether new sense; and, by the same token, 'metaphysics' had acquired an altogether new connotation, 'theology'.

Thus, Aristotle's 'first philosophy' was really a conflation of two totally different things, the science of Being and that of hypostatized Being – the one inviting, the other deterring, research; the one crying aloud for revision, the other thundering with the voice of Jehovah. But alas, so intertwined were the two in his work, and so intertwined were they always to remain in Scholastic philosophy, that, notwithstanding the *Critique of Pure Reason*, the English professor has failed to distinguish them even yet. Just as in sixteenth-century Padua, so in twentieth-century Oxford, any attack on one is taken for an attack on the other.[8]

Since there is actually no logical connection between the determination and the hypostatization of common denominators, I think it would be a very good thing if the two procedures were given different names; and, since there is a perfectly good name floating around in search of something to attach itself to, why not call the second 'ontology'? The usage is not traditional, but neither is the distinction, and until this is clearly drawn, there will be no end to the preposterous spectacle of philosophers throwing out the baby with the bath-water while theologians try to drown the poor mite in it.

However, Kant's onslaught upon 'transcendent entities' was by no means so ineffective in Germany as it was in the Home of Lost Causes. There, on the contrary, we find Hegel reporting as early as 1812, 'Even those who cling to everything else that is old regard metaphysics [i.e. ontology] as dead.' It was in order to show that the lesson had not been lost on himself that Hegel prefixed the word 'science' to each of his original titles, as Marx did the word 'critique'. German nineteenth-century philosophy began with the assumption that the single word we can *know* is that which science represents in terms of its common denominators: by the twentieth century it was only the *avant-garde* of Logical Positivism who had still to catch up with the news.

In point of fact, just as it was by eliciting an ethical ideal from the nature of scientific procedure that the English made their greatest contribution to moral philosophy, so it was by eliciting

---

[8] Needless to say there are distinguished exceptions to my generalizations about English philosophers – one has only to think of Muir or Mackinnin. I use the term 'English philosophers' here as it is normally used by the dominant coterie, to denote themselves.

If the reader suspects me of exaggeration, however, he need only consult a broadcast symposium, edited by D. F. Pears, *The Nature of Metaphysics* (London, 1957) – a symposium made particularly cosy and relaxed by the exclusion of metaphysicians. A discussion of Medicine from which doctors were excluded, or of Education in which no teachers took part, would be accounted surprising. But here it is the contributors who are happily surprised by their 'considerable measure of agreement'. The agreement comes out most strikingly in their common assumption that, deductive ontology being 'out', we have done with world-views; though one of them, in the *Encyclopaedia Britannica* article on 'Metaphysics', surmises that 'other patterns of synoptic world-views may emerge "in due course"' – a surmise that would have been prophetic indeed a couple of centuries ago.

The reader might also consult the chapter on 'The Nature of Philosophy' in D. J. O'Connor's *An Introduction to the Philosophy of Education* (2nd. edn., London, 1966), a standard work in British Training Colleges. Containing no thought, quotations or lofty dismissal of unspecified 'classical philosophers' that is not unimpeachably standard, this epitomizes the conflation of dogma and hearsay passed off on present-day students as 'philosophy' – and students who are expected to teach in their turn!

one from the nature of scientific faith that the Germans made theirs. For what did Hegel himself claim to demonstrate, if not the full implications of that assurance that nature will invariably conform to the principles of reason, *Variety*, *Affinity* and *Unity*?

It was because scientists had always held this assurance, Hegel inferred, that they had always applied the same criterion to species and organisms as they did to classifications and laws, naming those the 'higher' that realized the greater unity in variety. And it was because metaphysicians, sharing their assurance, had always applied it to the phenomenal world as a whole, that, no matter how bare their acquaintance with this world or threadbare the texture of their systems, they had regularly, from Aristotle to Spinoza, arrived at the same conclusion.

The conclusion was written into the premiss. It would be enough for a metaphysician to designate *Variety*, *Affinity* and *Unity* themselves the highest common denominators of the world, both to comprehend his own conceptual system as a particular instance and to see them most perfectly realized in that man whose conceptual, emotional, instinctive and physical powers were all diversified and integrated to the utmost. Von Humboldt, in short, was stating no more than the truth when he declaimed: 'The end of man, or that which is prescribed, not by vague and transient desires, but by the eternal or immutable dictates of reason, is the highest and most harmonious development of his powers to a complete and consistent whole.'

Hegel was not the only philosopher who, beginning where Logical Positivism ends, claimed to have established this ideal. Nietzsche did too. For to say that the only world we can know is that which science represents in terms of its common denominators is not to say that science alone represents it truthfully. So far is this from being the case, Nietzsche argued, that science, by its very confinement to common denominators, is reduced to a representation as little resembling the real as the lines on a map resemble the lanes on the ground. Its very strength is its limitation. Precisely because its data are 'intersubjectively testable', it must leave out of account every one of those unique, irrepeatable perceptions of unique, irrepeatable objects which constitute actual existence.

Abstraction begins with the concept, the word, and is indispensable to human survival. It is the scientist's duty to carry it as far as the esperanto of mathematical physics. But the truths of science can never add up to 'the true'. The search after truth itself demands that they should be complemented by those which the artist alone can record, and that a man's sensibility, therefore, should be as highly developed as his intellect. The ideal – Nietzsche borrowed Goethe's word, *Ubermensch* – would be scientist and artist in one, 'enormously multifarious and yet the reverse of chaos'.

I do no know whether either Hegel's or Neitzsche's demonstration is as conclusive as it appears, never having heard either discussed. But one does not have to be a professional philosopher to see that neither is refuted by the word 'metaphysics' and that both are of the utmost consequence. One would not even have to believe them more than 'the best and most irrefragable of human theories' to be equipped with a raft upon which to sail through life – a raft, moreover, so often sailed on in the past that there would be no lack of directions to follow. The aesthetic, educational and political wisdom of centuries would be at one's disposal, not excluding that of certain ontologists.

Ontology itself, after all, is not such a terrible crime. It is not as though a principle were necessarily false merely because somebody had hypostatized or personified it. Beds did not turn into chairs and tables the night Plato conceived the Form of the Bed; nor would Freud's highest common denominators be any less suggestive than they are, if a statue of Thanatos were put up in Piccadilly Circus to afford the devouter sadists a rendezvous for Black Mass. However it may have been in sixteenth-century Padua, Socrates has less to fear from ontology today than he has from its most inveterate foes.

Not many years ago, the All Union Conference of Soviet philosophers, having been reproached with failing to 'put themselves at the spearhead of the struggle against the decadent and horrible ideology of the bourgeoisie and deal out devastating blows against it', addressed a memorandum to their philosopher king in these terms:

> We promise you, dear Comrade Stalin, to take a leading part in the struggle against idealist, reactionary doctrines ... We promise you to transform our chairs into militant party collectives, exercising a continuing influence on the entire process of pedagogic teaching and displaying bolshevik vigilance and intolerance against every manifestation of bourgeois objectivism.

To prove its sincerity, the Philosophical Institute directed its members to 'lose no time in drawing up individual daily schedules of work for each particular worker in the sector concerned, setting a precise finishing-date for work on every single chapter or section of the projects under preparation'.[9]

Thanks to Locke, Mill and others, the English philosophical establishment is still under no such pressure as this. If it is ignorant, obscurantist and smug, it is not because the alternative is liquidation. Its members are neither forbidden to prosecute what enquiries they please nor required to reach predetermined conclusions. They are free to follow reason wherever it leads – and God forbid (supposing the responsibility His) that they should ever be less so. Nobody can foretell the long-term results of even the most apparently trivial piece of research; whereas we have only to read this (to a rationalist) appalling memorandum to see what can come of unscrupulous, precipitate thinking. It should be a salutary warning to those who reproach our teachers with want of 'commitment'.

If 'commitment' signifies, as it generally does, pitting any and every means to an undefined end against a society you can adduce no reason for denominating 'bad', there is nothing to be said in its favour, at least where philosophy is concerned. In the remoter fields of investigation – paleobotany, say, or Sanskrit lexicography – execrations, acclamations and war-cries may have a place; but where concrete issues of human life are involved, to proceed with less than the meticulous caution of engineers checking a space-craft would be tantamount to criminal negligence. Had Marx himself only scrutinized his Hegel more closely, or Bentham his Helvetius, these philosophers, instead of merely changing the world, might have changed it for the better.

Yet, wrong-headed as they are, the critics have some excuse. They, after all, have never set up to be political or moral philosophers; few of them have even attended a university course in philosophy; and if they did, they would be none the wiser. They would learn, at most, to denote the undefined end by an x and suppress the offensive 'hurrah'. Far from being given any reason for doubting their assurance, they would be assured that no reason could be given; and if they were so conscientious as actually to turn round thrice and pin-point dear Comrade Stalin by mistake, it would speak highly for the instruction received. That memorandum should serve as a warning to our academics as well.

The current philosopher is not dogmatic. He would be the last to claim final truth – or, indeed, any truth at all – for the materialist world-views on which Helvetius and Engels grounded their ethics. He is as scornful of materialist world-views as of others,

[9] The quotations are from Soviet documents, cited by G. Wetter in *Dialectical Materialism* (London, 1958), pp. 187, 192, 194-5.

and fond of dwelling on his modesty compared with those who sought to re-cast the sorry conceptual scheme entire. If he presumes Happiness Here an ethical criterion too self-evident for discussion,[10] it is not because he subscribes to a materialist definition of 'man'. He is perfectly right to deny that he has any reason whatever for his choice. He is only wrong when he infers that it is 'arbitrary'. It is no more arbitrary than the forbearance which – albeit again without reason – he continues to practise. He would object to being indoctrinated by Mao because he is indoctrinated by Mill: and it is only, I suspect, because he is so well and truly indoctrinated that he has evolved the theory of arbitrary decisions – to justify his indoctrination. It affords an excellent example of the procedure he ascribes to Aquinas and others, of 'finding bad reasons for what we believe on instinct' – though rarely before has the rationalist imperative been betrayed in the interest of betrayal itself.

The theory has palpable attractions. Its appeal is no harder to account for than that of Utility. Besides absolving its professor from any need to question his presuppositions and encouraging him to pursue any enquiry he can pass off as moral philosophy, it confers an agreeable sense of superiority over such as did feel the need. One can see why it is no longer an offence in English philosophical circles – it is *de rigeur* – to use the word 'philosopher' as a synonym for 'logomachist',[11] smile at the naïvety of men who saw problems where 'we' see none, or refer to philosophical problems themselves as unhappy afflictions any up-to-date practitioner could treat. The presumption that 'we', the enlightened, perceive the utter unsoundness and instability of all the arguments of the past, moreover, can be counted on to go down well in the lecture-hall – as, of course, can the proclamation of any 'revolution', even a revolution whose proudest claim is to 'leave everything just as it is'.[12]

True, the teacher who has never had to pose the initial problem of philosophy is not well-placed to explain or assess the solutions: but then, if he knows *a priori* that it is insoluble, why should he? Why should he even go to the length of finding out what they were? One can also see why our professors are for ever congratulat-

---

[10] To forestall the charge of 'vague, unsupported aspersions', I might instance S. Toulmin, *Reason in Ethics* (Cambridge, 1960).

[11] In P. Nowell-Smith's *Ethics* (London, 1954), the word 'philosopher' is rarely used in any other sense, and the usage is typical of those who speak of 'doing philosophy'.

[12] The phrase, so often cited, is Wittgenstein's – he, the anti-philosopher of genius being the doyen of what is known as 'the revolution in philosophy' and would better be known as the counter-revolution against Socrates.

ing each other on discoveries made a century ago,[13] and why their students, though fully conversant with the latest opinions on *x*, know Plato and Aristotle only by hearsay. That hearsay reports, handed down from one lecturing generation to the next, should likewise suffice for such old-world reactionaries as Kant, Hegel, Marx, Engels and Nietzsche, stands to reason. It would be too much to ask of philosophical revolutionaries that they should give us complete, correct translations.

I fear, all the same, that this betrayal will prove disastrous. For, no matter how content the don may be to leave everything just as it is, that question, 'What is the good?' will go on being both asked and answered, if not inside the Common Room, then outside, and if not by professional philosophers, by unprofessional. Not all are so well and truly indoctrinated that they can dodge it; nor, in spite of the example they are set, are all the young so wise in their own conceit that they would spurn any wisdom that came their way. On the contrary, nothing is more pathetic than their readiness to succumb to the first mystagogue or rationalist *manqué* who holds out some promise of genuine enlightenment – and nothing more contemptible than the *x*-monger's promptness to dispose of the promise without offering anything in its place. Let those who gloat over the gaping holes in such rafts as Marcuse's or Sartre's get down to building more seaworthy ones, or, better still, show where they have already been built.

We do not expect a philosopher to be a Wise Man himself. As Bradley protested long ago, to turn to him for advice on particular ethical problems would be as absurd as to 'go to a learned theologian, as such, in a practical religious difficulty; to a system of aesthetics for suggestions on the handling of an artistic theme; to a physiologist for a diagnosis and prescription; to a political philosopher in practical politics; or to a psychologist in an intrigue of any kind. All these persons *might* be the best to go to, but that would not be because they were the best theorists, but because they were something more.' The most we can ask of a philosopher is the *aspiration* to wisdom – the least, a respect for it in others.

It does not follow, however, because we have no right to require wisdom of a philosopher, that we have none to require knowledge of a teacher. What *have* we a right to require of him, if not that? The teacher is not appointed to solve the problems of philosophy

---

[13] Where, outside Oxford quadrangles, had that 'ghost in the machine' continued to walk as late as 1960, when Prof. Ryle's performance with bell, book and candle was hailed by round-eyed colleagues as 'one of the more important events in post-war philosophy'? (G. J. Warnock, *English Philosophy since 1900*, Oxford).

or science – he has problems enough of his own; he is appointed
to enable his pupils to think them out for themselves. But to think
a problem out for oneself, as every scientist knows, means to think
it out in the light of the hardest thought given it to date, and to
enable anyone to do such a thing means, first and foremost, to
expound the solutions already proposed. 'This is the function
of our own and every age', said Hegel, 'to grasp the knowledge
already existing, to make it our own, and in so doing develop it still
further.'

What, then, is one to say of an opulent, independent, by no
means unintelligent philosophical 'establishment', whose foremost
spokesmen, at a moment when science itself is posing the problem
of Socrates, Plato and Aristotle, of Spinoza, Kant and Nietzsche, of
Helvetius, Hume and Mill, assure us that all this is no concern of
theirs, that it is no use our looking to *them* for suggestions or clues,
that *they* are no better equipped than the man in the street or a
blundering amateur like myself to throw any light on the issue?
And what if the assurance is *true*? –

My disapproving of quacks, yes.

12 The Mechanical World-Picture

PETER ABBS

Introduction

In this essay I want to argue that, contrary to pervading interpretations about the freedoms of our society, we are living through a time in which *one* peculiarly narrow and particularly inadequate conception of man is dominant. I want to show that while this conception of man has only recently, in this century, become commonplace, it yet has its roots in the assumptions of the Renaissance Scientists, particularly in the works of Galileo, Kepler and Descartes. Finally I hope to indicate that the conception of man originating from the scientific renaissance, although now dominant, has become intellectually discredited and that a new world-picture both more accurate in describing man's full nature and more far-ranging in its implications is slowly and uncertainly emerging.

The theme of course is vast and it is therefore important at the outset that I make two points of clarification. First of all, it is important to be clear that for the most part I will not be talking about scientific epistemology *as such* but about the effects of science on man's understanding of himself and his relationship to society and nature. Secondly, it is important that it is accepted that I am attempting to delineate broad tendencies, general assumptions, commonplaces, and that while individual exceptions can always be discovered, they can never (while they remain exceptions) amount to a denial of a dominant drift. In this essay, then, I will be trying to lay down the important contours in the belief that if we get these right we can fill in the details in a more leisurely way and from our own experience.

*   *   *

It is a commonplace assumption that we are now living in an open society, a society in which a plurality of viewpoints, beliefs, values, styles of living co-exist. This view rests, most frequently, on the premise that the Victorian world with its unifying beliefs in Christianity, in Prescriptive Morality, in Empire, has under immense economic, political, and intellectual forces, been irreparably broken, and that we now find emerging through the fragments a less urgent but more tolerant society, allowing diversity and deviation, enjoying better material conditions and held together in times of crisis by the reasonable restraints of law and order. Ironically this notion of our society being free and diverse is so constantly promulgated by the Liberal Press, by a host of commentators, and by the all-pervasive suggestions of advertising, that it becomes extremely difficult to interpret the situation in any other way. And yet this is precisely what we must do. We must examine the prevailing orthodoxy. We must look critically at the fashionable portrait of our times because there are many reasons for believing that while it presents certain features which we can agree upon – in certain areas there *is* more tolerance, in certain ways the conditions of material life *are* better – it yet embodies a grossly inaccurate image of the complete reality. I believe the notion of a pluralistic society has become a standard cliché and is dangerously untrue. By pin-pointing certain pleasing surface features and by ignoring the larger truth, the cliché works in the manner of flattery, giving our society a false sense of security and a willingness to go along with whatever is instituted.

As with all clichés, we must subject this one to a series of questions. Why, for instance, it could be asked, if our age is so diverse, so free to develop political and intellectual alternatives, do our three main political parties offer policies which beyond their thin rhetorical differences become less and less distinguishable? Why in what the Press described as 'The Great Debate' (entry to the Common Market) did the three main political parties offer the same official policy? What sort of debate was it, when all the instrumental powers openly admitted their determination to achieve the same end? These questions could be applied with equal force to all the newspapers, from the gutter press to the 'quality papers'. Why, it needs asking, in ideological matters, do they so invariably present identical goals and support identical interests? If the picture of growing diversity, increasing liberty were true, we would expect the contrary. We would expect a multitude of papers representing a variety of different groups, interests and loyalties. Such a press existed for a time in the nineteenth century when non-conformists, free-thinkers, radicals, chartists, humanists, as well as the main political parties, had their own newspapers but no one can pretend anything like this exists at the moment.

If we turn, briefly, to our society, we encounter a similar situation. Where there was considerable variety, we find increasing uniformity: where there was a certain measure of independence we find a growing dependence. Throughout rural Britain, communities are disintegrating and with them their dialects and cultural heritage. Local farms, central to community life, practising various forms of husbandry, have been largely absorbed into highly mechanized holdings, based on identical business principles, and run with neither reverence nor craft. At the same time, a multitude of small rural schools have been closed and a few standardized schools (sometimes named 'campuses') erected in their place. As a consequence of these and similar pressures, children who once inherited a rich tapestry of songs, games and customs, now enter schools chanting the same commercial ITV jingles, artificially contrived and disseminated by those who serve the confined interests of the commercial élites. How then, when so much evidence points the other way, can the fashionable image of the pluralistic society hold sway? Is it an image created by the centralized mass-communications system in the same way as the copywriters create images, and for similar reasons – to seduce the reason and imagination of man into an acquiescent acceptance of what is?

The various areas I have touched upon, of course, require individual and elaborate studies, many of which have already been made. What I am concerned with here, however, is not the particular instant, but the general pattern: the narrowing down of political alternatives, the increasing centralization of power and industry, the diminution of freedom in the public sphere of life and the growing conformity in people's expectations and habits. The general drift of contemporary society can, I think, be only understood in its entirety, by reference to a dominant world-picture: and, having briefly glanced at our society, it is to this concept which I now wish to turn.

The concept of a world-picture is, I think, a clear one: it comprises the ruling principles which underlie a society and give it cohesion: it imparts to the daily tasks of life a unifying purpose and meaning. A world-picture is expressed most strikingly and dramatically in the various artefacts and symbols which a society creates thus, unconsciously, giving tangible shape to those more abstract principles and ultimate terms of reference which determine the actions and expectations of a people. Thus, Canterbury or Wells Cathedral is as expressive of the Mediaeval World-Picture as a towering office block or an airport or a University campus is of contemporary life. And, of course, as the shapes and rhythms and details of the buildings are utterly different and antithetical, so are the two corresponding world-pictures in their evaluation of man and the universe.

Introducing *The Elizabethan World-Picture,* E. M. Tillyard writes:

> The province of this book is some of the notions about the world and man which were quite taken for granted by the ordinary Elizabethan: the utter commonplaces too familiar for poets to make detailed use of except in explicitly didactic passages, but essential as basic assumptions and invaluable at moments of high passion. Shakespeare glances at one of these essential commonplaces, when in *Julius Caesar* he makes Brutus compare the state of man to a little Kingdom. The comparison of man to the state or 'body politic' was as fundamental to the Elizabethans as the belief in self-help was to the Victorians.

Or, it could be added, the belief in 'a rising standard of living' is to us. The essential basic assumptions of a society are, however, far from being self-evident maxims. They are more in the nature of categories which, once being accepted, mediate experience and define the sort of reality that is available to a society. Furthermore, as Tillyard demonstrates in his book, the assumptions constitute a sequence of evaluations which have deep historical roots penetrating down in to past cultures. The Elizabethan World-Picture penetrated down into the Mediaeval traditions and then forked, receiving sustenance from both the Hebraic and the Hellenic conception of life. The following passage which Tillyard quotes from Goodman's *The Fall of Man* demonstrates how in the Elizabethan age religious and philosophical traditions converged:

> For as it pleased God to ordain a ceremonial law differing from the natural law, according to the wisdom of his own institution, so assuredly the mind of man, *which delights in nothing so much as in mysteries,* may make whole nature a ceremony and all the creatures types and resemblances of spiritual things. (My italics)

One can see at once how in the passage the Biblical conception of a loving and wise God and the Platonic philosophy of Ideal Forms meet in an exciting state of confluence. It is also a text which illustrates vividly the differences between our world-picture and the Elizabethan. Reading the passage, one becomes quickly aware of a man who looks upon nature from within. He does not seek precise knowledge but metaphor, imagery, with which to embody the invisible realm of being. The mind is not viewed as a mechanical instrument but as a living power delighting in its own activity. In fact Goodman's description of the mind revelling in mysteries reminds one forcibly of Keats' notion of 'negative capability'.

Such definitions are foreign to our world-picture for we interpret the mind not spiritually, but mechanically. We see it as a mechanism, a complex engine, an advanced computer, surrounded by other mechanisms. As a result, we regard nature as an object about which we can gain knowledge and which we can manipulate to our material advantage. Our language accordingly is not evocative and symbolic, but precise and operational. And yet our way of interpreting mind and nature is by no means recent. Like the Elizabethan World-Picture it has its roots in powerful ideas which were current centuries earlier: ideas which, in fact, were largely responsible for supplanting the Elizabethan image of life as an immense chain of being with the notion that the world was more truly a complex mechanical apparatus working, without mystery, under definite laws: laws which could be tabulated without emotion or spirit in a language of precise signs, logical and mathematical. Our world-picture has its strongest roots in this intellectual and scientific tradition: in Copernicus, in Galileo, in Descartes: and later in Newton. It also has, like the Elizabethan, sympathies with other civilizations. Significantly, our world-picture has little in common with Hebraic culture, and much in common with Roman and Egyptian civilizations, civilizations which confirm its own abstract and mechanical characteristics.

A recent prestige advertisement in *The Times* for John Brown Ltd develops the connection between our prevailing values and those of ancient Egypt. Like many advertisements (read carefully) it is a revealing document: on either side of the copy a powerful Pharaoh faces the earnest profile of a John Brown engineer. Beneath the heading, *4,000 years of Progress* the copy runs:

His (the Pharoah Cheops) work force were slaves or peasants glad of regular food and shelter they received for their labours. Materials were no problem either – he simply took them from wherever he wanted. The achievement was staggering. The sheer size and geometric accuracy of this great monument is almost beyond belief... Today our techniques are a lot more sophisticated but the problems of planning and management are far more complex ... Today (John Brown) are proud to be playing a role in the latest Egyptian monument – the pipeline linking the gulf of Suez to the Mediterranean.

Without doubt the advertisement underlines the dominant unifying dispositions of the two civilizations: a driving obsession for power, for size, and functional accuracy, and for the construction of monuments which further define and perpetuate these concerns. The pyramid and the office blocks (many of them, like Centre Point, empty), the tall sharpened obelisks and the stationary modern rocket have striking similarities and symbolize very similar pursuits. William Blake realized that the Hebraic and the Egyptian represented antithetical visions and implicitly suggested the similarities between the Industrial Revolution and the building of the Egyptian monuments. In 1810 he painted *The Virgin and Child*, placing the expressive and vibrant figures of the virgin and baby against the stark monumental solidities of the Pyramids. Geoffrey Keynes comments, 'Egypt denoted slavery and materialism to Blake', as did the satanic mills of the Industrial Revolution and the theories of Newton.

In our own time in his great seminal work, *The Myth of the Machine*, Lewis Mumford has confirmed Blake's intuition by documenting the connection between Egyptian civilization and our own technocracy:

Most people think that the machine, at least in its complex forms, is a purely modern invention. Some people even date it from the eighteenth century and the so-called Industrial Revolution. I have a radically different view of the entire development both of technology and civilization. I believe I've discovered the first machine which remained quite undiscovered for many thousands of years and for a simple reason. Because this machine was based on the use of a large number of human beings assembled under the direction of a powerful king, a military force and a bureaucracy. The megamachine is the first real machine composed of individual parts: they are highly specialized for the performance of work and capable of doing machine-work of the highest precision and exactitude. Therefore the machine has been in existence for five thousand years, but only in this collective form was it enormously productive: a hundred thousand men assembled to produce the Egyptian pyramids, performed as a machine of ten thousand horse-power. The works performed by the megamachine – great irrigation works and dams, walled cities and marvellous feats of engineering – could never have been performed by a smaller and simpler community. The megamachine was responsible for the greatest achievements of civilization but from the beginning it was accompanied by forced labour, by war, by the extermination of enemy populations by the lifelong division of labour, by the suppression of the peasantry in the interests of a dominant ruling class. And this has remained the form of the megamachine right down to our own day.

Lewis Mumford's account introduces, as one would expect, details that the advertisement for engineering suppresses. If the '4,000 years of Progress' necessarily involved slavery, war, suppression and regimentation, then progress ought to have become a highly tainted and deeply ambiguous word, an apologetic word. It leads to the question – Is Progress worth such a price?

With this question in mind, we can begin our examination of the Mechanical World-Picture, for the concept of Progress is central to its philosophy. I want to begin by isolating four categories which seem to me to be essential terms of reference in nearly all contemporary political and ethical discussion and which derive, as I hope to show, from a false extension of traditional scientific method. That the categories are familiar and obvious is to be expected, indeed it indicates that they *are* the informing commonplaces of public life. But, as we shall see, although commonplace they are far from being self-evident maxims.

The Four Categories

1. THE BELIEF IN GROWTH

The concept of growth is fundamental to the Mechanical World-Picture. It is one of the incontrovertible absolutes against which the existing state of society can be evaluated by those who control it and through which future directions and efforts can be determined. Because growth – expansion, productivity – is an absolute, at no point can its path be impeded: yet at no point, can it be fully achieved for, in this context, growth is both an artificial and an infinite concept. Growth in nature is subordinate to design and purpose but, in the Mechanical World-Picture, growth usurps function and becomes an end in itself. In commerce, enough is never sufficient because it must be justified by being used to produce more. In everyday life, the rhythms of work and play follow the rhythms of commerce: so the consumer must constantly want more: each thing must induce a want for another: the individual must always seek to surpass his present state of material advantage and that of his neighbours. The common phrase 'higher standard of living' shows how insidiously the notion of living and of consuming have become one.

The examples one can find to illustrate this informing belief in growth are so numerous, so all pervasive, it is unnecessary to select. What I want to show, however, is that the idea of infinite Progress – for 'growth' is the gross materialistic version of this secular and abstract Victorian Deity – permeates our society. So I will leave to one side the advertisements, the newspaper editorials, politicians' speeches, business publications and brochures, and, quote, in turn, a television organizer, a scientist and an educationist.

> ...A seriously directed 'journalism' could interest and prepare people ... for the immense and relatively sudden industrial and social developments they *will have to accept*, could attune their minds and emotions to change, and *so minimize the frictions and inadequacies that today delay and frustrate Progress*.
>
> SIR GERALD BARRY, Granada TV (My italics)

> It may take many years before there is enough evidence to enable us to give a firm estimate of radiation risks (with reference to the population of Great Britain, the calculations by one group of research workers gives the figure of about 8,000 deaths from cancer every year). *Clearly we cannot wait for that* before embarking on any project involving nuclear radiations, and the community *will have* to reach a decision *about the level of risk* it is prepared to accept.
>
> PROFESSOR J. ROTBLAT, Letter to *The Times*, 1 June 1972
> (My italics)

> For modern education affects the economy in a number of ways; not only does it increase the flow of skills, but it assists people to acquire new techniques. Moreover it tends to destroy the traditional attitudes which so impede progress, and it links knowledge with methods of production.
>
> JOHN VAIZEY, *Education for Tomorrow*[1]

The controlling assumption behind each argument is identical: life, it is categorically insisted, must be regulated to fit the needs of Progress. In each case, the meaning of Progress is neither defined nor questioned and this is what one expects with an ultimate term of reference, or with what as we have seen, Dr Tillyard calls an 'essential commonplace'. Progress is seen to justify the actions and policies of modern societies, and the various sacrifices it demands, whether from human life or natural life, are seen in the manner of unfortunate necessities. In much the same way the Pharaohs' powerful bureaucracies must have regarded the human conditions of their slaves, as unfortunate but necessary, if the great abstract monuments to power were to be erected.

We can adequately define Progress in its present meaning as the ever increasing production of goods, the widening of markets

[1] Penguin Books.

(hence the Common *Market*) and the expansion of capital. Herman Kahn in his book *The Year 2,000* looks forward to the day when 'We can estimate that there would be about one family in twelve with an income of $50,000 ... (an income) that we now associate with being a millionaire.' There must, of course, always be this uneven distribution in order to create that inner empire of envy on which the outer structure rests. In an age of unrestrained expansion, the *general* task of advertising becomes three-fold. Firstly, it must equate new with better and more with richer. Secondly, it must humanize the hidden impersonal mechanisms and make them sound intimate and caring. Thirdly, it must ferment the envy of expansion and dissatisfaction. In performing these functions, advertising has become the official poetry and symbolism of the power élites. In as much as it has made the abstract and monotonous dictates of Progress seem infinitely desirable to the majority of people, we cannot deny it has been successful.

As I have already indicated, the desire for growth stretches beyond the economy and informs nearly every facet of modern life. As learning and scientific discovery are, and have been, essential to the industrial goal of endless expansion, so in Universities we find the proliferation of research programmes, especially in the Departments of Science, Medicine and Technology. In research, as in Commerce, one discovers the same hostility to any conception of meaningful restraint. Other societies have restricted inventions on the grounds that they would disrupt the community. Our society – in spite of Hiroshima, in spite of Vietnam – regards the notion of restriction as a sign of a reactionary, a closed and outmoded attitude to life. So we find modern discovery moving forward with Professor Beale of Edinburgh University asking, 'When will it be possible to change the heredity of living cells, in a controlled and predictable way?' or a Nobel prize winner urging his audience: 'Let us marshall all our scientific forces together in order to create life.' There is no questioning as to what the consequences of these experiments might be (though Mary Shelley in *Frankenstein* has given us dark warnings) or whether it is ethically right to embark on them. As in commerce and government the absolute category of Progress justifies the accumulation of knowledge and technique without so much as a glance at ethical, cultural and historical considerations.

In the realm of culture we discover to a very large extent the same pattern. Here, it must suffice, to refer to David Holbrook's essay on Ted Hughes and to point out the way in which the London intellectuals in the fashion of copy-writers are forever preoccupied with naming and celebrating the next fashion, the next trend, the next excess. Their love of the ever-more public and ever more literal spectacles of cruelty, of absurdity, of sexuality, is nothing but an ugly and inverted form of Progress and shares the same anti-human frame of reference. As a consequence, they not only make no attempt to criticize society, they actively prepare people to accept the brutality, the ugliness and inhumanity of the mechanical system.

THE BELIEF IN MEASUREMENT

The Mechanical World-Picture has its roots in the philosophies of Galileo, Copernicus, Descartes and Kepler: their discoveries (and later, Newton's) in physics, in chemistry, in anatomy and astronomy were largely the result of observing the world analytically, of calculating and measuring, of inferring and deducing. The discoveries were so dramatic and so useful, that there developed a pronounced tendency to regard the inner realm, the emotional and imaginative energies of man, as at best irrelevant, at worst falsifying. It was Kepler, for example, who observed:

> the mind has been formed to understand not all sorts of things, but quantities ... the further a thing recedes from quantities the more darkness and error inheres in it.

This dogmatic insistence on quantification – and with it the virtual exclusion of subjective life – became quickly a major assumption of scientific method, and has become a major assumption of contemporary life.

In a recent article in *The Times Literary Supplement*, for example, Dr Tallentine proclaims:

> To a culture accustomed to precise measurements of quantities, even as such vast ones as interstellar distances, the idea that qualitative inquiries must also yield to final numerical solution is not alien.

Inasmuch as Dr Tallentine is describing another absolute of the Mechanical World-Picture, he is correct.

We can see this concern with measurement everywhere: in the talk about viability, in the schemes for 'industrial rationalization', in the antics of Cost Benefit analysis, in the insistence that statistical evidence is necessary to clinch any argument. Efficiency, like growth, has become an absolute, regulating and justifying all manner of social policies – many of them, inhuman.

The belief in order and measurement, which was common to

the seventeenth-century scientists, quickly culminated in casting the world in a new image. Kepler wrote, 'My aim is to show that the celestial machine is to be likened not to a divine organism but rather to a clockwork.' Over the centuries this image of the universe, further confirmed by Newton, and later socially embodied through the Industrial Revolution in vast systems of mass-production and human regimentation, has become the prevalent way of regarding life. Thus Singer concludes his *Short History of Scientific Ideas to 1900*:

> Thus we part with our story of classical science. Its task was to describe the world in mechanical terms in the hope of reaching a unitary view.

The unitary view depending on mechanical models, allowed no place for the inward and passionate, or the symbolic and cultural nature of man. Hence, under the sway of scientific ideas these unique characteristics of man have, for want of being developed, largely atrophied. Interpreting ourselves as machines we have become machines.

When the inner energies are equated with darkness and error, we find a society that gives unconditional praise to the external and predictable. In his book, *Beyond Dignity and Freedom*, B. F. Skinner writes: 'It is the autonomous inner man who is destroyed – and that's a step forward.' His aims – far from unfashionable – are celebrated in the modish paintings of our time. Quite appropriately, in a colour supplement, Andy Warhol claims: 'I would like to be a machine.' Elsewhere he explains: 'The things I want to show are mechanical. Machines have less problems ... Some day everybody will think just what they want to think, and then everybody will be thinking alike.' Given the projected image of man as an efficient machine, Warhol's conclusion is absolutely sound. I hope it is clear from these examples that a belief in measurement is another absolute of the Mechanical World-Picture.

THE BELIEF IN SIZE

Another belief, central to the Mechanical World-Picture, consists of a belief in large and centralized organization – for, it is claimed, only through enlarging firms and institutions can the goal of increasing efficiency and increasing productivity be realized. Certainly this would explain why industrialism begins with the entrepreneur and a plethora of small businesses, continues with a smaller number of larger firms and completes itself with a few giant multi-national corporations. Thus in *The Times* today one frequently finds side by side a bitter and bewildered letter by a small businessman who finds his business, under present economic conditions, disintegrating, and a full page advertisement in which a vast impersonal company intimately proclaims: 'YOU KNOW US FOR OUR SIZE'. The progressive movement into larger organization is not confined to industry. It can be seen at work politically: at a national level Britain has now transferred certain powers to Brussels: at a local level, regions have been reorganized for greater efficiency, with the result that fewer will represent more. It can be seen at work in Education, where, although a recent *Times* survey pointed to 'a direct connection between the incidence of disorder and the size of the school', the policy of closing small schools and replacing them with large, continues. More immediately, more tangibly, we can see in the high office buildings, in the tower-block flats, in the unshapely sprawl of cities and towns, the belief in size firmly embodied all around us.

Inevitably size brings with it the need for elaborate control. While every person must be neatly classified, and have a clearly defined function, he must also be expected to serve his organization. To this end, the individual, for his own material and social well-being, is encouraged to identify with the firm. In the most subtle manner, he is asked to discard his own individual conscience in order that he may incorporate the firm's values and make them his own. The self-made man gives way to the corporation-made man. The individual, in so far as he is attached to the bureaucracy, becomes an adjunct to the machine.

Reviewing a recent book *Brain of the Firm: The Managerial Cybernetics of Organization*, R. L. Grimsdale wrote:

> The firm and its environment form a system of immense complexity and it is to the properties of large systems that attention must be now directed. The dimension of the problem must be appreciated and techniques for coming to grip with systems of almost indescribable complexity must be developed.

As with Progress, it is assumed that systems of immense complexity are inevitable and that it is the task of society to make men fit the dictates of the system. At no point in the review is size questioned: because, along with efficiency and growth it constitutes another absolute of the Mechanical World-Picture. What techniques will be finally employed to persuade men to identify with the impersonal institution it is impossible to determine. Certainly they will not be violent and explicit but indirect and psychological. It is worth pointing out here that, even now, a University Research Programme backed by a general grant from business, is endeavouring to create a drug – or a 'social medicine' in the language of bureaucracy – which will induce a state of happiness in the workers as they increase their firm's productivity. As the review says: *techniques must be developed.*

On a world-wide scale, can there now be much doubt that America and Russia have similar long-term goals and that the 'cold war' has been partly fabricated as both an invaluable distraction and as a means by which both sides can quietly tighten and increase their control over their respective Empires?

Consider, for example, the full implications of the following report in the Business News of *The Times*:

> The Nixon visit to Moscow will almost certainly result in an expansion of trade and cooperation in the field of advanced technology. Computers and their allied electronics will be a key area. The Soviet economy has failed to reach satisfactory growth and productivity rates; and Russian planners have long recognized that basing 'extensive' growth upon increasing labour inputs into existing production lines is no longer viable.
>
> The computer ... has a fundamental and unavoidable role to play. 'Intensive' growth depends upon computers....
>
> ... Basically, the Soviet plan it to set up a hierarchy of computerized or automated management systems. This would begin at the enterprise level, merge into industrial branch systems ... and then merge into a yet higher level at the planning commissions of the republics and the all-union government in Moscow.
>
> The concept of a hierarchy of computerised management systems was first formulated in the late 1950s by the cybernetician, Academician V. Berg. He argued for its feasibility by pointing to the computer network of the United States Strategic Air Command.
>
> ... All that the businessmen have to do (if the politicians can create a satisfactory climate) is to work out some means of financing it all.

Here, ravelled in one ball, uniting East and West, one discovers, once more, the three absolutes of the Mechanical World-Picture: expanding growth, measured efficiency and centralized control. The passage also reveals that these inter-related and ultimate values are shared by businessmen, by practical scientists and by politicians: each working for each other; together forming a formidably powerful alliance. This explains why, in an advancing technocracy, we observe a number of political languages, a number of political parties and newspapers but only *one* politics, only *one* public philosophy. It also explains why, in spite of the paraded images of diverse richness, we witness daily a growing uniformity at all levels of life.

What, we may ask, is the ultimate end of the 'one politics'? Again the article provides an answer. The ultimate end is to establish the pyramid of power: centralized control through the devotion of a bureaucracy, through persuasion techniques, and through the mechanical power of the computer. This brings me to the last element of the Mechanical World-Picture: the belief in power.

THE BELIEF IN POWER

It is significant that the military forces did not only protect Egyptian civilization, they also provided a regimented labour force which during peace-time could extract gold and erect monuments, as well as a powerful inner bureaucracy understanding and respecting the various levels of hierarchical organization. High military scribes not only attended the war councils, they also, at the end of a hereditary Dynasty, occupied the actual seats of power. In a similar way, military forces have established and secured the powerful modern nations and been helpful in establishing their political and social structure. Arnold Toynbee has stated this unambiguously enough, and in doing so he only states what we must all know: 'The application of successive Western technical inventions to the art of war is what has given the West its modern ascendancy over the rest of the world.' It is no exaggeration to say that in Russia, and in America, today, the interests of the military, the scientific, political and the economic all but coincide. To establish this we need not examine the Pentagon or the Armaments Industries or the Vietnam War – we need only to glance at current political language where we find totally different areas of activity being smoothly drawn together: 'space-military programme', 'military-political', 'Freedom Academy of cold-war specialists'. Qualitatively different objects are slickly stapled together to form demented compounds. The terms reveal the way in which the controllers of modern society interpret every aspect of life in terms of power and aggression. It is in keeping with this situation that the Gross National Product, an abstraction that is constantly dangled like an ideal before us, and which measures the might of nations, *includes* the production of the most evil weapons. As Charles Carter declares in his book *Wealth*:

A country will be counted richer by the national-income statisticians if it produces more atomic warheads, tanks or napalm. Spending on arms is a *major interest* of the great powers.

If we return to the quotation concerning Russia's need for computers, we observe that the actual social system which the ruling power hopes to create is derived from the US Strategic Air Command. The military system, depending on efficiency, on regimentation and hierarchy, is seen by the technocratic power élites as the best model for political man. This alliance between the military and the political and industrial is not a new phenomenon, but the scale on which it exists is new. Now all human life is dependent on the dictates of a tiny minority.

In the past, war has provided a situation for scientific experimentation as well as vast and insatiable markets for many manufactured products. Furthermore the regimentation of people and the mass-production of goods necessary in war-time conditions have been invariably extended beyond their need and provided patterns for peace-time existence. Once, in the First and Second World Wars, the large assembly lines had been erected, once the systems of mechanization had been imposed, there was no return to the simpler, more diverse, and, from a cultural and human standpoint, richer methods of production. As Lewis Mumford has demonstrated in his book *The Pentagon of Power*, the powers which individuals, in times of crises, had corporately surrendered to their Governments, were often never returned.

It is in this belief in power that we find the energizing and largely unconscious drive of the Mechanical World-Picture. Without this, it could not continue. Without this, it could not become the path that all countries seek. To quote Arnold Toynbee again:

> Here we have an explanation of the present-day sanctification of the word 'science'. Science – married to technology, has generated material power: this material power has been forged into potent weapons: and the desire, partly rational and partly irrational, to possess these weapons stimulates a desire to master the science to which the weapons manifestly owe their origin.

The Glorification of the World-Picture

A world-picture permeates a society and, by providing ultimate terms of reference, invisibly unifies it. As we have seen, a world-picture is also embodied in the artefacts which, in turn, unconsciously urge people to perceive and understand experience in certain ways. Long before conceptual articulation is possible, a child has certain expectations about the nature of society – which he has learnt from his games, his rituals, his toys, his complex inherited world of symbol and artefact.

To restrict the present discussion for one moment one can see for example that certain modern dolls tend to develop particular expectations about life in those who play with them (and are very cleverly designed to do so). Thus the Barbie and Cindy doll is made with a gyrating adolescent body and an accompanying world of necessary objects, a boyfriend with a fashionable car, a dream house, a fashion shop, a dress for every day of the week, and a host of other gadgets and possessions. What, it must be asked, does a child learn by playing with such a doll? She learns as a child that overt sexuality and intense consumption are what matters. As an infant she is learning to see life as if she were an adolescent consumer. What is more, the doll, by providing everything at a literal, life-like level, does not develop her powers of improvisation, empathy or imagination. The child is imprisoned inside a very narrow world – and in these confines her expectations and assumptions about life are developed. This is, I realize, of course, a highly specific example – but it is not difficult to relate such dolls to other prevailing influences in advertising, entertainment and comics, which surround the child.

The Mechanical World-Picture is constantly being affirmed in our society, daily resurrected in the papers, in the magazines, on television and on public hoardings. It is the set task of the publicists and copywriters to constantly fabricate new fantasies, new images, new symbols. No sooner has there been some technological feat than the publicity industry convert it into a symbol. In this respect, advertising can be regarded as the sustained labour to glorify the absolutes of Progress and Power. In fact, so necessary and so powerful has advertising become that it is reaching the point where it actually defines the conditions for the presentation of information and entertainment. Jingles, images and slogans become part of news programmes. As Charles Parker suggests in his essay, the mass media contracts to a closed ritual: a set of slickly produced symbols and a number of clever performers, and this in turn makes it all the more difficult for people to find and name the alternatives. Tragically, intellectuals in the west, instead of resisting the debasement of meaning brought about by the conditions of the entertainment industries, have, for the most part, desperately swum with the current. As Ian Robinson shows, the poet has learnt, like the politician, to become a performer. He has been willing to parade his schizophrenia, paranoic or suicidal tendencies in the space between glossy advertisements. By disregarding any notion of ethical coherence or human dignity and meaning, the intellectual has provided explicit justification for a society which is only held together by the relentless drive for more power and more profit. At the same time, the intellectual by his acts and choices has been responsible for the suggestion that culture is part of the glittering package and inseparable from it.

Mario Amaya, in *Pop as Art*, explicitly makes this point:

> This leads to a certain sort of performance-artist, who works almost in direct relationship to the commercial art world, who produces for exhibitions rather than for himself, who tries to anticipate the expectations of powerful critics and dealers, and who must create attention at all costs or perish in a sea of thousands of other artists, all fighting to reach the raft of success.

Here, without moral criticism, it is explicitly stated that the artist fits himself to the prevailing orthodoxy in order to achieve success. Furthermore he writes:

> Such artists accept the despicable, with a terrible sang-froid, and in a way that implies they are neither hating nor loving, but just having. Instead of taking up the fight against mass-think, they have reflected it, parrot-like in their own works, over and over again...

They are 'having' their world in the same sense as the consumer who blankly absorbs the surfeit of products produced by the mindless system of mass production. The image of man (where it exists) in contemporary art is, as a result, either brutal (as in Bacon) or mechanical (as in the Pop Artist). In many contemporary films the same image of man can be discovered, often linked, it would seem, with the sadistic desire to shock and hurt the audience. The conclusion that Masud Khan draws in his study of pornography provides, I believe, the framework for understanding the failure of present culture to be a renewing energy in our lives:

> It is my contention that with the Industrial Revolution and the advent of scientific technology in European cultures man began to consider himself neither in the image of God nor of man, but in that of a machine which was his own invention, and pornographic ecriture and imagery try to make of the human body an ideal machine, which can be manipulated to yield maximum sensation.

Such an interpretation confirms our central analysis of a dominant Mechanical World-Picture. Art following the impetus of mass production has recreated Man in the image of the Machine.

The Signs of Disintegration

It is in the nature of a world-picture that it becomes so solidly embodied, so much a matter of unthinking and unfeeling routine, that it continues to exist long after it has any moral or intellectual justification. At this critical point in time, the ruling minorities, whose power and prestige rest, finally, on the energizing assumptions embodied in the dominant *Weltanschauung*, unable to rely on the active goodwill of the populace, have to resort to constant publicity, an endless flow of propaganda and reassurance. The tone of the civilization becomes desperate and frenetic as it becomes experientially more unreal and insecure. At the same time there is an effort to suppress or isolate the increasing number of criticisms rising from all parts of society. As many tensions are created which are not truly acknowledged and which therefore cannot be confirmed and helped at a public level, there develops a propensity to seek out answers which would appear to give immediate satisfaction and gratification: 'therapies' of violence, drug-taking, sexuality and psychosis. It is impossible to be certain, but Western civilization could now be very close to this precarious position.

It is instructive to notice that at the high point of the Elizabethan World-Picture, alternative conceptions of the nature of the world were already in circulation. Tillyard writes:

> Recent research has shown that the educated Elizabethan had plenty of text-books in the vernacular instructing him in the Copernican astronomy, yet he was loth to upset the old order by applying his knowledge. The new commercialism was hostile to Mediaeval stability.

Long before the Elizabethan World-Picture had finally crystallized, the seeds of an alternative world had been widely scattered. And *this* world, emphasizing free competition and expansion, understanding causality and valuing rational enquiry, and finally freeing itself in the nineteenth and twentieth centuries from metaphysical and moral Christian presuppositions, is, as we know, our present inheritance. It is this inheritance which is now in question. For in the same way as the revolutionary ideas and concepts of Galileo, Descartes and Copernicus burst through the confining shape of the Mediaeval inheritance, so now a new flux of living ideas threaten to end the dominant world-picture of our day. As Marjorie Grene claims:

> To put finally to rest our Newtonian delusions, to renew our

conception of nature as *living*, and to see ourselves once more as living beings in a world of living beings, still constitutes the major task of philosophy in the twentieth century.

As I wish to show later, the Romantics from Blake onwards attacked the stultifying nature of the Mechanical World-Picture, but from about 1900 many scientists began to find it likewise inadequate and distorting. Before discussing their growing dissatisfaction with traditional mechanism, I would like to briefly return to the four categories of the world-picture in the order that I have presented them and to summarize the ways in which they fail as guides to social action.

The Inadequacies of the Four Categories

GROWTH

Ironically, it can be concluded that the metaphor of growth has a certain unintended accuracy. Throughout nature, growth is related to function and design. It is found that where growth usurps function (as in cancer) it becomes a form of disease and destroys the whole body. Our society by raising economic growth to the order of a final end has not only destroyed the diversity of individual cultures and natural life and erected in their stead an oppressive uniformity, it has also put the very survival of man in question. Apart from being repulsive in itself, a rising standard of consuming, as many ecologists have pointed out, cannot be continuously maintained in a world which is finite. Ultimately then, growth, in its current meaning, must be equated with the philosophy of egoistic hedonism and with eventual genocide.

MEASUREMENT

If, as T. E. Hulme claimed, Romanticism can be called 'spilt religion', the belief in the universal validity of measurement can be named 'spilt science'. Because the philosophy of science on which the Mechanical World-Picture is based, rejected the realm of being, it fell into the grievous error of assuming that all aspects of life could be precisely tabulated and measured. One invariably discovers the same assumption informing present-day computer-worship. Here it must suffice to say that measurement alone can never answer the moral and aesthetic question of *worth*. Cost Benefit Analysis cannot estimate the beauty of a church or the value of a species of wild duck. Moral, spiritual and aesthetic questions (real because they are experienced as such) can only be understood and answered in the unique act of each man's living. What is measured is always greater than the measurement for life transcends the abstract, though useful, schemata of man's practical reason. Unfortunately, the Mechanical World-Picture was responsible for equating helpful systems of measurement with the immeasurable reality.

SIZE

The comments made on growth apply equally to size. In natural life, bigger is never of itself a sign of better. In human life we know that excessive numbers – whether in states, corporations, or football matches – create difficulties, disturbances and disorders. In organizations, large size results in the institution being artificially elevated above the individuals who compose it. Size stifles individual creativity and encourages all that is passive and commonplace. As Carl Jung has pointed out, such an emphasis on the uniform and collective can lead to a serious psychological regression in the individual psyche which makes it possible for people to accept or condone deeds of violence and perversion which, in other conditions, they would regard as loathsome and inhuman. One need not here list the atrocities committed in the name of collective man in our own 'enlightened' century. Technocracy in its uncritical drive for efficiency and production has failed to consider the effects of size on the quality and meaning of human life.

POWER

In 1793 William Blake engraved for his work *The Gates of Paradise*, a picture in which a man stands at the foot of a ladder which stretches from the earth to the moon. Below the picture he put the caption 'I want. I want'. The scientific pursuit of knowledge was never wholly free from the psychological and military pursuit for power and domination. Leonardo da Vinci was exceptional in that when he discovered the snorkel he refused to reveal the discovery on the grounds that 'the evil nature of man' would exploit the contraption by using it as a means to sabotage shipping. An equivalent decision today would be labelled 'reactionary' and false to progress. This is largely because the accumulation of knowledge and technique has been seen to be necessary to an ever-expanding economy, providing it with new possibilities for extending production and profits, as well as centralized power to be used against those who might oppose.

In technocracy, power comes to exist for itself and is seen to stand in no need of moral or intellectual justification. A man in our society becomes powerful not because of who he is or what he has achieved, but according to what capital he owns. Power becomes divorced from meaning, from moral intention. In a small way, this can be seen, for example, in Lord Thomson, who wishes to acquire more and more newspapers *not* in order to disseminate a particular philosophy or to create a certain style of newspaper but merely in order to possess. Where power exists for a purpose, it provokes evaluation, it calls forth rational debate: but where it exists for its own exercise and its own perpetuation, it becomes a negative force emptying life of meaning. In this context, power promotes not only vulgar opportunism but also a pervasive sense of unreality, of ultimate purposelessness.

Such a cursory examination of the four absolutes of the Mechanical World-Picture reveals that they all share one quality: the absolutes are means not ends. In each case we can legitimately ask what progress, efficiency, size, power is *for*.

And to ask the question, with full consciousness of what we are doing, is to begin to free our minds from the prison of prevalent assumptions. And the first question invites a second: in becoming ends for determining action, have not the categories been responsible for distorting and, in certain cases, inverting all those human values and aspirations which should be at the centre of any culture worthy of the name?

The Seeds of a New World-Picture

1. CHANGES IN MODERN SCIENCE

It is now necessary to consider the nature of the ideas which threaten the autonomy of mechanism. We must begin by mentioning a startling change in scientific understanding itself. The physicist Heisenberg, having established that the observer actually influenced the behaviour of a particle when it was both small and fast moving, concluded in *The Physicist's Conception of Nature*:

> Science no longer confronts nature as an objective observer, but sees itself as an actor in the inter-play between man and nature... In other words, method and object can no longer be separated. The

Scientific world view has ceased to be a scientific view in the true sense of the word.

Such a position constitutes a startling reversal of traditional scientific method where since the time of Descartes an absolute division between subject and object had been axiomatic. Under the Descartian assumption, man had become, as Blake and Coleridge claimed, a passionless spectator looking upon an alien and inert universe. With Heisenberg's Uncertainty Principle, establishing that, at least in one area of physics, there could be no sharp distinction between the observer and the observed, man and the universe are brought together in a living relationship. The 'subjective' is granted a reality: and the 'objective' modified in terms of the realization. Adolf Portmann, in the tradition of Whitehead and Bergson, has said: 'Nature comprises every aspect of life — subjective experience no less than structure.'

It is perhaps worth mentioning here that if such a conception of man and nature is emerging from some of the purer forms of scientific enquiry and philosophical speculation, it is also close in understanding to that powerful conception of art which sees art as essentially the reconciliation of the inward and outward universe through the creation of the symbol. In the creation of significant art there is constant interplay between the outer and the inner, between the material suggesting certain actions and the creator's intention searching to become more lucid, between what is given and what must be created. The resulting work is not the actual experience but the symbol, both concentrating and transcending the experience, existing formally in the world where it waits to be interpreted through the viewer's inner powers of feeling and imagination.

I am not suggesting that such a view needs a scientific foundation for its justification, or that the principle of nature comprising both subjective and objective aspects provides such a justification. But it does seem to me that there is a common ground here between the scientific and the creative: and that this, as it arises genuinely, can only be a valuable sharing. Certainly, under the influence of the Mechanical World-Picture, many of the arts have deteriorated so much that they can only be regarded as anti-art, anti-life: optical art, kinetic art, pop art, the documentary novel, mechanical architecture, literal 'acting out' theatre, the computer poem and electronic music: all these forms demonstrate only too frequently the imaginative impoverishment brought about by a dominant philosophy which had no place for the expressive, the symbolic and decorative faculties of man.

In a different context, in ecology, we find that, again, a number of scientists are discarding the absolutes of the Mechanical World-Picture. Traditionally, scientists have been valued in society for their 'neutrality', for their freedom from the passionate urges of ideology. In the last thirty years this neutrality has become exploited so much by technocracy that it has ceased to be neutrality and has become implicit support of the status quo. The lofty role of political neutrality has deteriorated to that of being an expert advising the political and military establishments. In many ways, the *Blueprint for Survival* can be seen as a rejection of such a passive, if highly rewarded, function.

But the content of the ecologists' manifesto is even more important and revolutionary. It could be said that the *Blueprint for Survival* not only questions but seeks to reverse the four absolutes of the Mechanical World-Picture – at least in as much as these absolutes are used by the commercial and political powers to justify economic expansion. In this book, 40 scientists argued for a decentralized society, stabilized by a 'stationary condition of capital'. And, not unlike Heisenberg, the book offered under the name of science a radically different conception of the universe:

> There is no valid distinction between the laws of God and Nature, and Man must live by them no less than any other creature. Such a belief must be central to the philosophy of the stable society, and must permeate our thinking. Indeed it is the only one which is *properly scientific.*

Here, again, in a more practical and didactic context, we find Heisenberg's notion of life as an interplay between different worlds: in this case, the divine, the personal and the natural: and as co-operation takes the place of control so does diversity take the place of unity. The drive for a 'standard world' – 'a global-suburb', sharing one language, one currency, one system of values is rejected for a variegated world, rich with different cultures, languages, beliefs, traditions. (However one must add here that the *Blueprint* has little understanding of what culture means.) These ideals can only be achieved by ending the insatiable drives of modern commerce, by slowly dismembering the vast systems of mass production and establishing a pattern of decentralized communities. For scientists, who are, indeed, flattered and promoted by technocracy, to support so wholeheartedly a conception of society that many years ago William Morris was advocating is, indeed, a departure whose full significance is yet to be realized.

In the acceptance of subjectivity as an informing reality, in the understanding of nature as manifold, in the attacking of the gods of Progress and Productivity, it does not seem over-rash to suggest that a number of scientists (how small does not matter) and philosophers are slowly articulating an image of the universe radically different from Renaissance science, which may, in turn, provide elements of a new and more comprehensive world-picture: a world-view which is not, to posit the minimum, in conflict with cultural views of man. Is it unreasonable to hold that here may lie some of the scattered seeds of a new development? The hope is the more founded because there are places in our society where such seeds can lodge and take root. I want now to consider some of the places the seeds might settle and germinate in as well as further possibilities for renewal.

2. EDUCATION AGAINST MECHANISM

The metaphor of growth is also frequently used by those educationists and teachers who are concerned with the imaginative process. Here the word has an utterly different denotation from the one we have been considering. Growth, as used by English and Art teachers, refers to that movement of the child into himself and into the world which is made possible through the imaginative act: growth denotes a dynamic teleology: a developing self-realization. Yet such imaginative creation is, of course, not to be understood as an isolating and exclusive activity – for creation cannot sustain itself without a supporting community or culture. The stronger that community (beginning with the family and moving outwards, and backwards into the past), the stronger the inherited culture, the greater the possibilities for imaginative and cultural achievement. Children who are deprived of a significant and living culture are deprived of ways in which to interpret and experience and express the world in which they live. In our own mass-produced culture – of television and TV comics – the comfort and certainty of the stereotype quickly contracts the mind to a terrifyingly low range of possibilities and expectations, many of them sentimental, others, sadistic. The realization that the aims of the teacher and the aims of modern commerce are for the most part incompatible has brought education into a critical relationship with the society it ostensibly serves.

It could be said that in many ways the conflict is one between different conceptions of growth. For commerce, growth is, as we have seen, a quantitative notion: growth is the continuous drive to increase production, consumption, and capital for their own sakes. Commerce has thus come to require two qualities in man, an outer competitiveness (necessary to secure rising levels of production) and an inner passivity (necessary to secure rising levels of consumption). For educationists, in contrast, growth is an inward and qualitative concept, implying a development of the whole person for his own sake. There can be no reconciliation between such radically different conceptions, and it is possible, as universities are seen to betray their moral and cultural responsibilities, that those teachers committed to creative and imaginative work will become a powerfully articulate voice for social change.

3. THE RESISTANCE OF THE SMALL COMMUNITY

However, the possibilities of education are not only defined by the schools, they are also defined by the surrounding and indigenous communities. And, here, sporadic though the eruptions are, one can detect another source of dissatisfaction within our society, for it is becoming clear to a number of small communities that their deepest interests and the interest of Progress conflict. Adorno has said, 'Industrial Production can increasingly dispense with accumulated experience.' Local traditions and loyalties, local beliefs and forms of speech are seen by the advocates of commerce as impediments lying irritatingly in the path of an international and mobile technocracy. Because all the rewards of technocracy lie in the present and the glittering promise of tomorrow, the past becomes equated with all that is outmoded and static. At best, history, where it does not conflict with present interests, survives as sentiment. In this respect, the Youth Movement is one with technocracy. In *The Greening of America* Charles Reich maintains: 'The most basic limitations of life all vanish, leaving open a life that can be lived without the guideposts of the past.' Under such pressures to forget, the act of remembering becomes subversive. It is symptomatic of our condition that old people who instinctively return to their own childhood, who no longer produce or extensively consume, find themselves in institutions. Yet a rejection of the past, whether the individual's past or the general historical past, is, as a single moment of introspection reveals, dangerously false. Without memory, without accumulated and well-tested experience, without the slow accumulation of knowledge and wisdom, without a past, what can the present be? It can, as people who have lost their memory have testified, be nothing more than a vague and random collection of sensations. Significantly, it is this sort of experience – the experience of unreality, absurdity, nausea – which one finds recorded obsessively in modern literature and art. Again, is it not possible that the worship of mobility, of 'rationalization' schemes, of instant answers, develops in a people a psychological *aimlessness* which unconsciously seeks meaning and confirmation in the extreme 'solutions'? A living culture, a living community, in contrast to technocratic society, maintains its roots in the past even while it moves, as indeed it must, towards the future: and the individuals within that culture and community have a place which is their own and time which is a heritage.

It is not surprising then that a number of communities find themselves resisting the economic imperialism of our day. The recent opposition of local communities to oil drilling in Dorset, to Lord Harlech's Pop Festival in Lincolnshire, to the takeover by the army of a loch in Scotland, has been noticeable both for its spontaneity and unity. In a more intense, more articulate and more developed way, movements like Cymdeithas Yr Iaith (Welsh Language Society) express coherent forms of protest and cultural renewal. On a political level, these movements can only achieve their aims of cultural determination through a vigorous policy of regionalism and certainly an important part of such politics would be the insistence on the need to re-establish a widespread poly-technics. Our present uniform system of mass-production, contrary to advertising propaganda, creates an intolerable monotony, both in the condition of the worker and in the products manufactured. It may be true that within the range determined by mass-production there are a number of choices (though even here the choice is often between labels and packages): but it is the range itself that is so severely restricted. The answer to our centralized system of mass-production is, as the *Blueprint for Survival* indicates, firstly to establish a decentralized system of production, which is then further modified by the reintroduction where it is both possible and valuable, of traditional methods of craft and creation. In agriculture, this would largely mean a return to the small farm and with it all those forms of husbandry which have been developed through centuries of farming experience. Such a momentous change of direction would also restore dignity to labour – a dignity which has been lost under unchecked industrialization, and the lack of which forms a major source of contemporary boredom and passivity. A decentralized poly-technics would, inevitably, as it developed, restore style, beauty and visual variation to a civilization now oppressed by utilitarian ugliness.

In his lecture, *Art and The People*, given in 1883, William Morris declared that in a sound society, committed to the fulfilment of man, two questions would have to be asked of anyone wishing to produce or manufacture: 'First, will the thing being produced be useful to the world? Second, will the making of it give healthy and pleasurable occupation to the makers?' His simple questions were, and remain, subversive. They also point to another form of society, which Morris celebrated in his lectures, a society where production and need, beauty and function, work and pleasure, would be no longer dissociated but reconciled.

It should not be regarded as surprising that many of the alternatives to over-industrialized society are to be found inside the tougher and more alert side of the Romantic Revolution, for, historically, one can see that this revolution in sensibility was an attempt, by stressing the inward, the intuitive and imaginative faculties of man, to correct the mechanical and brutalizing excesses of industrialism. If Romanticism was guilty of idealizing the Medieval world, it was yet aware that without a past transmitted to the present through an enduring community, without a heritage of symbol and artefact, there could be no human life worth the living. In a more practical manner, William Morris, was responsible for renovating many of the traditional crafts – printing, stained glass, dyeing, weaving, paper making, embroidery – which had disappeared under the levelling action of industrialism. Furthermore, Morris saw in the Medieval Guild system, a society in which moral and aesthetic notions – notions of justice, beauty and worth – regulated production; his historical knowledge provided him with ways of seeing beyond his society and of grasping the potential alternatives to it.

The Romantic's response to the beauty and immensity of nature can also be seen as countering the narrowly exploitive disposition of the industrialists, a disposition which has lead to the contemporary anxieties about pollution. In 1871 William Morris said:

> Is money to be gathered? cut down the pleasant trees among the houses, pull down ancient and venerable buildings for the money that a few square yards of London dirt will fetch; blacken rivers, hide the sun and poison the air with smoke and worse, and it's nobody's business to see to it or mend it: that is all that modern commerce, the counting house forgetful of the workshop, will do for us herein.

If the claim I am making for the Romantics is true it is not surprising that their belief in the interdependence of man and nature has been recently resurrected by the ecologists and declared fundamental both to science and to securing the continuance of life on our planet. But the Romantic spirit transcends the position of the average ecologist in that it attempts to apprehend life as a creative whole: and in this belief, as I have argued elsewhere, lies its greatest contribution to the twentieth century.

In a letter written in 1914, D. H. Lawrence defines this particular aspiration:

> I think there is a dual way of looking at things: our way, which is to say, 'I am all. All other things are but radiation out from me' – The other way is to try and conceive the whole, to build up a whole by means of symbolism, because symbolism avoids the I and puts aside the egotist: and, in the whole to take our decent place. That was how man built his cathedrals. He didn't say 'out of my breast springs this cathedral'. But in this vast whole I am a small part, I move and live and have my being.

If the various positive intellectual, political and cultural energies which I have too briefly touched upon in this essay should at some point in the forseeable future connect, there could occur an explosive fusion which would generate further energy and bring about unified political action. It is conceivable that this fusion would be so powerful, so compelling that it would provide all the elements of a new world-picture, a world-picture which having human and cultural premises at its centre, would provide an ideal framework for a more humane, imaginative and beautiful civilization. Without some such hope, however slender it may seem, our world would remain, as it is now, intolerably dark.

Index